Attracting Butterflies & Hummingbirds
to Your Backyard

Attracting Butterflies & Hummingbirds to Your Backyard

Watch Your Garden Come Alive
with Beauty on the Wing

SALLY ROTH

RODALE

RODALE

WE INSPIRE AND ENABLE PEOPLE TO IMPROVE THEIR LIVES AND THE WORLD AROUND THEM

**Library of Congress
Cataloging-in-Publication Data**

Roth, Sally.
    Attracting butterflies and hummingbirds to your backyard : watch your garden come alive with beauty on the wing / Sally Roth.
        p.   cm.
    Includes bibliographical references (p.   ) and index.
    ISBN 0–87596–861–9 (hardcover : alk. paper)
    1. Butterfly gardening.   2. Gardening to attract birds.   3. Hummingbirds.   I. Title.
QL544.6 R68   2001
638'.5789—dc21   00–012911

Distributed in the book trade by St. Martin's Press

2 4 6 8 10 9 7 5 3 1   hardcover

EDITOR: Susan B. Burton
COVER AND INTERIOR BOOK DESIGNER: Michele Raes
INTERIOR ILLUSTRATORS: Leigh Wells (butterflies and hummingbirds), Mary Woodin (garden designs and how-to art)
FRONT COVER PHOTOGRAPHERS: The Image Finders/Jim Yokajty, Ralph Paonessa
BACK COVER PHOTOGRAPHERS: William B. Folsom, Visuals Unlimited/S. Masloski
PHOTOGRAPHY EDITOR: Lyn Horst
PHOTOGRAPHY ASSISTANT: Jackie L. Ney
LAYOUT DESIGNER: Keith Biery
COMPUTER GRAPHICS SPECIALIST: Dale Mack
RESEARCHER: Sarah Wolfgang Heffner
COPY EDITOR: Sarah Sacks Dunn
MANUFACTURING COORDINATOR: Patrick T. Smith
INDEXER: Lina Burton
EDITORIAL ASSISTANCE: Kerrie A. Cadden, Claudia Curran

Rodale Organic Living Books
EXECUTIVE EDITOR: Kathleen DeVanna Fish
MANAGING EDITOR: Fern Marshall Bradley
EXECUTIVE CREATIVE DIRECTOR: Christin Gangi
ART DIRECTOR: Patricia Field
PRODUCTION MANAGER: Robert V. Anderson Jr.
STUDIO MANAGER: Leslie M. Keefe
COPY MANAGER: Nancy N. Bailey
BOOK MANUFACTURING DIRECTOR: Helen Clogston

On the cover: Monarch butterfly (see page 279) and blue-throated hummingbird (see page 202)

For my beloved Angel Man, Jimmie Epler,
and for Ruth Husk, a real country girl

RODALE
ORGANIC GARDENING STARTS HERE!

Here at Rodale, we've been gardening organically for more than 50 years—ever since my grandfather J. I. Rodale learned about composting and decided that healthy living starts with healthy soil. In 1940 J. I. started the Rodale Organic Farm to test his theories, and today the nonprofit Rodale Institute Experimental Farm is still at the forefront of organic gardening and farming research. In 1942 J. I. founded *Organic Gardening* magazine to share his discoveries with gardeners everywhere. His son, my father, Robert Rodale, headed *Organic Gardening* until 1990, and today a fourth generation of Rodales is growing up with the magazine. Over the years we've shown millions of readers how to grow bountiful crops and beautiful flowers using nature's own techniques.

In this book, you'll find the latest organic methods and the best gardening advice. We know—because all our authors and editors are passionate about gardening! We feel strongly that our gardens should be safe for our children, pets, and the birds and butterflies that add beauty and delight to our lives and landscapes. Our gardens should provide us with fresh, flavorful vegetables, delightful herbs, and gorgeous flowers. And they should be a pleasure to work in as well as to view.

Sharing the secrets of safe, successful gardening is why we publish books. So come visit us at the Rodale Institute Experimental Farm, where you can tour the gardens every day—we're open year-round. And use this book to create your best garden ever.

Happy gardening!

Maria Rodale

Maria Rodale
Rodale Organic Gardening Books

CONTENTS

WELCOME TO A WORLD OF WONDERS

"How can I get butterflies to come to my yard? And maybe hummingbirds?" asked my friend Larry, a self-proclaimed city boy, on a fine spring morning.

While I've lived nearly all of my 40-something years in the country, Larry has lived all his life with neighbors. His favorite getaways are to the grand cities of the world, where he revels in the culture, admires the architecture, and gets to know the locals.

Me, I head for the hills when vacation rolls around, getting as far off the beaten track as I can. We're incongruous pals, but the friendship has shown me that even the most citified soul still hungers for nature.

It was fun to help him pick out plants and place nectar feeders, and it was even more fun to watch the "city boy" spending hours in his new garden, pulling weeds, planting seeds, and enjoying the flowers.

When I visited Larry in early summer after a few weeks away, I was surprised to stumble over a big comfy chair parked smack-dab in the middle of his living room, far from its usual place in the designer-perfect furnishings.

"What's the chair doing here?" I asked peevishly, rubbing my stubbed toe.

"Best view of the hummingbirds in the garden," he answered proudly.

Soon after the hummingbirds became regulars, a crop of creepy crawly caterpillars (black swallowtail butterflies-to-be) showed up on his parsley plants. When Larry greeted them with delight instead of disgust, I knew he was reclaiming that side of his spirit—the one we all have—that hungers for connection with the natural world.

The desire to bring butterflies and hummingbirds to your garden starts with appreciation of their beauty, and that's reason enough to invite them home. But their presence adds much more than just ornament. Even the little things are a joy to discover—the way a butterfly cleans its face as fastidiously as your pet cat, or how a hummingbird follows a regular path from one favorite flower to the next.

Connecting "Why" with "How-To" I've paid close attention to these

winged friends all my life, from as far back as I can remember, when I first watched them in my mother's gardens. I've observed butterflies and hummingbirds in the gardens I made in the East, the Northwest, and the Midwest, and I've enjoyed those I met on travels or in friends' gardens. This book is a way to share what I've learned.

Food is the way to a hummingbird's heart, and it works magic with butterflies, too. Throughout this book, you'll find many possibilities for plants to add to your garden, as well as ideas for more unusual menu items that hummers and butterflies enjoy. Understanding the "why" behind the preferences of butterflies and hummingbirds makes it much easier to accomplish the "how-to." For instance, daisies attract butterflies because they offer a secure platform for butterfly feet to grab hold, and native plants are important to keep in our gardens because they're intimately connected to the needs of butterflies and hummingbirds, having evolved alongside them. Follow the advice in these pages and I guarantee your yard will be humming and fluttering with lively wings before the first summer is over. To help you attach names to your delightful friends—whether they're hummingbirds, butterflies, or caterpillars—you can consult the field guide to scores of likely species in Chapters 9 and 10.

The Discoveries Never Stop

Once you have butterflies and hummingbirds in your yard, you'll soon find yourself wondering "Why'd they do that?" about a dozen times a day. Behavior is just as fascinating to me as beauty, so you'll find lots of pointers in this book for helping you figure out what your friends are up to. You'll soon see that there's always something new to discover! I'm still learning.

While Larry was learning the delights of nature from the comfort of his cozy chair in the city, I was on vacation in the wilds of Glacier-Waterton International Peace Park in the snow-covered northern Rockies. Sliding down a slippery trail in howling wind and blowing snow to get a better view of mountain goats at a salt lick, I paused on the icy path—just as a hummingbird zipped out of a towering pine tree and began plucking tiny insects from a spiderweb 2 feet in front of my nose!

I learned three things from that sighting: first, that these tiny birds are a lot tougher than I'd given them credit for; second, that apparently insects are the food of choice when nectar flowers are hidden under snow; and third, that even with years of experience, it's darn tough to tell one female hummer from another.

I can't tell you just which hummingbird species I was looking at in Glacier. But I can tell you that even if you can't pin a name on the hummingbirds and butterflies you see, watching them is always a thrill, whether you're nature girl or city boy.

CHAPTER 1

Butterflies and Hummingbirds:

THE BASICS

It's always cause for celebration when a hummingbird or butterfly shows up to grace the garden. Whether we're lucky enough to host them every day or we're honored by just an occasional visit, these amazing animals add such life to our surroundings that we want more, more, more.

Lucky for us gardeners, the very thing we love best—flowers!—is also tops on the list of attractants for all hummingbirds and many butterflies. Flowers produce nectar, and that's a mainstay of their diet. If flowers could talk, they'd tell us that they appreciate the attentions of these creatures, too. Without the probing bill of a hummingbird or the delicate proboscis of a butterfly, many flowers would go unfertilized. The pollen that sticks to the nectar seekers gets passed along to the next flower in turn, which leads to fertilization, seed production, and a new generation of flowers.

Beyond planting butterfly and hummingbird flowers, you'll need to fulfill a few other basic needs to attract these cheerful visitors to your garden. Supplemental foods, water, and shelter will help your butterflies and hummingbirds feel so much at home that they'll choose your yard as the place to raise their families.

GREAT BUTTERFLY EXPECTATIONS

No matter where you live, you'll see a bounty of butterflies in your yard once you take steps to make it more alluring. Even in seemingly inhospitable areas—the desert, the seacoast, the Far North, the treeless Plains—well-adapted butterflies thrive. Butterflies are abundant: Millions of individuals from more than 700 species of butterflies flutter around north of Mexico.

What butterflies you'll see, and when you'll see them, depends on where you live. Many species are wide-ranging, but some prefer particular habitats: woods, open fields, muddy riverbanks. Your style of gardening and the types of natural environments around your neighborhood can affect the types of butterflies you'll see. But no matter what your home habitat, rest assured—you'll see plenty.

HUMMINGBIRD HOPES—QUALITY, NOT QUANTITY

With hummingbirds, it's a different story. These jewel-like birds aren't common everywhere in North America. Only a few species make the trek to the northern stretches of the continent. British Columbia and other western Canadian provinces are visited by a few species, including the glorious Anna's, the tiny calliope, and the black-chinned hummingbird—and the lovely rufous hummingbird even makes it as far north as Alaska.

If you garden in the West, here's your chance to feel smug. The majority of hummingbirds that frequent the United States travel and live in the West—from the eastern foothills of the Rockies, west to the Pacific Coast, and down to Mexico. The Southwest gets the lion's share, but a decent number of species frequent the far west into Canada. East of the Rockies, we see only a paltry few species of hummers on the wing.

All is not lost for the eastern half of the country. The indefatigable and abundant ruby-throated hummingbird brings the scintillating buzz and whir of hummingbird wings to gardens of the East. Hummingbirds are a true rarity only in the wide stretches of the Great Plains, especially the northern plains. If you live in this part of the country, don't lose hope. Hummingbirds can stray far and wide, and if you provide a welcoming garden, anything is possible!

The male broad-billed hummingbird is a rare sight, except in the hummingbird hot spots of the Southwest, where it delights visitors to guest ranches.

HUMMINGBIRD INVENTORY

Which species of hummingbirds you'll see at flowers and feeders depends on the natural breeding and wintering ranges of the birds, as well as the migration routes they travel. Hummingbirds have a habit of turning up in unexpected places, so keep binoculars and a field guide at the ready.

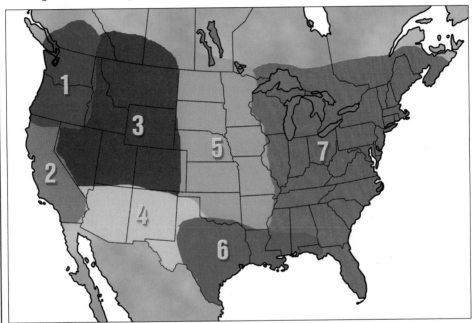

1. Pacific Northwest (Oregon through British Columbia)	Allen's (through mid-coastal Oregon), Anna's, black-chinned (not along coast), calliope, rufous (through coastal Alaska)
2. California	Allen's, Anna's, black-chinned, calliope, Costa's, rufous
3. Rockies	Black-chinned, broad-tailed, calliope, rufous
4. Southwest	Allen's, Anna's, black-chinned, blue-throated, broad-billed, broad-tailed, calliope, Costa's, magnificent, rufous, violet-crowned, white-eared
5. Great Plains	Broad-tailed (rare), ruby-throated (somewhat rare), rufous
6. Texas/Gulf Coast	Black-chinned, broad-billed, buff-bellied, magnificent, ruby-throated, rufous
7. East of the Mississippi	Ruby-throated, rufous (rare)

How Many Hummingbirds

An all-American phenomenon, hummingbirds are unique to our connected continents. Scientists recognize 339 species in North, Central, and South America (and the islands off those coasts).

If you can't make it to Costa Rica—a hummer's haven—your best chance to see a multitude of these little dazzlers is in the American Southwest. In this corner of the United States, 21 different species zip in and out of the country.

One of the best hummingbird hot spots is in the mountains that rise from the southern deserts of Arizona and New Mexico. Guest ranches in this area cater to besotted hummingbird lovers who travel many miles to catch a glimpse of the birds so rare in other places.

Of the 21 species that visit the United States from their usual winter homelands in Mexico and southward, only about a dozen nest here and in Canada. If you live east of the Mississippi River, only a single species—the ruby-throated hummingbird—will nest in your area.

Though hummingbirds of any kind are scarce in the Great Plains east of the Rockies, hummingbird hopes are on the rise. The natural grasslands of the landscape are not particularly welcoming to hummingbirds, but as gardeners there plant more trees, shrubs, and flowerbeds and hang out feeders, the birds may extend their ranges.

More hummers than you can count are often the case at a feeder, especially during migration, when the high-octane birds zoom in to refuel. Here, broad-tailed hummers load up on carbs.

PEAK SEASON

In the cold-winter regions of North America, both hummingbirds and butterflies reach their highest numbers in mid- to late summer. New broods of both the pretty winged insects and the bright little birds are now on the wing, spending their days visiting flowers and other food sources. On a fine summer day, you may see a dozen big, bold-colored swallowtails gliding from flower to flower, joined by monarchs, skippers, delicate hairstreaks, and myriad other butterfly beauties. Hummingbirds may dart in and out to fill their bellies with nectar from flowers and feeders, or even perform fantastic aerial dances to impress an intended mate. If you look closely, you may spot munching caterpillars.

Butterflies are fewer in spring and fall in cold-winter regions, when temperatures are

chilly and flowers are fewer. But these two seasons often bring a burst of hummingbirds, as wintering migrants move up to breeding grounds in spring, and then head south at the end of the season.

My small backyard in Indiana hosts only half a dozen ruby-throated hummers during the summer nesting season, but at either end of that time period, my gardens are abuzz. I'd estimate that 20 hummingbirds may visit on an average day during spring migration. In fall,

A single Mexican sunflower (*Tithonia rotundifolia*) plant has hundreds of blossoms, enough for butterflies and hummingbirds both. Monarchs find it irresistible.

when numbers swell because of new progeny, a single feeder may have 20 ruby-throats circling around impatiently like airplanes waiting for their chance to land. Multiply this number by five feeders, add in hummingbird-friendly flowerbeds, and it's a good guess that more than 100 hummingbirds may stop here on any given day during fall migration.

Butterflies and some hummingbirds fly all year round in the mild areas of the United States, where winter is a page on the calendar, not a foot of snow at the door. The warm weather means the flowers and other foods are available all year. In such a Shangri-la, hummingbirds may raise three batches of nestlings in a single year. The tiny black-chinned hummingbird often accomplishes this feat in hospitable coastal California. In the colder stretches of this bird's range, one or occasionally two broods is the norm.

Warm-area butterflies also raise more progeny in mild winter areas, and they stay put during the winter months. With no cold to kill them, adults keep flying until a predator scoops them up or they die of old age, usually a matter of less than a year.

A Matter of Degrees

To figure out when the peak season for spotting butterflies and hummers happens in your neighborhood, consider your latitude (how far north or south of the equator you live) and your altitude (how far above sea level you are). Spring arrives later and autumn chills are earlier in high-altitude or northern regions. In those areas, the arrival of spring's first butterflies and hummingbirds occurs weeks later than in the warmer climates of the lowlands or in southern regions.

Butterfly Seasons

The first butterfly of spring is as delightful a surprise as the first flowers. Early butterflies and early-blooming perennials often appear together, after a few days of early spring warmth have stirred them from dormancy.

Not all butterflies emerge at the same time. Some butterflies make their first appearance in early spring, more appear in late spring, and by summer, all resident species are a-flutter. Keep in mind, though, that even these generalizations are a matter of perspective. The dainty spring azure butterfly, a tiny creature no bigger than your thumbnail, flits about in earliest spring. If you live in Georgia, that could mean February; in Virginia, perhaps March or April; and in the Rockies, early spring may come in May.

The mourning cloak butterfly is a lovely exception to seasonal rules. This velvety brown beauty with a bit of lacy "petticoat" trim peeking along its wings pays little attention to a schedule. Famed for early appearances, the mourning cloak is often on the wing

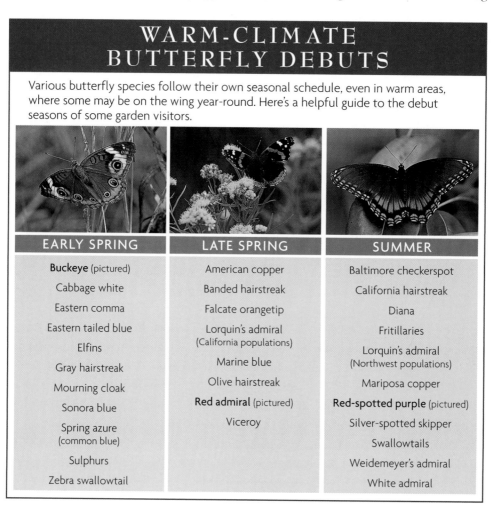

WARM-CLIMATE BUTTERFLY DEBUTS

Various butterfly species follow their own seasonal schedule, even in warm areas, where some may be on the wing year-round. Here's a helpful guide to the debut seasons of some garden visitors.

EARLY SPRING	LATE SPRING	SUMMER
Buckeye (pictured)	American copper	Baltimore checkerspot
Cabbage white	Banded hairstreak	California hairstreak
Eastern comma	Falcate orangetip	Diana
Eastern tailed blue	Lorquin's admiral (California populations)	Fritillaries
Elfins		Lorquin's admiral (Northwest populations)
Gray hairstreak	Marine blue	
Mourning cloak	Olive hairstreak	Mariposa copper
Sonora blue	Red admiral (pictured)	Red-spotted purple (pictured)
Spring azure (common blue)	Viceroy	Silver-spotted skipper
Sulphurs		Swallowtails
Zebra swallowtail		Weidemeyer's admiral
		White admiral

In the right light, the male black-chinned hummingbird shows a flash of rich violet at the lower edge of his throat feathers. On its way to and from breeding grounds west of the Rockies, the tiny bird hums its indefatigable way along a route that stretches from Mexico to as far as British Columbia.

even in the heart of winter—whenever the weather warms up enough to coax the sleeping adult from its hiding place. Unlike most of our familiar garden butterflies, it is not a nectar seeker, so it isn't dependent on flowers for life-giving sustenance. On warm winter days, it can sip sap or old fallen fruit. Should the weather turn cold again, it simply goes back to sleep until the next warm spell.

Miracle Migrants

Over the millennia, the travels of hummingbirds have become perfectly timed to the blooming seasons of the flowers upon which they depend. It's not the thermometer that tells hummingbirds when it's time to move southward—these little birds can withstand mighty chilly temperatures—it's the food supply. Unlike many song-birds, hummers can't switch to seeds or berries when insects and flowers are nonexistent.

To cope with the cold season, which puts an end to the insects and nectar flowers that hummingbirds rely on, these feathered sprites fly south. The rufous, black-chinned, calliope, and ruby-throated are the long-distance champs among North American species. These resilient birds make journeys of thousands of miles, leaving breeding grounds as far north as Alberta, Nova Scotia, and Alaska for a winter vacation in warm, welcoming Mexico and southward.

It's hard to believe that a bird that weighs less than an ounce can travel these incredible distances using just wing power. Hummingbirds manage to do it twice a year—and at speeds that can reach 50 miles an hour in a tailwind.

5 SIMPLE STEPS TO SUCCESS

Once you start noticing butterflies and hummingbirds around your neighborhood or in your yard, you're sure to be hooked. You'll want to see more and get a better look at each of your guests. Food is the first step to gaining the attention of your favorite visitors. For hummingbirds and most butterflies, that means offering nectar in feeders and with flowers. To encourage your guests to linger long enough for you to get to know them, you'll want to take a few other simple steps to make your garden a well-rounded habitat for long-term appeal. Here's what you'll need to make your yard an oasis.

1. **Nectar.** Nectar flowers that appeal to the specific needs of hummingbirds and butterflies are the foundation of an inviting garden. Watching hummingbirds zip from flower to flower is naturally entertaining. Most butterflies seek their sweets from flowers, not from sugar-water feeders. However, hummingbirds quickly zoom to nectar feeders, so be sure to include them in your garden plan. Check out Chapter 2 for all you need to know to make your garden a nectar mecca.

2. **Water.** It's a treat to watch a hummingbird wriggle through a spray of water or splash on a wet leaf. Butterflies appreciate moisture, too. Some of them are so fond of it that they alight

Flowers hold no attraction for the beautiful red-spotted purple butterfly, but overripe fruit or a humble mud puddle will gain its gratitude. Black and iridescent blue on top, this species gets its name from the colors and pattern on its underside, which you'll see only when its wings are folded.

en masse at mud puddles day after day, like social drinkers crowding the bar at the neighborhood pub. Because of their delicate structure and specialized flight, a regular birdbath won't do the trick. You'll need custom-tailored water features to draw them in, and we've included instructions for how to construct these quick and easy projects in Chapter 3.

3. **Supplemental foods.** Some of the most beautiful butterflies, including the glorious red-spotted purple, don't live on nectar from flowers. They prefer a more varied menu of items that can be, um, interesting. Soft or overripe fruit is the most palatable on this list by human standards and a surefire attraction for many species, including mon-

'Homestead Purple' verbena and bright reddish orange dahlia blossoms signal abundant nectar to both butterflies and hummingbirds in this small garden.

archs. If you're not too squeamish to supply horse manure and other delights, some unusual visitors may come your way. Learn the ins and outs of offering these delectables in Chapter 4.

4. **Shelter.** Windy days and chilly weather are hard on the delicate wings and cold-blooded bodies of butterflies, and hummingbirds also suffer in these conditions. A garden design that includes open space surrounded by sheltering hedges—with a mix of sun and shaded spots—will keep your customers lingering in even less-than-perfect weather. Plants with large leaves provide built-in umbrellas should the need arise. Butterfly hibernation areas for the long winter's sleep will also help make your yard a home. Chapter 5 explains how to create these essential sheltering spots.

5. **Nest sites and host plants.** Give hummingbirds and butterflies long-term assistance by including homesites for their future generations. Suitable shrubs, vines, and other plants—plus a few inspired handmade contraptions and a handout of nesting materials—will keep nesting hummers happy. Food for caterpillars known as "host plants," will give a big boost to butterfly populations. In Chapter 6, you'll discover how to provide all these things for your winged guests.

In the pages to come, you'll learn exactly how to put these steps into practice and make butterflies and hummingbirds flock to your yard. You'll also end up with a garden that's beautiful, satisfying, and, best of all, filled with fascinating, colorful, and lovely living creatures.

CHAPTER 2

Flowers and Feeders for

NECTAR

Watching a clump of butterfly weed covered with butterflies or a hummingbird dipping its beak into a flower or a hummingbird feeder is a delight for us humans. However, to the animals and plants involved, it's just the day-to-day business of staying alive.

Hummingbirds, butterflies, and gardeners make a perfect combination because the flowers you plant are an irresistible attraction to the guests whose attention you want to capture. You don't need an acre of perfectly tended perennial borders, either—even a single potted plant on the porch will bring nectar seekers to your neighborhood.

"Nectar" is nothing more than sugar water, whether you cook it up yourself and serve it in a plastic feeder or you let the flowers themselves produce the sweet stuff to entice butterflies and hummingbirds to their blossoms. Even the sweet sap from trees or the juices from fruits are appealing to some species, as you'll learn in Chapter 4. But since your satisfaction is a big part of the reason you grow a garden, you'll want to make sure your space includes flowers that satisfy your soul as well as the more earthly appetites of your winged visitors. "Limiting" your garden to hummingbird and butterfly flowers isn't much of a restriction at all because there are hundreds of fine garden plants that will bring them flocking. In Chapter 7, you'll find garden designs with guaranteed appeal for any size space, from a container collection to a shady side yard.

NECTAR FROM FLOWERS

The natural relationship between hummingbirds, butterflies, and flowers is a simple one: The hummingbirds and butterflies get food and the plants get pollinated. Most types of flowering plants can't self-pollinate (meaning they can't fertilize their own flowers to ensure a new generation of plants). The plants depend on pollinators such as insects, animals, and even the wind. Wind distributes the pollen of grasses, including corn, many trees, and some other plants. Plants without airborne pollen need other help for pollination, and that's where nectar comes in. The sweet, sticky liquid is the bribe that lures these ouside pollinators to the blossoms.

Bees, wasps, and other insects are the pollinators for many flowers and for most fruit and vegetable crops. Other flowers—especially deeper, tubular ones—depend on pollination by visitors with longer tongues: butterflies and hummingbirds.

Picking the Right Nectar Plants

So how can you tell which flowers to plant to have the most success in attracting butterflies and hummingbirds? One way is to study the flowers. Nectar-producing flowers are not all created equal. Some have clusters of teeny blossoms with nectar so close to the surface that you may be able to see it if you peer into a flower. Queen Anne's lace and dill are two examples. These plants tend to attract small, short-tongued insects like ants, flies, wasps, and beetles. Even with their short tongues, these insects can easily reach the droplet of nectar in the tiny blossoms. Butterflies may join right in at the banquet alongside the smaller insects, as long as the blossom supports their weight. Tiny butterflies like blues and hairstreaks often sip from Queen Anne's lace, for instance, while larger monarchs avoid these flimsy flowers but do frequent small-flowered but sturdier goldenrods.

The plants we think of as classic nectar flowers—like honeysuckle and columbine—hold a larger amount of sweet liquid in their tubular flowers. The flower's reproductive parts are positioned perfectly at the top of the blossom. When the hungry visitor reaches down into the nectar fountain, it brushes against the reproductive parts, inadvertently picking up pollen to transfer to another flower and dropping off pollen that it accumulated elsewhere.

TOP 10 FLOWERS

Yellow cosmos
(*Cosmos sulfureus*
'Klondike' Series)

Attracts butterflies
and occasionally
hummingbirds

Orange, red-tinged,
and yellow flowers on
branching plants

Annual

Simple to grow
from seed

Sow in full sun, in
average to lean soil

Blooms summer
through fall

It's a win-win relationship between hummingbirds and flowers, and this Anna's hummer is wearing the evidence. Notice the yellow pollen dusted on the bird's beak. The clinging pollen grains will be deposited on the next flower the bird thrusts its bill into, neatly accomplishing the act of pollination.

Clues to Watch For You can usually identify a good hummingbird or butterfly flower by looking at its shape or blossom arrangement. For hummingbird flowers, check the blossom for a fringe of stamens (the flower's male reproductive parts) extending past the opening of the floral tube. Botanists describe this characteristic as "exserted stamens;" in my everyday language, this phrase translates simply to "sticking out really far." When the hummer comes close enough to dip its beak into the nectar, the pollen on the anthers (capsules that bear pollen) at the stamen tips dusts the bird's head. After sipping the nectar, the hummer will move on to another flower, unwittingly drop off some pollen on the stigma (the top part of the flower's female reproductive structure). As it does so, it picks up more pollen, and continues the process from flower to flower.

Plants with clusters of flowers are generally good for attracting butterflies because the blossom clusters offer more than a single sip of nectar. Daisy-type flowers are especially appealing because the yellow "button" in the middle is really a conglomeration of tiny petal-less flowers packed tightly together. Watch a butterfly sip from a daisy, and you'll see it insert its proboscis into one tiny flower after another.

HUMMINGBIRD FEEDING HABITS Put yourself in the shoes of the nectar-seekers you wish to tempt. Pretend you're a hummingbird. Feel those whirring wings, that urge to zoom, that need for room to move. What looks like a good flower to put your beak into? How about that nice deep one that promises a honey-sweet treat at its tip? It's the one no other creature could possibly have emptied of nectar before you got to it—it's made just for you! Hummingbirds also prefer flowers that are arranged around the stem so that the tubes point outward or upward, without nearby leaves or branches that could interfere with their whizzing wings. Salvias, penstemons, and agaves do the trick quite nicely.

HAVING BRUNCH BUTTERFLY-STYLE Okay, now pretend you're a butterfly. Your wings are fragile, your flight is soft, you're a klutz compared to an acrobatic hummingbird. You need someplace secure to latch onto with your clinging feet. Your nectar straw is a skinny

Butterflies like flowers that offer them a place to linger while they dine. For large species like this monarch, a flat shape offers secure footing while it probes each of the tiny nectar-holding flowers that make up a daisy, like this bright zinnia. A cinch to grow, zinnias are a must in the nectar garden.

little thing, so you can slip it into the tiniest spaces, like the tubes of a daisy, as well as into wider flowers—as long as you can reach their length.

The three flower shapes that seem to suit butterflies best are daisy-type flowers, spikes of closely placed small flowers, and flat- or round-topped clusters of small flowers. Some single large flowers and a few pea-type blossoms also attract them. Examples of good flower choices for butterflies would be a daisy platform, a flat-topped yarrow cluster, a branching cluster of asters, a goldenrod spray, or a gayfeather spike.

Hummingbirds eat like kids in front of the refrigerator— open mouth, insert food. They don't need to perch to enjoy a good meal, but they do need hovering room.

See how easy it is? Once you understand how butterflies and hummingbirds feed and fly, you'll find it's simple to identify a perfect match just by looking at the flowers. You'll go to the garden center or the native plant sale, hold up a plant, and say, "Ah! Butterfly flower!" without consulting any list at all.

To help you in your quest for hummingbird and butterfly flowers, throughout this book I've included lists of flowers that attract each. Some lovely plants even fill the bill for both creatures. Don't limit yourself to plants in my lists, though—there are so many possibilities that I can't name them all. The only list that really matters is the one that works for your garden!

If you're a beginner at butterfly and hummingbird gardening, start with the tried and true "Top 10 Flowers" that I've highlighted throughout this chapter. Choose ones that will thrive in your garden and fit your style.

An Eye for Color
Flower shape isn't the only quality that attracts butterflies and hummingbirds; they notice color as well. They even have different color preferences. Red grabs the eye of hummers, while purple tempts butterflies. Knowing this will help you set the color theme of a hummingbird or butterfly garden, but don't limit yourself too much—both butterflies and hummingbirds will visit suitable nectar flowers of any color of the rainbow.

RED SENDS THE SIGNAL The flash of a red flower glows against greenery like a neon beacon in the gloom. The color announces "nectar here!"—and hummingbirds have learned to heed the call. I can't think of a single red or orange-red American flower that doesn't appeal to hummingbirds. The only plants with blossoms of this color that fail to attract them are imports from other lands, where hummingbirds never existed, or hybrid flowers created by plant breeders. The most perfect red rose, for instance, has little nectar magnetism to hummers.

Red has such strong appeal that hummingbirds will investigate practically anything of that hue, whether it's a child's bicycle or a dog's toy. Orange, orange-red, and certain shades of pink also hold allure for hummingbirds.

BLUE IS BEAUTIFUL, TOO I'm obsessed with the color blue, so my gardens are always full of a multitude of flowers in my favorite color. I've noticed blue is a hit with hummers, too, as long as I stick to the basic flower shapes and arrangements that suit their feeding and flying needs. I look for tubular flowers, outward-facing blooms, and vertical spikes free of entanglement. The hummers in my yard flock to my blue salvias and delphiniums.

Blue salvias, native to the Americas, are a natural choice for hummingbirds because their azure blossoms light the way for hummers on the route back to South America. Many perennial blue salvias come into bloom very late in the season. In the plants' natural haunts, that bloom period is perfectly timed to the arrival of fall migrants and winter resident hummingbirds.

Red is for hummingbirds—and so is blue! Native late-season salvias, like this Mexican sage (*Salvia leucantha*), usher the birds southward in fall.

In my own garden, the October-blooming, rich cobalt blue Brazilian salvia (*S. guarantica*) can be counted on to succor at least a few straggler ruby-throated hummingbirds that pass through after the rush of migrants.

My observations are borne out by the experiences of early hummingbird watchers almost a century ago in the Southwest. Over a 30-year period in the early twentieth century, Arthur Cleveland Bent collected hundreds of anecdotal references for his series of books on American birds. He relates an experiment in which curious researchers draped bits of red and blue cloth on desert vegetation. They found that both colors attracted equal attention from the hummingbirds found there.

No matter what the reason, the blue flowers in my all-blue and mixed-color gardens are always a success with hummingbirds. I just make sure to cultivate plants with blossoms whose shape promises a nectar feast.

TESTING THE THEORY It's easy and even fun, though mildly mean-spirited, to experiment with the theory of whether particular colors attract hummingbirds.

Tie a red bandanna to a bush in hummingbird season and watch what happens. Then try the same experiment with a strip of green or yellow cloth fluttering from a shrub. You'll see that color does make a difference in what hummingbirds investigate first—the green or yellow cloth won't attract much attention!

Your hummingbird companions may show great interest in your orange-handled pruners or your neighbor's red baseball cap, as well. After the eruption of Mt. St. Helens in Washington State in 1980, the early scientific investigators experienced first-hand what colors hummingbirds like. The curious birds in search of a snack tickled the scientists through the ventilating grommets of their orange jumpsuits.

BEST COLORS FOR BUTTERFLIES Butterflies seem to be less color-centered than hummingbirds, but they still show a strong preference—for purple. That purplish magenta hue that is scorned by some snobbish gardeners is one of our fluttering friends' favorites, perhaps because it's the natural color of many nectar-rich, butterfly-perfect, native American wildflowers.

Purple coneflower (*Echinacea purpurea*), a standard in just about every perennial garden bed these days, is actually an American native, along with its close relatives, Tennessee coneflower (*E. tennesseensis*) and pink coneflower (*E. pallida*). The coneflowers are favorites with butterflies, too, and many nurseries feature all three varieties.

Butterflies also favor many verbenas, meadow phlox (*Phlox maculata*), garden phlox (*P. paniculata*), eupatoriums (*Eupatorium* spp.), and more asters than I could possibly include here—there are more than 400 native North American species!

Butterflies like yellow, too, perhaps because many ideal butterfly wildflowers also sport golden petals. Think of all the yellow daisies that bloom during the weeks of late summer, the time when butterfly populations are at their peak. Consider the goldenrods that drench every bit of bare ground with a buttery yellow feast for migrating monarchs. Even our all-American sunflowers are just as popular with butterflies as they are with birds. Try out a few!

TOP 10 FLOWERS

Phlox
Meadow phlox
(*Phlox maculata*),
Garden phlox
(*P. paniculata*)

Attracts butterflies
and hummingbirds

Pink-purple species
are highly attractive;
many cultivars
available

Perennial; tall phlox is
hardy in Zones 5–8,
garden phlox in
Zones 4–8

Self-sows moderately;
seedlings may bloom
an intense purple-pink
instead of the color of
their parent

Plant in sun to shade

Blooms in summer

DOUBLE-DUTY FLOWERS

It's fun to find plants that combine attributes that appeal to both hummingbirds and butterflies. Look for tubular, clustered or daisylike flowers that are red or purple. It's not guaranteed—I still can't figure out why butterflies don't flock to many salvias—but it often works. Here are some of the most popular double-duty flowers for hummingbirds and butterflies. Some are annuals, some are perennials, and a few are even shrubs!

HUMMINGBIRD ATTRACTANT	+ BUTTERFLY ATTRACTANT	= DOUBLE-DUTY PLANT
Spikes of tubular flowers	Purple color	Anise hyssop (*Agastache foeniculum*) Blazing stars (*Liatris* spp.) Butterfly bush (*Buddleia davidii*) Lilacs (*Syringa* spp.) Penstemons (*Penstemon* spp.) Salvias (purple-flowered cultivars of *S. nemorosa* and *S. × sylvestris*)
Red color	Daisylike flower	Dahlias (*Dahlia* spp.) Mexican sunflower (*Tithonia rotundifolia*) Common zinnia (*Zinnia elegans*)
Red color	Wide tubular flower	Hibiscus (*Hibiscus* spp.) Hollyhock (*Alcea rosea*) Mallows (*Malva* spp.) Daylilies (*Hemerocallis* spp.) Lilies (*Lilium* spp.)
Orange to red color	Flat, clustered flowers	Butterflyweed (*Asclepias tuberosa*)
Clusters of tubular flowers	Purple color	Wild bee balm (*Monarda fistulosa*) Meadow phlox (*Phlox maculata*) Brazilian vervain (*Verbena bonariensis*)

Disregard the anti-magenta sentiment popular in some gardening quarters—it's a favorite color for nectar-seeking butterflies like this western tiger swallowtail. If you let tall meadow phlox sow itself, it will eventually revert to the favored butterfly color, no matter what the blossoms of the parent plant look like.

Plant the Rainbow So, should an ideal butterfly and hummingbird garden contain only red, purple, yellow, and blue flowers? Certainly not. Hummingbirds and butterflies generally investigate any spot of their favored colors first, but flowers of other colors are just as welcome for their nectar. Once they find nectar, the color of its "container" doesn't matter in the least to a hungry butterfly or hummer.

When you're trying to boost your flying visitor populations, it makes sense to use the strongest magnet you can. Splash your garden with flowers of their favorite colors—or with decoy objects—interspersed with your favorites. This will strengthen the floral magnetism of all your plantings, no matter what color they are.

Keep in mind that planting clusters of flowers will work best—these creatures seem most attracted by big splashes of their favorite colors, not just single flowers here and there.

COLOR DECOYS An old trick I learned from my mother some 40 years ago is highly effective at tempting hummers and butterflies to your garden. When Mom wanted more hummingbirds to come a-calling, she borrowed some fake flowers from a dusty bouquet that she stored in a hidden corner.

Resort to trickery to bring more butterflies and hummingbirds to your garden! They're so attuned to the nectar signal of colored blossoms that they will investigate any object that flashes the right sign. A purple gazing globe will draw investigating butterflies; a red bandanna does the trick for hummers.

She placed the garish red plastic posies strategically throughout her gardens to draw the birds to blossoms featured in her quiet color schemes. Once the birds homed in on the nectar-less red plastic, they quickly moved on to the real nectar flowers in less gaudy shades of pink, white, and lavender. After a few days, the birds had made the gardens part of their feeding patterns, and my mother rounded up the faux flowers and returned them to the bouquet until next year.

I put the trick to good use every time I want to increase the hummingbird appeal of a new garden. I pick up silk flowers at the thrift store and spread them around—it's a small investment that pays off big-time.

My own butterfly-attracting scheme came about unintentionally. A friend gave me a deep purple gazing globe to add my garden and I created a place of honor for it in the center of my vegetable garden: I placed a low pedestal and the violet globe in the center of sweet white alyssum planted in a diamond shape. Almost immediately, tiger swallowtails began fluttering around the globe, trying to get a purchase on its slippery slope. Were they just trying to get a look at their beautiful selves? No, the color of the globe fooled them into investigating. They soon moved off to a nearby butterfly bush, whose blooms exactly echoed the color of the gleaming glass globe.

The moral of these stories is that if the top-attracting colors are scarce in your garden, don't hesitate to add a colorful piece of sculpture, a red flag, or anything else that will lure butterflies and hummingbirds to your yard for a closer look. Once they arrive, they're sure to find some nectar plants that suit them.

STARTING A BUTTERFLY AND HUMMINGBIRD GARDEN

Before you head for the garden center and load up your car with plants, you'll want to make sure you have their new home ready and waiting. Start small at first, until you get an idea of how much of a garden you can reasonably care for. You may find that your garden beds seem to get bigger and bigger every year as you create more room for other plants you want to try.

Instant Color with Containers
The easiest way to begin is with containers of plants—a hanging basket you pick up on the spur of the moment or an arrangement of annuals in a big pot for the front step. Container gardening is a cinch because it almost completely eliminates the most time-consuming chore of gardening: weeding. Keep in mind, though, that when you grow plants in a container, they're to- tally dependent on you to supply their nutrients and their water, if rain is irregular. Potted plants dry out quickly, so you may need to water as often as once a day in dry weather.

You want plants that bloom for weeks or months in a container, so annual flowers are the way to go. (Most hardy perennials bloom for only about 2 weeks.) Strictly speaking, many popular "annuals"—including impatiens, heliotrope, and ageratum—are really tender perennials, which die in autumn in cold regions only because of the cold, not because their natural lifespan is at an end. Tender perennials are indefatigable bloomers, too.

With all the wonderful already-in-bloom annuals available at garden centers for less than the price of a fast-food meal, there's no need to grow your own. Buying multipacks of plants gives you instant effect, instead of waiting 10 weeks or more for seeds to sprout and grow until they're at the blooming stage.

TOP 10 FLOWERS

Cardinal flower
(*Lobelia cardinalis*)

Attracts hummingbirds
and butterflies

Tall stems of deep red
flowers with pretty
fringed petals

Perennial; Zones 3–9

Easy to propagate
from cuttings

Plant in sun to shade,
in average to wet soil

Blooms late summer
through fall

Many garden centers and nurseries sell pots of flowers that are ideal for hummingbirds and butterflies. But it's easy and fun—and usually cheaper—to exercise your creativity and make your own. You'll need a container, soilless potting mix (read the bag to find out how much you need for your size of pot), and the flowers of your choice. To help feed the plants, mix a scoop of compost with the potting mix.

Tear open the corner of the soil mix bag, add water, and wait until it's absorbed before you pour the moistened growing medium into the pot. Squeeze the sides of the plastic plant packs to pop out each flower and snuggle them into the soil mix. Cram them in together, planting their rootballs closely. Since you'll be supplying fertilizer, you don't have to worry about each plant having enough soil space to satisfy its nutrient needs. Fill the pot with soil mix to about 2 inches from the top, to make a reservoir for watering.

For a container that looks good to your eye as well as to hungry guests, include plants of various growing habits: upright types such as *Verbena bonariensis*, sprawlers such as sweet alyssum, and mounded plants such as 'Lemon Gem' marigolds.

Use the wiggle method to see when the pot needs water—if the soil mix feels dry when you wiggle your finger 1 inch into it, give the pot a generous drink. Fill it to the brim with water, let it drain, and then fill again. Apply an organic fertilizer like fish emulsion at watering time about once a week, or as recommended on the package, to keep your beautiful container collection flourishing.

To enjoy winged visitors at your window, fill a window box with hummingbird favorites such as cypress vine, fuschia, and parrot's beak.

Making a Garden Bed If you have a sunny spot to make your first garden, you're in luck, as most butterfly and hummingbird flowers are best suited for sun. If shade is your lot in gardening life, don't despair. You can still make an appealing planting, though your choices are slightly fewer.

After you decide where you want the garden bed, you'll need to get rid of any existing vegetation. You can smother the grass or weeds with layers of newspaper, chopped leaves, or even old pizza boxes, but that method takes at least a season to kill off the underlayer. I'm not that patient so I use the strip-it method to clear space if I'm making a new bed in what is now lawn. It's a lot faster to do than it is to describe, and it's surprisingly easy. Just loosen the edge of a strip of grass by slicing under it with your shovel in a straight line about 18 inches wide. Then get down on your hands and knees and begin to roll up the grass, exactly as you would do with a rug. Lawn grass has shallow roots that knit together, so once you loosen one part, the rest follows with gratifying ease. Keep a long-bladed weeding tool handy to pry out any dandelions or other deep-rooted weeds that get in the way of stripping off the sod. Repeat the process until you have a bed just the right size for the plants you have chosen.

When the bed is bare, loosen the soil with a shovel, dig in some aged manure or compost to make your worms happy and your plants thrive, and plant your flowers. You can pop potted perennials, annuals, shrubs, and other plants into place. For added fun, grow some plants from seed; many excellent butterfly and hummingbird flowers are foolproof. Sprinkle zinnias, cosmos, bachelor's buttons, cleome, and other fast-blooming annual seeds on loosened, moist soil, cover lightly, and keep weeded. I usually don't bother with weeding until my annuals are about 4 to 6 inches high, because the plants grow so fast they can outrace most competing weeds. Perennials grow much more slowly from seed, so I start them in pots to eliminate weeding chores. I use small plastic pots, recycled from plants I bought for the garden, and fill them with a half-and-half mix of garden soil and potting mix. Then I sprinkle a few seeds into each pot, sift a scant handful of soil over the top, and spray with a fine mist nozzle. I start perennial seeds in spring and keep the pots grouped outdoors, so that I can water them regularly in one fell swoop. In fall, I transplant the perennials to the bed where they will bloom the following spring.

TOP 10 FLOWERS

Goldenrods
(*Solidago* spp.)

Attract butterflies, especially monarchs

Arching yellow-gold plumes

Perennial; Zones 5–9

Spread aggressively; plant on a bank or in a meadow

Plant in sun to shade, depending on species

Bloom summer through fall

Smothering the grass to make a new garden bed, instead of stripping the sod, takes time but not much labor. Because you will be laying down a thick layer of paper that plant roots can't penetrate, you won't be able to plant seeds in a bed like this for at least the first year. It's a fine method for an instant garden of potted perennials or shrubs because you can make individual holes in the layer to pop the plants into.

Take your collection of newspaper and cardboard to the new bed area instead of the recycling center, and lay them out. Overlap the pieces, making sure every inch of space is thoroughly covered. Wet thoroughly with a hose.

In a year, the earthworms and other organisms in the soil will have gotten a good start on recycling the paper into soil, and the vegetation beneath it will be dead or nearly so. If you just can't wait a year to plant the bed, use a sharp-bladed shovel or sharpened trowel (or even a sturdy chef's knife) to cut holes for planting through the layers of paper.

In either case, cover the new bed, with or without plants, with something that looks better than a mass of sodden newspaper. I usually use grass clippings, chopped leaves, or store-bought bark mulch, but aged manure or compost will also work well if you have enough to go around.

The decomposition of the organic paper and mulch layers will make your soil hospitable to the plants, but you can also spread compost around the plants in later years to boost fertility levels. Grass sometimes has amazing regenerative powers, so keep your eyes open for any intruding through the holes where you planted your flowers, and give it a quick, merciless yank.

Something from Nothing: That's Compost

Your new garden will yield a daily harvest of weeds, dead flowers, and other organic debris that can become the basis for better soil, whether you garden in pots or on a half-acre. Combine the leftovers from your garden with the leftovers from your kitchen, add scraps of paper, grass clippings, and anything else that began its life as a plant (no matter how far removed it is in its present form), and you have the basic recipe for making compost, an essential ingredient for healthy, flourishing gardens.

A blanket of compost gives plants all kinds of good things. It supplies some nutrients and it stimulates the activity of organisms in the soil—which are what make nutrients available to plant roots. Compost even gives plants a dose of antibiotics to keep them healthy. The organic

TOP 10 FLOWERS

Butterfly Weed
(*Asclepias tuberosa*)

Attracts butterflies and hummingbirds

Rich orange flowers; cultivars also available in red, yellow, and even pink shades

Perennial; Zones 4–9

Avoid transplanting; grows from a taproot

Plant in full sun, in very well-drained soil

Blooms in summer

A SIP OF SWEET STUFF

Want to get a taste of the sweet stuff that hummingbirds seek? It's simple to do! In case you didn't learn this trick as a child, here's how to sip nectar from a flower.

1. Find a vine of white-and-yellow flowered Japanese honeysuckle. It shouldn't be hard to locate—this vine has become a common weedy presence in many areas.

2. Pick a white flower. (The yellow ones aren't as fresh.)

3. Hold the little green cap at the end of the flower between the thumb and forefinger of one hand, and hold the white tubular part of the flower gently between the fingers of your other hand.

4. Pinch off the green cap with your fingers—not your fingernails—being careful not to pinch through the single white filament attached to the cap.

5. Slowly draw cap and filament (the pistil of the flower) away from the blossom.

6. As you draw the pistil slowly through the flower, it will collect the nectar, which hangs as a bead of liquid at the tip of the flower where you pinched off the cap.

7. Quickly touch your tongue to the nectar drop. Mmm! Delicious!

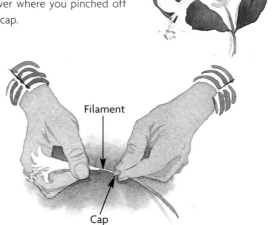

Filament

Cap

---

matter it contains is like dessert for earthworms, which will wiggle up from deeper soil levels to get at the stuff, thus opening up air spaces that make it easier for plant roots to grow.

But there's a selfish reason to make compost, besides the benefits it brings to plants. Turning what had been garbage into something that makes your garden grow will give you a great feeling of personal satisfaction, too.

I'm a big fan of lazy composting, which means I don't even build a layered pile. When I have a handful of just-pulled weeds, I lay them beneath plants in the garden, tucked discreetly out of full view, of course, where they quickly rot back into soil. Ashes to ashes, as they say. Even kitchen scraps get similar treatment: I scatter them beneath a concealing layer of weeds, or pull some soil over them to hide them and hasten decomposition.

Every scrap of stuff that is or once was a plant makes ideal raw material for the compost pile. Leaves, grass clippings, spent plants, potato peelings, newspapers, and the like will undergo a miraculous transformation from unwanted trash to precious compost in just several short weeks—and no, you'll never have too much of this good thing!

If you want to make compost in quantity, then build a pile. It can be a casual mound, or contained in any of the commercial or homemade compost bins and barrels. Nitrogen-based materials, usually green in color, and carbon-rich matter, usually brown, are the main ingredients, layered at about a 1:4 ratio. That means for every inch of fresh grass clippings, weeds, or fresh manure you pile on, add 4 inches of straw, dead leaves, or crumpled strips of newspaper. Don't bother getting out a measuring stick to make sure you're doing it right—your pile will tell you when things are out of kilter. If you notice a whiff of ammonia in the air, add brown materials; if the pile seems to take forever to break down, add more green.

Avoid using any materials in your compost pile that are animal-based, other than eggshells. Meat scraps, bones, and animal fats not only take a long time to decompose, they'll attract visitors you probably don't want to encourage, like flies, rodents, and your neighbor's dog. Keep weeds that have already gone to seed out of your compost pile, too, unless you want to take the risk of inadvertently sowing a patch of pests when you spread the finished compost on your garden.

Keep your pile moist to keep it cooking by spraying it with the hose when rain is scarce. Turn it occasionally with a pitchfork if you want it to cook faster; the air you introduce will encourage the growth of the organisms doing the work of decomposition.

When your former weeds and scraps have transformed to crumbly black soil-like material, your compost is done. Collect the finished stuff, which will be at the bottom of the pile, and give your plants a treat by spreading it around them.

You can use compost on any plant in your garden, from established trees to a bed of annuals. Anything with roots benefits from this versatile and valuable addition.

Perennial Favorites

Perennial flowers are the foundation of any hummingbird and butterfly garden because they return year after year. Many are early bloomers, offering nectar when migrant hummingbirds return or spring butterflies emerge.

While butterflies sample a huge variety of perennials, hummingbirds tend to favor some over others. Salvias are always a prime target. So are columbines (*Aquilegia* spp.), speedwells (*Veronica* spp.), penstemons, foxgloves (*Digitalis* spp.), and delphiniums. Penstemons thrive in the West, but many are finicky for gardeners in other areas. In the East and Midwest, try substituting the oddly named Maryland figwort (*Scrophularia marilandica*). Hummingbirds never overlook this tall plant with small brownish-purple flowers, but humans hardly notice it in the garden until fall, when its seedpods add a delicate touch.

For butterflies, rely on daisies and you can't go wrong. All members of the huge daisy or Composite family are attractive to butterflies. You could fill a garden—shady or sunny, dry or wet—with asters alone and please these winged insects. That might be a little humdrum and far too easy, so dress it up a bit! Add the fluffy spikes and clustered flowers that butterflies adore, like milkweeds (*Asclepias* spp.), goldenrods (*Solidago* spp.), ironweeds (*Vernonia* spp.), and the interesting members of the genus *Eupatorium,* which includes many late-season bloomers like Joe-Pye weed (*E. purpureum*), spotted Joe-Pye weed (*E. maculatum*), and blue mistflower (*E. coelestinum*).

Caring for perennials couldn't be simpler. Once planted, they'll come back reliably year after year. You can snip off faded flowers if you like, which often stimulates another round of bloom if your growing season is long enough. I usually leave seedheads in place because I like the bonus of seedlings that occasionally spring up from fallen seeds. If you garden in a cold climate, you can cut back the frost-killed stems of your perennials in fall or in late winter, before the plants start to push out new shoots at the soil surface. I let mine stand through the winter because I find it more interesting to look at the forms of the dead stems than at bare ground. Leaving the plants standing also helps ensure their own survival by acting as a catch-all for fall leaves, which collect among their stems and insulate the crown of the plant from cold and frost-heaving. Many perennial daisies, as well as other perennials, also attract birds to their seeds through fall and winter.

TOP 10 FLOWERS

Purple coneflower
(*Echinacea purpurea*)

Attracts butterflies

Purple daisies with glowing orange centers

Perennial; Zones 3–9

Tough and reliable

Plant in sun in average soil

Blooms summer through fall

A GALLERY OF BUTTERFLY PERENNIALS

Here's a rundown of examples of perennials that butterflies love, organized by flower shape: daisylike flowers, spiky flowers, clustered flowers, and large single flowers. To attract the widest variety of butterflies, choose some from each group for your gardens or containers.

DAISYLIKE FLOWERS	SPIKY FLOWERS	CLUSTERED FLOWERS	LARGE SINGLE FLOWERS
Asters (*Aster* spp.)	Anise hyssop (*Agastache foeniculum*)	Yarrows (*Achillea* spp.)	Hollyhock (*Alcea rosea*)
English daisy (*Bellis perennis*)	**Delphiniums and larkspurs** (*Delphinium* spp.) (pictured)	Alliums (*Allium* spp.)	Japanese anemone (*Anemone × hybrida*)
Cupid's dart (*Catananche caerulea*)	Blazing stars (*Liatris* spp.)	Thrifts, sea pinks (*Armeria* spp.)	Daylilies (*Hemerocallis* spp.)
Chrysanthemums (*Chrysanthemum* spp.) (pictured)	Cardinal flower (*Lobelia cardinalis*)	**Milkweeds** (*Asclepias* spp.) (pictured)	Hibiscus (*Hibiscus* spp.)
Coreopsis (*Coreopsis* spp.)	Great blue lobelia, blue cardinal flower (*Lobelia siphilitica*)	Astilbes (*Astilbe* spp.)	**Lilies** (*Lilium* spp.) (pictured)
Pinks (*Dianthus* spp.)	Penstemons (*Penstemon* spp.)	Wallflower (*Erysimum cheiri*)	Mallows (*Malva* spp.)
Coneflowers (*Echinacea* spp.)	Selfheal (*Prunella grandiflora*)	Eupatoriums (*Eupatorium* spp.)	
Fleabanes (*Erigeron* spp.)	California fuchsia (*Zauschneria californica*)	Candytufts (*Iberis* spp.)	
Blanket flowers (*Gaillardia* spp.)		Phlox (*Phlox* spp.)	
Helenium (*Helenium autumnale*)		Sedums (*Sedum* spp.)	
Sunflowers (*Helianthus* spp.)		Goldenrods (*Solidago* spp.)	
Mexican hats (*Ratibida* spp.)		Verbenas (*Verbena* spp.)	
Coneflowers (*Rudbeckia* spp.)		Ironweeds (*Vernonia* spp.)	
Scabiosa, pincushion flowers (*Scabiosa* spp.)			
Silphiums (*Silphium* spp.)			

When you see the first signs of life among your perennials in spring, extend your garden by dividing larger clumps into several smaller plants. Many perennials have a gratifying habit of expanding outward as their roots spread. Slice off pieces from the "mother plant" with a shovel, making each division about 4 inches across, and replant separately.

Instant Flowers I love the anticipation of watching perennials inch up from the ground in spring, then slowly grow to full bud and bloom, but I also crave the instant gratification of annuals. There's a huge demand for annuals these days, and garden centers across America are ready to accommodate. You can walk into any garden center and find dozens of different kinds of annuals, all in full flower and ready to be popped into the ground.

No matter what the reason, the ready supply of annuals is great news for hummingbird and butterfly aficionados because annuals are tops at supplying months of nectar flowers. Whether you grow them from seed or yield to temptation and load up the SUV with a dozen flats in full bloom, annuals are unbeatable at supplying instant color. In just a single afternoon, you can transform a bare garden into a bright spot, snuggling colorful annuals into beds, containers, and hanging baskets.

Choose your annuals by the flower structures and colors that hummingbirds and butterflies like, and use the arrangements suggested in Chapter 5 to create the perfect spot. Keep in mind that as far as butterflies and hummingbirds are concerned, any "arrangement" is a good one as long as they can easily reach the flowers. The suggested garden designs in Chapter 7 start with accessibility of nectar flowers, but also include a sensibility to our human sense for aesthetics.

The mission in life of an annual flower is exactly the same as the mission of every other living thing: to perpetuate the species. Annuals do it by cramming as many flowers as possible into their brief one-season lifespan, producing zillions of seeds so that their progeny will have a fighting chance. Once most of their flowers have matured into seeds, their work is over, and the parent plant is ready to retire. For annuals that bloom early in the year, such as bachelor's buttons, that time can come when there's still plenty of good growing time left. The sneaky little trick to keep annuals blooming is to remove seeds as they form. Gardeners call this deadheading, and it works wonders to keep annuals going. Just use your fingers to snip off dead flowers when you see them on your daily garden strolls.

TOP 10 FLOWERS

Columbines
(*Aquilegia* spp.)

Attract hummingbirds and butterflies

Long-spurred blooms in a great variety of colors

Perennial; Zones 3–9

Plant in sun to shade, depending on species

Bloom spring to summer

Nearly all annuals have shallow roots, so you'll need to water them when rain is scarce, unless they're naturally drought-tolerant. Pull out the hose and soak the bed whenever you see the first sign of wilting plants. Annuals usually bloom prolifically without the benefit of fertilizer; in fact, they may bloom better in lean soil.

True annuals—not the tender perennials we often think of as annuals, like impatiens and zonal geraniums—are the easiest plants of all to grow from seed. They reach blooming size in just several weeks. Remember those marigolds you planted in a paper cup for Mother's Day when you were in kindergarten? Teachers know that kids want sure, swift results. If you've never started plants from seed before, try sowing a packet of bachelor's buttons, cosmos, marigolds, cleome, zinnias, or any other true annual. When friends compliment your beautiful garden, just smile and look humble.

Because of their propensity for overcompensation, annual flowers often become a permanent fixture in the garden as seeds dropped from the parent plant sprout the following fall or spring. Self-sown plants are a boon to busy gardeners! Learn to recognize the seedlings so you don't inadvertently smother them with mulch or hoe them off. If they

ATTRACTIVE ANNUALS

Want instant gratification? Try a few of these annuals to lure hummingbirds, butterflies, or both into your garden right away.

ANNUALS FOR HUMMINGBIRDS

Snapdragon
(*Antirrhinum majus*)

Spiderflower, cleome
(*Cleome hassleriana*)

Garden balsam
(*Impatiens balsamina*)

Impatiens
(*Impatiens wallerana*)

Monkey flowers
(*Mimulus* spp.)

Texas sage
(*Salvia coccinea*)

Scarlet sage
(*Salvia splendens*)

ANNUALS FOR BUTTERFLIES

Bur marigold
(*Bidens ferulifolia*)

Shepherd's needle
(*B. pilosa*)

Yellow cosmos
(*Cosmos sulfureus*)

Snow on the mountain
(*Euphorbia marginata*)

Blanket flower
(*Gaillardia pulchella*)

Candytufts (*Iberis* spp.)

Sweet alyssum
(*Lobularia maritima*)

Marigolds (*Tagetes* spp.)

Verbenas (*Verbena* spp.)

ANNUALS FOR HUMMINGBIRDS AND BUTTERFLIES

Annual phlox
(*Phlox drummondii*)

Mealycup sage
(*Salvia farinacea*)

Mexican sunflower
(*Tithonia rotundifolia*)

Brazilian vervain
(*Verbena bonariensis*)

Common zinnia
(*Zinnia elegans*)

come up in dense groups, you needn't bother with thinning the extras—let the plants do the work! They will compete with each other until the strongest survive, while the weaker siblings yield the growing space. If you want to spread out the bounty, transplant some seedlings elsewhere when they are about 4 inches tall. To transplant, carefully pull up a seedling from moist soil after a rain or a watering, make a hole with your finger in moist soil, and tuck in the root of the young plant. Firm the soil around it, give it a drink, and there you go. You can also use a trowel for transplanting if you like.

Permanent Plants Perennials and annual flowers are the prime sources of nectar, but some woody vines, shrubs, and trees also have great nectar flowers for hummingbirds and butterflies. Butterfly bush (*Buddleia davidii*) is a classic butterfly plant, and a red buckeye (*Aesculus pavia*) tree is a favorite of the hummingbirds that frequent my yard. Including permanent plantings in your yard is also important for establishing the flight paths that hummingbirds become accustomed to, and they provide windbreaks and nesting or perching places. In Chapter 5, I'll return to this topic in detail when I describe how you can create a year-round sheltering habitat for hummingbirds and butterflies.

The Benefits of Native Plants A garden filled with well-known butterfly and hummingbird plants will give you many weeks of wonders, but there are plenty of excellent, less-common nectar flowers to discover, too.

A good place to begin branching out is with native plants. Tens of thousands of fine annuals, perennials, shrubs, vines, and trees cloak the wild places of the United States, yet garden centers stock only a small fraction of those. By attending native plant sales and exploring catalogs of nursery specialists, as well as trekking your favorite wild trails, you will uncover some treasures that thrive in your little corner of the world. Take a field guide along when you go exploring in the wild, and jot down the names of the plants you like so you can track them down from commercial growers. Many excellent small nurseries specialize in regional native plants, and larger nurseries and garden centers are beginning to increase their offerings, too.

TOP 10 FLOWERS

Scarlet sage
(*Salvia splendens*)

Attracts hummingbirds

Fire-engine red
flower spikes

Tender perennial
grown as an annual

Excellent in containers
or garden beds; dwarf
cultivars do well in
window boxes

Plant in full sun, in
average to lean soil

Blooms early summer
through fall

A meadow planting offers plenty of open space for dancing wings. Choose a wildflower mix that's made for your area of the country, and you'll discover that many of the plants have great appeal to a large number of butterfly species and to hummingbirds—the pollinators the plants intend to attract.

Avoid the often very strong temptation to pull up a plant from the wild. Remember that other folks may come this way, too, and they will also enjoy seeing it. Unless the area is threatened by development or owned by you or a friend who has given you permission, there's no good reason to decimate the wild stocks of our natural plant treasures when you can buy the same plants for just a few dollars without harming the native populations. Wouldn't you rather enjoy your garden with a clear conscience?

This is particularly true if you live in a desert area, a coastal region, the high mountains, or some other out-of-the-mainstream climate. The bulk of commercially available garden plants featured in catalogs adapt well to the "average" garden—one that isn't plagued or blessed with the vagaries of an intense climate. No matter where you live, you'll find it gratifying to learn about and adopt into your yard and gardens the native flora that flourish naturally in your area.

Each region of the country has its own wild jewels. Mountain gardeners can choose from a slew of penstemons, columbines, and other fanciful native wildflowers. Desert folk can decorate with ocotillo (*Fouquieria splendens*) and prickly pear (*Opuntia* spp.). In the Northwest rain forest, dwellers can enjoy the delights of salmonberry (*Rubus spectabilis*) and fringecups (*Tellima grandiflora*). And these are just the merest scratch on the surface of the American wildflower treasure trove.

NECTAR FEEDERS

You'll love watching butterflies and hummingbirds visiting the flowers in your garden or flitting among the blossoms on the potted plants on your deck and patio. But if you'd like the jaw-dropping experience of seeing a hummingbird at very close range, put out some nectar feeders, too. Serve sugar water in a feeder just outside your window, and you're practically guaranteed great views of visiting hummingbirds. They'll quickly become regular customers, and they may guard their constant food supply like a dog with a bone, chasing off all interlopers.

Serving sugar water for butterflies, on the other hand, doesn't do much good. Nearly all butterflies that seek nectar at flowers are uninterested in nectar feeders. Only those species that take their nourishment at sources other than flowers are apt to be customers at a sugar-water feeder. This guest list includes some real beauties, like the red-spotted purple and the subtly colored question mark, as well as the monarch, which eagerly visits nectar flowers and nectar feeders alike. However, because of inherent difficulties in design, butterfly nectar feeders are usually not a worthwhile addition. Many models actually trap and drown—or damage the wings of—fragile visitors.

Hummingbird feeders are high-maintenance contraptions, but they're worth every bit of bother. You can expect to clean and refill the feeder every 3 days, and probably once a day after you develop a regular clientele.

These feeders are an exception to the old rule, "You get what you pay for." Some of the least expensive models that are available at birding centers are much more fuss-free than the higher-priced designs you can buy from catalogs or "boutiques."

Use common sense when you go shopping for a feeder, and try before you buy. Keep in mind that the tube you're unscrewing in the store will be full of sloshy, sticky sugar water when it's time to do the chore at home. If you can take apart the feeder with a minimum of effort and spill, you've found a good one. If the drinking ports are hard to reach for cleaning, or the whole shebang falls apart in your lap, keep looking.

Types of Feeders Once you start comparison shopping, you'll see that hummingbird feeders come in two basic models. One is the classic vertical tube reservoir, with drinking holes at the bottom. The other is what I call the flying saucer shape, a wide, flattened disk that holds

TOP 10 FLOWERS

Red buckeye
(*Aesculus pavia*)

Attracts hummingbirds

Red to orange-red flowers held in upright clusters

Small tree; Zones 5–8

Grows to 20 feet tall, good for small yards

Attractive foliage

Plant in sun to shade, in humus-enriched soil

Blooms in early spring

water horizontally and seats customers around the rim of the "saucer." Being a klutz, I prefer the vertical model, which I can carry without tilting a trail of sugar water across the floor. A quick twist of the cap and swish with a bottle brush, and I'm ready to refill.

If your fine-motor skills are better than mine, the saucer-type model may suit you to a T. There are no nooks and crannies, so you don't need a special brush to clean the reservoir— a dish sponge will do. And because the holes are above the water, the feeder won't drip on hot summer days. (Heat expansion can cause vertical models to develop a slow drip-drip-drip at feeding ports.) You can also find artsy hummingbird made of glass or ceramic. Opaque models are a frustration because you won't be able to tell when your feeder needs refilling until the lack of hummingbird traffic alerts you.

Putting Out Your First Feeder
If this is your first feeder, don't be shy— buy that big red plastic strawberry-shaped feeder and hang it proudly. The more red, the better is the rule for hummingbirds. Don't worry for now about aesthetics: After the hummers find your feeder, you can replace it with a more discreet model.

Larger feeders need refills less often and accommodate more hummingbirds at one time. Transparent feeders let you see at a glance when refills are needed.

Hummingbirds have become accustomed to feeders all across the country. If the birds are anywhere in your neighborhood, they will instantly adopt a newly hung feeder. If your feeder hangs for longer than a week with no takers, you may have hidden it too well. Move it to a more prominent location out in the open and wait for the action sure to come.

Stick-on window feeders that hang from suction cups are a thrill, especially outside kids' rooms. The suction cups can't support much weight, so the reservoirs are small and they need frequent refilling. However, because the birds drain these so quickly, you won't need to scrub each time you refill. It's easier to carry the sugar water to the feeder in a big measuring cup and fill it on the spot than to carry the tiny filled thing back outdoors, dripping as you go. To save time and effort, refill your feeders outside.

Extra-Sweet Treat

Increasing the sugar-to-water ratio in your nectar solution can put your feeder in the top spot on your area hummingbirds' list of nectar hot spots. If this is your first feeder, or if you're trying to steal the hummingbirds from your neighbor's yard, try a 3:1 solution of water to sugar in the feeder. The sweeter-than-standard mix will definitely hold their attention and keep them coming back for more.

As weather turns cold, flower nectar tends to drop in sugar content as the plant pulls resources into survival, and hummingbird metabolism needs extra fuel to keep that little body warm. During the cold spell you can offer a stronger solution, too, of 3 or $3\frac{1}{2}$ to 1.

Keep the extra-sweet treats for occasional use only. A steady diet may not be the best thing for your hummers' health. Revert back to good old 4:1 after a few days to stay on the safe side.

Feeder Recipes Over the years, I've developed a minimum-effort recipe to mix up a batch of sugar water. One batch makes enough to fill an empty 8-ounce feeder, with a little extra left over that I pour into any feeder that is low. Here's how I do it.

1. Boil water in a teakettle or saucepan.
2. Pour $\frac{1}{2}$ cup of granulated white sugar into a 3-cup, heatproof glass measuring cup.
3. Pour 2 cups of boiling water into the cup. Stir until sugar totally dissolves.
4. Cool, and fill feeder.

The recipe results in a 4:1 ratio of water to sugar, the recommended concentration for hummingbird attraction and good health. If you're mixing a larger batch, just multiply the measurements accordingly: 1 cup sugar for 4 cups of water, $1\frac{1}{2}$ cups sugar for 6 cups of water, and so on.

Don't use honey to make your mix. Hummingbirds reportedly may suffer a tongue fungus from honey—and when your tongue is twice as long as your body, that could definitely be a problem. Stick to sugar, and all will be well.

If you appreciate convenience, and don't mind paying a little extra to get it, look for superfine sugar, sold in well-stocked supermarkets and at restaurant-supply outlets. It dissolves instantly in cold water, saving you the step of boiling the water. You can also buy premixed packets of nectar, at even higher prices, to stir into water.

I'm a penny-pincher, so I go the frugal route and use plain table sugar in my feeders at home. However, when I'm heading for a camping trip, I stock up on nectar mix so I can quickly fill my feeder at the campground—it's a great way to see hummingbirds when you travel to a new place.

COLOR TO DYE FOR Okay, listen up! You've probably heard that red dye in nectar solutions is a bad, bad thing. Perhaps you've even heard that the dye can damage a hummingbird's kidneys. Well, the experts say that's not true. So don't worry—you can relax. The plain truth is it doesn't matter—healthwise—to hummingbirds whether or not you color their water.

Apparently the myth about red food coloring gained headway when Red Dye #2 was pulled off the FDA's list of approved additives to human food several years ago. Suddenly we feared all red dye, and hummingbird nectar caught some of the fallout.

Though red-dyed water may help hummers notice a new feeder more quickly, it really isn't necessary. Recent research has shown that hummers will find nectar even without a big flash of red to steer them to it. A discreet bit of red near the feeding hole is all you need. For more punch, you can wire a fake flower near the opening, but you may not need that, either.

So, if you like the convenience of ready-mix nectar powders and all you can find is the red variety, don't worry. You aren't harming your hummingbirds by using it.

This rufous hummingbird has nothing to fear from the red dye in its sugar water. The rumor of hummingbird ill effects is not supported by scientific evidence.

Crafty Alternatives

Back in the dark ages before plastic, folks fed hummingbirds from just about anything they could rig up. Brown bottles were the container of choice among the naturalists who roamed the Rockies 100 years ago. The original contents of the bottles, possibly Dr. Quack's Cure-All Elixir, didn't matter a bit to the hummingbirds, who later feasted on the sugar water that refilled the bottles.

Test tubes are a time-honored alternative, and still easy to come by from biological supply houses like the ones you'll find listed in "Resources and Recommended Reading" on page 287. See the illustration on the opposite page for details on setting up a test-tube feeder.

When I was a kid, I didn't know you could buy hummingbird feeders, so I made my own from a hamster water bottle. It worked, though poorly. At well-stocked bird supply houses and discount stores, you may find a screw-on cap that converts a clean, recycled plastic soda bottle into a nectar feeder. It may not be the most aesthetically appealing choice, but it's a fun project to do with kids. You can even use a tall, skinny jar, such as olives or cocktail onions come in, to make an impromptu feeder.

If you want to let your inner craftsperson out to play, feel free to experiment with any water-holding containers you like. As long as the nectar is fresh and stirred to the right ratio, hummingbirds don't care whether they're drinking from your prized Waterford crystal or a plastic cup.

Cleaning Your Feeders

Disgusting black gunk builds up quickly around the feeding ports of sugar-water feeders, and sometimes inside the reservoir. This residue is just a slight case of mold, and is easily remedied with a swipe from a bottle brush or other similar scrubbing tool.

Good housekeeping is important because bacteria and other pathogens can build up in the sugary solution and possibly cause ill effects in the birds that feed upon it. You can recycle old toothbrushes or other bristled tools as feeder scrubbers, or pour a few rice grains into your feeder with some water and shake it to remove the gunk. However, for quick and easy cleanup, nothing beats a few specially designed tools. I highly recommend investing in a set of three brushes offered by Duncraft (see "Resources and Recommended Reading" on page 287). You'll save a million bucks' worth of frustration.

Clean and refill your feeder every 3 or 4 days, even if it doesn't look like it needs it. Sugar water can go bad, especially in hot weather, and hummingbirds will then avoid it.

I don't usually bother with soap when cleaning my feeders, but if you use soap, be sure to rinse until the water runs totally clear to remove all residue.

To make a hummingbird feeder out of a glass test tube, wrap wire around the lip of the tube, attach it to a branch, and use a funnel to fill the tube with sugar-water solution.

Make your life easier by investing a few dollars in cleaning tools designed to make feeder maintenance swift and easy. A long-handled bottle brush makes quick work of any scum and mold that may be lurking in the nooks and crannies of a feeder. A few seconds of swabbing, a quick rinse, and you're ready to refill and rehang the feeder.

Success in All Seasons

Nectar feeders are so popular with hummingbirds that you're practically guaranteed a steady stream of customers once you open one for business. So why stop with just one? Hang a feeder in front of every window in the house that you spend time looking out of—the window over the kitchen sink, the window at your desk or sewing table, the window at the breakfast table, the window at your favorite reading chair.

Sugar water is a fine supplement in a garden that has waves of bloom, when nectar flowers may be in short supply. The feeders also help accommodate a rush of birds during migration in spring and fall.

Ask your local chapter of the Audubon Society or a nearby nature center or state park when the hummingbirds tend to arrive in the spring. Here in extreme southwestern Indiana, it's easy to remember. It's a red-letter day, all right: April 15, income tax day. At least the annual ritual of putting out the feeder somewhat softens the blow of the tax collector.

If you live where winters rarely get cold enough to freeze water, leave your feeder up year-round. You may have wintering hummingbirds ranging nearby. In cold-winter areas, keep your feeder up until the sugar water threatens to freeze. You won't prevent hummingbirds from migrating! The birds go when the seasons change and the hours of daylight kick their traveling instincts into gear—not when your feeder runs dry.

Another good reason not to take feeders down early is because some individual birds may be on a delayed flight. Juvenile hummingbirds especially may show up weeks and even months after the bulk of the adult birds have left. A sip of sugar water can save these stragglers' lives, supplying them with crucial fuel for the next leg of the trip.

Simple sugar water may have played a big part in some major changes in hummingbird behavior. Several species are expanding their ranges, and experts attribute it at least partly to the popularity of putting out hummingbird feeders.

Clearly a Danger Make sure your feeder is very close to or safely distanced from windows, or your hummingbirds could literally run into trouble. Head banging is a common, though unpleasant, sport among these fast fliers who may suffer knockout blows—or worse—from colliding with a pane of unyielding glass.

Placing the feeder less than a foot from the window decreases the chances of any fatal encounters because the birds can't build a lot of speed in that short distance. Should new arrivals misjudge the space, you can try to prevent accidents by moving in the opposite direction. Place the feeder at least 6 feet away from the window so that eager beavers won't smack themselves silly.

Other hazards can await hummingbirds that come to your feeders. Don't place feeders near roads, where hummers could run into cars. Keep them away from water, too, where frogs may make a meal of the feathered mites. If you have a pet kitty, keep her in the house. Shoo stray cats whenever you see them, and if you can't keep them away, place your hummingbird feeder in an open area where the birds will be able to spot a stalker.

Recycle a soda bottle into a budget-priced nectar feeder by adding a screw-on accessory, available for less than $5. Yellow "bee guards" deter pesty insects.

TOP 10 FLOWERS

Spider flower,
cleome
(*Cleome hassleriana*)

Attracts hummingbirds

Available in rose,
purple, pink, white,
or a color mix

Annual with a long
bloom season and
interesting spidery
seedpods

Self-sows generously,
producing stout,
branching plants

Plant in sun

Blooms summer
through fall

One of the most curious dangers hummers face is the old-fashioned screen door or window screen. If one of the long-billed birds gets curious about something it spots in the house (probably that red sweater you left on the chair), or if it incautiously fails to notice the screen, it could wind up hanging from its impaled beak. Avoid panic if this happens at your house. Gently hold the hummer's body horizontal with the base of its bill, and have a helper clip the screen to free the bird and avoid damaging its bill.

Nectar Feeders for Butterflies

The nectar flowers you so thoughtfully plant in the garden will attract big swallowtails and dainty hairstreaks, the rapid-flying skippers, the bright coppers, and all the other nectar-flower butterflies. However, many lovely butterflies would rather eat overripe fruit, tree sap, or substances that seem bizarre to our human taste buds, like manure and carrion.

These species that don't visit flowers—including the comma, the question mark, and the red-spotted purple—are the ones you will attract with a butterfly nectar feeder. Monarchs may also sample the fare you offer in a nectar feeder.

Unfortunately, the nectar feeders on the market leave something to be desired. One popular seller, designed to look like a giant daisy, appears to be a sensible feeder at first sight. There's a reservoir for nectar, places to set fruit, and a moat to fill with water to keep out crawling insects attracted to the offerings.

It's the moat that causes the problems. Smaller butterflies manage to get themselves trapped in the space, then flutter their wings madly trying to escape, which results in irreparable damage to those fragile structures. Tragic, and avoidable.

I have my best luck with a simple homemade butterfly nectar feeder. I use a thin, green plastic-fiber kitchen "scrubbie" saturated in sugar water and placed on a plastic saucer nailed to a post. It may not be fancy, but it works. Of course, it also draws swarms of bees, wasps, and ants, but I like watching insects of all kinds and have no deadly allergies to stingers, so I don't mind them.

Until someone invents a foolproof butterfly nectar feeder, stick to alternative offerings when it comes to butterflies. Chapter 4 has lots of suggestions for bringing beautiful non-nectaring butterflies to your yard with safe fruit feeders and other tempting provisions.

Nectar Feeder Wannabes Sweet stuff is a major attraction to many kinds of animals (did somebody say chocolate?) besides hummingbirds and butterflies. Wasps, bees, ants, and other insects love the sticky liquid of a sugar water feeder, and will do everything they can to gain access.

Cheap plastic "bee guards" will keep many insects out of your feeders, but not the ants, which can march right through the holes in these protective grids. To deter ants, you'll need a barricade. Some folks smear their feeder hook with petroleum jelly. If you try this route, use a thick layer at least 3 inches wide; otherwise the ants may form a bridge of bodies to reach the prize you're offering.

ANTI-ANT MOAT

A plastic cap and electric drill (or even an ice pick) are all you need to make a utilitarian ant guard for your nectar feeder. Here's how to do it.

MATERIALS

Plastic cap from a spray bottle of nonstick cooking spray, paint, hair products, or household cleaners
Caulk

---

1. Thoroughly wash and rinse the plastic cap.

2. Drill a $\frac{1}{16}$-inch or smaller hole in the center of the cap, making the hole just wide enough to accommodate the wire of your nectar feeder. Or use an ice pick to puncture a hole in the cap. Aim for a tight fit so that the cap fits securely on the wire and doesn't slide.

3. Thread the wire that's attached to your butterfly feeder through the hole in the cap so that the cap is in an upside-down position a few inches above the feeder.

4. To guard against leaks, dab a bit of caulk around the wire in the hole.

5. Fill the feeder and hang it.

6. Fill the cap with water to create an anti-ant moat.

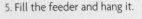

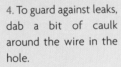

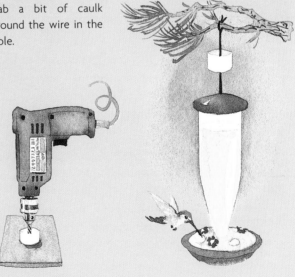

Painted lady butterflies will visit nectar flowers like this ageratum, but they'll also feed at butterfly nectar feeders, either store-bought or homemade.

A better solution—and a less messy one—is to slip a moat between the feeder and the hook. You can buy such an attachment for a few dollars, or make your own as shown on page 51. You can also buy or make a bell-shaped guard, which looks like a miniature squirrel baffle, and coat it with petroleum jelly on the underside to repel those pesky ants.

Hummingbirds don't seem to mind drinking from a feeder that has a few bees or wasps hanging around. I've even watched the birds insert their beaks right through a cluster of drinking honeybees, with no apparent fear on the part of either creature.

Ants, however, aren't acceptable dinner companions to hummingbirds. When these busy insects gain access to one of my feeders, the hummingbirds desert it. I wonder if this might be an instinctive reaction to the fact that ants are predators of young hummingbirds in the nest. Amazingly, when the teeny-tiny babies are newly hatched and helpless, ants may attack and polish them off.

It's not only insects that raid hummingbird feeders. Other determined nectar drinkers are much more of a disturbance. Orioles love nectar, and you can buy special large-capacity feeders just for them. In recent years, other birds including woodpeckers, house finches, wood warblers, and 50 or so other species have become confirmed sugar addicts.

A little sip is one thing, but wholesale guzzling is quite another—and if one of these greedy neighbors finds your nectar supply, you'll find yourself refilling your feeders at a frenzied pace. The sugar water may not be good for these birds, and visits from such large guests mean that hummingbirds can't get to the feeder. When a downy woodpecker or other bird seems to show signs of liking my nectar feeders a little too much, I discourage constant visits by shooing the bird away when I spot it.

You may encounter difficulties from other uninvited guests at your

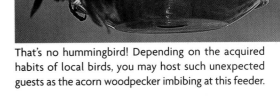

That's no hummingbird! Depending on the acquired habits of local birds, you may host such unexpected guests as the acorn woodpecker imbibing at this feeder.

nectar feeders. Opossums and raccoons may snitch their share occasionally, but these big animals have too hard a time clinging to a feeder to become serious pests.

Though it may be frustrating to have your hummingbird feeders usurped by other birds, insects, or foraging furry friends, these creatures are all just doing what comes naturally. I like to offer a handout to any creature that will take me up on it because it gives me the opportunity for closer observation, as well as the fun of connecting with a wild thing. If you fill your garden with nectar plants as well as nectar feeders, there should be plenty for everyone.

CHAPTER 3

The Lure of

WATER

Supplying places where hummers can sip and splash in the water and puddles where butterflies can soak up moisture will make your garden a magnet for these favored guests. Even though most of their diet is in liquid form, all butterflies and hummingbirds also need water. Hummingbirds will leave the neighbor's nectar feeder to play in your sprinkler. Water features and mud puddles will attract species of butterflies that you don't ordinarily see at your flowers. Most of the anglewings—a group of species that seek out water—dine on sap, fruit, and other nonflower nourishments; flowers and their nectar hold no attraction for them.

Adding butterfly drinking stations can lead to glorious exhibitions when great quantities of butterflies congregate for a drink. A single cloudless sulphur, with its elegant green-tinged yellow wings, is a fantastic sight, but when a dozen of these beauties get together, the effect is breathtaking.

Water features can bring hummingbirds and butterflies close enough to get some great pictures. Set your camera up on a tripod, attach a shutter release cable, and set the camera to focus on the spray or puddle. Then move back a discreet distance to wait for your subjects to arrive. Be sure the camera is out of the path or drift of wet spray to prevent moisture damage.

HUMMINGBIRD DELIGHTS

It was a midsummer morning when I had my first hummingbird-water experience. I was watering plants, using the ineffective but satisfying method of dousing them with sweeps of spray from the hose. As I idly aimed the hose toward a bed of red zinnias, a loud buzz interrupted my reverie and made me duck involuntarily. When I realized it was only a resident hummingbird, I went back to watering.

Almost immediately, the hummingbird was back, and this time he zoomed right through the spray. Making tiny squeaking sounds that I could interpret only as delight, the male ruby-throat swung back and forth through the spray, occasionally wriggling in mid-air as if to better enjoy the bath.

After several minutes of water play, the hummingbird retired to the wire fence where wild morning glories grew in a tangle of abandon. There, he ruffled his wings and chest and preened himself back into shape just like the robins that visit my birdbath.

The bird's antics so charmed me that I went to the nearest store that afternoon to splurge on an oscillating sprinkler—a giant step forward in watering technology for me! A penny-pincher at heart, I turned on the sprinkler for only an hour every morning. My frugality served me well, as I learned later that this was the perfect technique for attracting hummingbirds. The tiny birds are creatures of habit, and the eight birds that regularly visited my yard for nectar quickly became accustomed to the bathing schedule.

Nature's Birdbaths A traditional birdbath is far too deep for a tiny hummingbird. In the wild, these birds find bathing spots that contain just a shallow skim of water. Leaves are a favorite birdbath for hummingbirds. Stroll through your garden after a heavy rain or during a gentle shower and you may spot a hummingbird bathing on a leaf of a shade tree or in a large-leaved shrub.

These bathing beauties use every plant in my garden that has smooth-surfaced leaves that don't shed water instantly after a rain. Slightly concave surfaces and nearly horizontal leaves seem to have the strongest appeal. The young tuliptrees (*Liriodendron tulipifera*) in my Indiana garden with their large, slightly cupped leaves are a favorite impromptu bathhouse for hummingbirds. Hummers also bathe on the leaves of dogwoods, eastern redbuds (*Cercis canadensis*), spicebushes (*Lindera benzoin*), and sugar maples (*Acer saccharum*) around my place.

I don't know how to duplicate the already perfect conditions of naturally wet foliage, so I rely on the real thing. You'll provide plenty of hummingbird bathtubs by including just a few trees and larger-leaved shrubs in your garden; even young trees and shrubs will do the trick quite nicely.

Design a garden with hummers in mind by including a shallow pool and a mister. Splashes, sprays, drips, and gurgles alert hummingbirds to come to the bath. Be sure to set a bench nearby so you can watch their antics as they bathe.

Spritzes and Sprays

Watch how hummingbirds behave on rainy days, and you'll learn how to use water to attract them to your garden. When rain comes in a deluge or with strong winds, there's nary a hummingbird to be seen. The delicate birds know that the force of heavy wind and rain could dash them right out of the air. During a light shower, however, hummingbirds often fly about as if it were a sunny day, with an occasional pit stop to shake water from their ruffled feathers.

To imitate the light showers that delight hummingbirds, shop for devices that provide water in a mist of spray or a spritz of small droplets. You can spend as little as a couple of bucks for a plastic hose nozzle to do the job, or as much as ten times that for a commercial mister head that's tailor-made for hummingbirds. If you have more to invest, a patio misting system that emits sporadic clouds of very fine spray will attract hummingbirds and also keep your outdoor living spaces tolerable in high summer heat.

HOSE NOZZLES Many types of hose nozzle attachments will supply the gentle spray your hummingbirds crave. For a low-tech bath that doesn't require you to hold the hose, you can loop the hose over the crotch of a tree to spray outward or downward; or, lay the hose on the lawn and anchor it with a rock to point the nozzle upward.

Although this water garden is a lovely feature, it won't attract butterflies or hummingbirds to bathe or drink because the water is too deep.

LAWN SPRINKLERS Lawn sprinklers also make fine hummingbird baths. With our raised consciousness about water scarcity—not to mention the ominous ticking of the water meter—no gardener would want to leave a sprinkler running all day. That's no problem, however, as using it for even half an hour at approximately the same time every day will quickly train hummingbirds to arrive at bath time.

Hummingbirds do well with sprinklers that aim their spray in the same direction for several minutes at a time (or until you change the setting). The wildly fluctuating oscillating sprinklers that whip around in every direction aren't a good choice if your goal is to attract hummers.

With many models priced at less than $10, a lawn sprinkler is a low-cost way to set up a summer-long hummingbird bath. Nearby plants will also benefit from the extra water. You can move the sprinkler around from time to time to water various areas of your garden. Hummingbirds will quickly adapt to the new location as long as there is ample room on both sides of the spray for them to fly freely through the spray.

An advantage of lawn sprinklers over hose nozzles and misters is that the spray covers an area large enough to accommodate several hummingbirds at once. During migration and when young leave the nest, your sprinkler may attract several birds at the same time.

COMMERCIAL MISTERS If you want to have some extra fun watching hummers bathe, try one of the innovative water devices designed especially to lure the birds to your yard. Most of these devices consist of a mister head attached to a flexible tube that fastens to your garden hose. In just a few minutes, you can thread on the connections and set up the mister.

Only a little water flows through the mister, so your water bill won't skyrocket. If you have a little mechanical ingenuity, you can even hook up a mister to the recirculating pump in a water garden or small garden pool. That way, water is drawn from the pool, sprayed through the mister, and returned to the pool, losing only a small amount to evaporation or

Games of tag through the spray of a sprinkler may be an everyday occurrence in a hummingbird-friendly yard. Listen for the high-pitched twittering calls of your resident hummers to alert you that the action has begun. In my garden, water play is popular with juvenile birds near the end of summer.

wind drift. Of course, you'll need to aim the mister over the water in the pool so that the spray is also recirculated.

These mist-head attachments vary somewhat in construction and price, but you can figure on spending about $20. Look for them at garden centers and bird-supply stores, or order by mail from the suppliers listed in "Resources and Recommended Reading" on page 287.

WATER FOR BUTTERFLIES

Water can break a butterfly's fragile wings or damage the wing's protective scales, so they steer clear of deep or rushing water. A butterfly bath should be just a foot deep—a butterfly's foot, that is, not yours!

Entice butterflies with shallow watering holes. Use your creativity: A thin film of water on a garden wall, mud puddles, and a slight indentation on your patio filled with rainwater all can be havens for thirsty butterflies.

The Pavement Trick
A few years ago I accidentally discovered an easy way to supply butterfly water. It was a mild, windless midsummer's day—perfect butterfly weather. After an unaccustomed bout of weeding on a brick patio, I turned on the hose to wash away

the debris on the bricks. Before I had even finished washing the patio, I noticed gorgeous red admiral butterflies alighting on the wet bricks behind me. Several red-spotted purples soon joined them with their wings wide open as they drank, showing their lovely blue-splashed black velvet topsides and hiding their red-spotted purple undersides.

Spritzing a walkway or patio—whether it's made of concrete, tile, or gravel—takes just seconds and will attract butterflies as long as the moisture remains. After my initiation into butterfly watering, I made it a habit to wet down the pavement every afternoon so I could sit back in my lawn chair and watch the action.

Saucer of Stones

Because large expanses of pavement collect solar heat in a hurry, causing a thin layer of water to dry as quickly as a just-washed blackboard, I experimented with other methods to find a longer-lasting butterfly drinking station. The most successful was another simple solution—a clay plant saucer filled with river stones and gravel. I soaked the stones, allowing a bit of water to collect in the bottom of the saucer but making sure the tops of the stones were

This red-spotted purple butterfly may look like it's nectaring, but in fact it's just basking in the sun. Uninterested in nectar, it will quickly come to wet paving or puddles.

A cluster of butterflies at a wet spot is called a "puddle club." Here, sulphurs take advantage of the moisture and nutrients they can extract from the damp earth. Tiny blue butterflies, red admirals, and big, beautiful swallowtails are other top clients at bare-dirt puddles. A bit of manure mixed in makes it even more inviting.

exposed for perches for the butterflies. Then I placed the saucer in a partly shaded area to slow down the sun's drying action.

The butterflies that frequent my yard soon learned where they could find a steady water supply. Because the stones hold moisture overnight, I can count on finding the saucer splashed with colorful visitors when I make my morning garden rounds.

Water doesn't interest all butterflies, but enough species seek water to make it worth investing a few dollars in a container and 5 minutes in filling it. You may see admirals of several kinds, plus representatives of the anglewing family: tawny emperors, golden-brown questionmarks, and pert little hackberry butterflies. Red-spotted purples and classic monarchs also alight.

The Mud Puddle Scene

A dirt road that's pocked with potholes is prime butterfly-watching territory after a rain. Wherever a pothole holds water or mud, butterflies are likely to congregate. Watch butterflies at a mud puddle, and you'll see their delicate proboscises probing the mud just as if they were searching for nectar in a flower. The butterflies ingest both the water that's in the mud and small amounts of minerals from the wet earth.

Dozens of species of tiny blue butterflies, plus bright yellow and orange sulphurs and pristine whites, are regulars at the damp dirt social hall. Many stunning swallowtails visit puddles, and tiger swallowtails are particularly common mud-puddle patrons. I've seen spectacular groups that included all species of the "black" swallowtails native to my area—

spicebush, black, and pipevine swallowtails, as well as dark-phased female tigers—all drinking side by side. Monarchs, red-spotted purples, and admirals may also partake.

Observing the clientele at a mud puddle is a great way to get to know butterflies. They sit still for long periods, allowing you plenty of time to thumb through your field guide and pin down an identification—not to mention practice your photography skills.

More Wet-Soil Attractions
In nature, butterflies gather at the edges of lakes, streams, and even along sandy beaches—wherever the soil is wet with water and nutrients. Here are some other hints for creating a wet spot that will attract butterflies.

- If your garden includes a constructed or natural stream, create a small area along its banks that will resemble a butterfly's natural haunts. Remove vegetation, add sand to lighten the soil if you like, and let the watercourse saturate the soil.
- Resist the urge to sweep collected water from around your pool. Your local butterfly puddle clubs may adopt areas at the perimeter of the swimming pool where water splashes out when people jump in.
- Let the faucet drip a little. An impromptu mud puddle often forms beneath a busy garden faucet between filling watering cans and buckets.
- Fill your birdbath often. Another potential butterfly hot spot is beneath the pedestal birdbath because of frequent cleaning and refilling.
- Make the most of any wet place in your garden by stripping the plants from the soil surface so that the mud is freely available to winged visitors. If you need to navigate the area yourself, settle a few stepping-stones for a mud-free path.

GUESS WHO ELSE MAY COME TO CALL

With a hummingbird spray or mud puddle set up in your yard, you'll probably attract other fascinating guests besides hummers and butterflies. Look for robins, hermit thrushes, bluebirds, and many other birds. I rig up one of my fine-mist hummingbird heads so that it sprays over a pedestal-type birdbath; hummers fly through the spray, while songbirds enjoy a bath-with-shower combo.

Several species of wasps may visit your mud puddles to collect the raw materials to make homes for their larvae. You may feel a tad nervous about the idea of attracting wasps to your yard. The fact is, wasps will rarely bother you unless you interfere with their work. Keep a respectful distance of at least 2 feet from their workplace, and they are unlikely to threaten you. Before you bend for a really close look, watch for a few minutes to see in what direction their flight path lies. Position yourself out of the line of traffic, and keep a careful eye on the insects. If they train their uncanny gaze on your face, that's a signal to back off.

BUTTERFLY SOCIAL CLUB

Making a mud puddle can be as simple as excavating a depression and watering it often to keep the mud wet and inviting. If you want to save yourself the trouble of frequent mud puddle waterings, you can make a more permanent feature by burying a shallow receptacle beneath the soil. If you build your puddle in midsummer, the height of butterfly season, you may have clients the very first day.

MATERIALS

Shallow plastic lid from a storage box or trash can
Sand
Water

---

1. Select a sunny site surrounded by open lawn or near the edge of an open patio area. To have the best chance of attracting butterflies, the spot should have a clear approach from all angles.

2. Remove the sod or other vegetation from an area about 3 feet in diameter. If you're taking out sod, just slip a shovel blade beneath the roots along one edge, and peel back.

3. Dig a hole just deep enough to accommodate the lid, but leave the rim barely exposed. This will prevent the surrounding soil from wicking away the moisture in your mud puddle.

4. Settle the container into the depression so that it is fairly level. Adjust the depth of your hole if necessary.

5. Mix sand with the soil you removed from the hole to achieve a light consistency of about half-and-half. If your soil is naturally light, use less sand; if your soil is clay, pour in the sand with a liberal hand.

6. Fill the lid with the mixture of sand and soil. Make a slight depression (about 2 inches deep) in the center, and gradually taper the soil level until it almost reaches the top of the rim around the edge of the lid. Keep the rim barely exposed.

7. Turn your hose nozzle to a medium-strong spray and sat-urate the soil in the lid until it's as wet as a very moist sponge.

8. Position a garden bench near the puddle so you can enjoy the view when butterflies discover the new spa. A mud puddle is a great place to practice butterfly binocular viewing, or to photograph your visitors.

You'll need to re-soak the puddle from time to time to keep the mud well moistened—but don't keep it soaking wet. Butterflies prefer a more solid footing as they line up along the edges of a wet mud puddle.

Sand-soil mix   Plastic lid

CHAPTER 4

Tempting Butterflies with

TREATS

Not all butterflies get their nourishment by delicately sipping nectar from flowers. Many species meet their needs for nutrients by dining on overripe fruit and items that people prefer to avoid thinking of as food. As W. J. Holland wrote in the 1916 *Butterfly Book,* "Some insects have very peculiar appetites and are attracted by things loathsome." Those things include sweat, manure, and animal carcasses. Don't worry, though: You can attract these butterflies to your yard quite easily—without having to put up with a manure pile.

Serving up simple fruit feeders and planting fruiting plants will attract beauties like the red-spotted purple and tawny emperor to your yard. Butterflies will feast on almost any kind of fruit, large or small, sweet or tart. Even that rotting fruit on your counter is a tasty treat to a fruit-loving butterfly. They'll also feed on sap and fungi. You may serve as a butterfly feeder yourself on a hot day in the garden as hackberries and red emperors alight on you for a delicate sip of sweat when beads of perspiration collect on your bare skin.

THE NUTRIENT NICHE

Rotting fruit and other repulsive items may not be our idea of a tempting menu, but nature wastes nothing. All materials that are organic in origin contain the basics of life-sustaining nutrition—carbohydrates, proteins, and (in some cases) fats, plus a complement of trace elements. While we may turn up our noses at manure, many insects have no qualms about eating it to provide their bodies with necessary nutrients and liquid.

The ethereal flight and exotic beauty of butterflies are entrancing, but remember: These extravagant winged creatures are really just insects in dress-up clothes. Like their relatives, the flies, wasps, and beetles, many butterflies are just as fond of the sweet or fermented juices and the liquefying flesh of decaying pears, apples, crabapples, melons, and just about any other fruit you can name.

Think about it—in the wild, rotting fruit would soon bury the trees it fell from if it didn't decompose. By extracting liquids from the fallen crop, butterflies and other insects aid in the decomposition process—which is just a basic form of recycling! Ashes to ashes, dust to dust, and rotting fruit to butterfly body; it's a miraculous system.

Showing the bright markings that give it its name, a red-spotted purple butterfly finds a soft spot in a pear skin to insert its proboscis and sip sweet juice.

Fruit for Butterflies No butterfly garden should be without fruit. This sweet, juicy food is amazingly popular with some butterflies. I've seen monarchs and red admirals cross desolate stretches of a shopping mall parking lot just to reach the fallen fruit of a single crabapple tree.

Any fruit you have on hand will attract feeding butterflies, as long as it's very ripe or, even better, rotting. In my southern Indiana garden, the butterflies prefer pears, apples, crabapples, and bananas. They'll also sample other offerings, including fruits that grow on vines and bushes like grapes, berries, melons, and tomatoes.

The riper the better is the rule when it comes to feeding fruits. Butterflies have a hard time eating solid foods. Overripe to rotting fruits are more appealing because of the juice and soft, deteriorating flesh. Slice a fresh pear for the fruit feeder, and it may draw only one or two butterflies. But let that pear sit until it looks like unappetizing brown mush, and it's likely to become a magnet for fruit-eating butterflies.

I discovered the butterfly appeal of watermelon when I was carrying a leaking half-melon to the compost heap from the refrigerator, where it had outlived its welcome. Before I took five steps from the kitchen door, I had monarch butterflies fluttering around my heavy offering. The smell so ex-

Fruit holds great appeal for red-spotted purples, red admirals, and other nonnectaring butterflies, whether it's on the ground, in a feeder, or on the tree.

cited them, apparently, that they alighted even while I was still carrying the melon. Ever since, I have included watermelon in my summer fruit feeders.

I use the sniff test to gauge butterfly appeal. If the fruit smells "off" to my nose, chances are the butterflies will adore it; if it holds that sweet, sickly smell of fermentation, it's even better! Butterflies' preference for rotting fruit is a budget-saver for us. Most supermarkets will give you fruits that are past their prime for human consumption at very low cost or for free. Plus, you won't feel so guilty about wasting that last banana or letting the cantaloupe sit on the counter a few days too long if you share the overripe bounty with your garden guests.

I was feeding fruit to butterflies in my childhood, though it wasn't until later that I realized it. When I was a kid, the neighbor boy and I would sling leftover tomatoes from the garden; first at the shed wall, then at each other. The rottener, the better, was our motto, and how we reeked afterward! Yet after our tomato wars, the scene of the crime was always alive with butterflies fluttering at our homemade "catsup." Little did we know we had provided a perfect all-you-can-eat buffet for the winged crowd.

FRUIT PLANTS FOR BUTTERFLIES You can encourage more butterflies to visit your garden by adding fruit trees and bushes. The butterflies will eagerly eat overripe fruit directly from the branches, or snack upon it on the ground.

One summer I inadvertently turned my compost heap into a giant butterfly feeder. Brown rot, a disease that turns fruit all brown and mushy, had infected my peaches. Counting the crop as lost, I raked up all the dropped peaches and dumped the wheelbarrow loads of fruit on the compost heap to add to the mix. The next day, when I flung an armful of weeds onto the heap, I startled an entire tribe of colorful butterflies. They took to the air in alarm, momentarily forsaking the fruity feast when the weeds sailed toward them.

If your tomatoes crack in the garden after a spell of heavy rain, keep an eye out for butterflies visiting the fruit. Lovely question marks with their tawny wings and delicate lilac edges favor tomatoes; so do hackberries, tawny emperors, and other anglewings.

Plants that hold their fruit even after it's ripe help you keep the garden tidy and still feed the butterflies. Many apple cultivars, especially old-fashioned heirloom types, keep the apples on the boughs well into winter. Crabapples, too, may stay on the tree rather than litter the ground. Small brown Seckel pears hold their harvest for a remarkably long time as well. The fruit may remain on the branch so long that it creates a different kind of feeding station for butterflies—the neighborhood saloon.

TOP FRUIT PLANTS FOR BUTTERFLIES

Apple
Banana
Cantaloupe
Cherry, sweet or sour
Fig
Grape
Nectarine
Pawpaw
Peach
Pear
Persimmon
Tomato
Watermelon

Whether fermented on the tree or on the ground, alcoholic fruit is a big hit with butterflies. It's easy to tell whether your fruit has fermented just by watching the behavior of the butterflies dining upon it. If they sit still without flying away when you come close, they're probably drunk. Inebriated butterflies may also bumble into each other or blunder into the fruit when coming in for a landing. It's a good thing they're not behind the wheel!

One of the best butterfly fruit trees is the American persimmon (*Diosporos virginiana*), which bears a heavy crop of small, round, orange fruits in fall. It's also a favorite with the fruit-loving birds called cedar waxwings. When the waxwings settle onto a branch of my persimmon tree, they dislodge the tawny golden orange anglewing butterflies into a clear blue autumn sky. Glorious!

Fruit Feeders

Simple homemade contraptions are perfectly adequate for serving butterflies their daily fruit. My favorite device costs about 10 cents from my favorite thrift shop. I buy a plastic dinner plate or saucer, and screw it to the top of a flat-topped post, a deck railing, or a fence in a shady spot, and serve up the fruit. You will get the best view of your feeder guests if you put the feeder close to eye level.

Start your fruit feeding sparingly. A single pear cut in half or a leftover slice of watermelon is plenty for starters. Once butterflies discover your offerings, you can increase the amount and variety. I like to offer a sampling of various fruits to see which attract the most species and which kinds the butterflies visit most often.

OTHER VISITORS Other insects will also swarm to overripe and rotting fruit. If you've ever had to shoo away yellow jackets from a Labor Day picnic, you know that wasps are fond of fruit. So are ants, beetles, flies, and other six-legged creatures.

Setting up a fruit feeder can be the start of a consuming interest in entomology (the study of insects). Dining insects focus intently on eating and usually allow you to observe them closely, a fascinating study for grownups and kids alike. Watch the

Watermelon is a real picnic for a mob of butterflies. Hackberries, commas, question marks, red admirals, and red-spotted purples may come for lunch.

trail of ants leading to the feeder and you'll see that those returning to the nest have abdomens swollen to translucence with fruit juice, while those just arriving are their normal, svelte selves.

Moths may visit your fruit feeder after dark. Take a flashlight and investigate in the evenings to see what you find lurking at that rotten banana. You'll be delighted to discover that tiny moth eyes shine in the dark. If you see triangular moths with mottled gray

BUTTERFLY FRUIT FEEDER

Even if you've got only 10 minutes to spare, you've got time to set up this easy fruit feeder for butterflies!

MATERIALS

Plastic plate

2- or 3-inch galvanized, brass, or stainless steel round-headed screw

Galvanized, brass, or stainless steel washer

Flat-topped wooden post, about 5 feet long

1. Drill a hole in the center of the plate to accommodate the screw. (Keep the plate flat on a board as you drill to help prevent splitting.) Also drill a starter hole in one end of the post.

2. Dig a hole in your lawn or garden and install the post about 12 inches deep, packing dirt firmly around the base.

3. Set the plate on the post. Insert the screw through the washer and into the hole and tighten the screw. Be careful not to overtighten or you may break the plate.

4. Set a few pieces of fruit on the plate, well separated.

or brown wings, you probably are hosting some of the magnificent group called under-wings. Gently lift a wing and you may get a peek of brilliant red, orange, or yellow decorated with snazzy black stripes.

The sweet smell of rotting fruit may attract beetles at night, too. The eyed elatior beetle is a regular visitor at my fruit feeders. This interesting character sports a pair of startling white-rimmed eyespots on its gray wings.

If you wish, use a homemade bee guard like the one shown on the opposite page to keep stinging insects away from your fruit feeder. (Once they discover that they can't reach the fruit, bees and wasps will go elsewhere to look for food.)

FRUIT FEEDER MAINTENANCE Eventually even the most delicious rotten fruit loses its appeal. When all that remains is a curled, dried-out husk of the original offering, it's time to clean house. I do a weekly cleanup of my fruit feeders, mostly for the sake of appearances, by using a strong stream from the garden hose to wash off leftovers. I remove the remaining residue with a swish of my hand over the wet plate, and it's ready to receive its next delectable offering.

Dishwater gray when their wings are closed, *Catocala* underwing moths reveal breathtaking color when they show what lies beneath, a good reason to check your fruit feeders with a flashlight after dark. Slow to take alarm, underwing moths like this *Ilia* species remain feeding while you feast your eyes.

FEEDER INSECT GUARD

A piece of window screen guarding the fruit in your fruit feeder will frustrate any insects with small mouthparts. Butterflies can extend their proboscis through the guard to find the fruit, but the bees and wasps won't be able to reach! (Ants may still be a problem.)

MATERIALS

Fiberglass window screening
Strip of ½-inch mesh hardware cloth, 3 inches wide
Twist-ties or pieces of flexible wire
Duct tape

1. Measure the perimeter (around the edge) of the plate.

2. Cut a strip of hardware cloth to the length of the perimeter, plus 2 inches.

3. Bend the hardware cloth into a circle, overlapping the ends an inch. Hold the ends in place with twist-ties or wire.

4. Cut a piece of screening large enough to wrap over and around the edges of the hardware cloth circle.

5. Stretch the screening over the circle of hardware cloth.

6. Wrap screening over the edges of the hardware cloth circle. Use duct tape to fasten the screening to the inside edges of the circle. Trim the excess.

7. Set the bee guard over the filled fruit feeder.

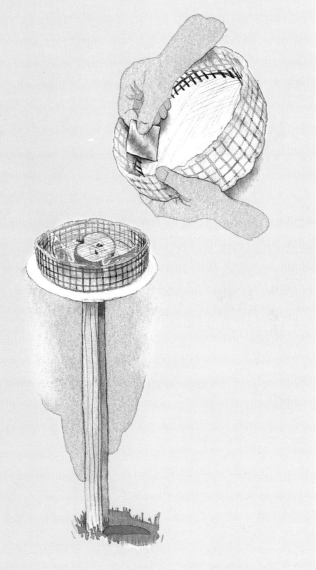

The lovely and common question mark butterfly will spurn your flowers, but you may spot it sipping sap from a freshly cut tree stump or where sap trickles from a live tree. Look twice to find such visitors; when their wings are closed, the dull undersides are very hard to see against wood or bark.

Sap Faintly sweet to the human palate, tree sap is a huge draw for the same butterflies that adore fruits. It also attracts hummingbirds and songbirds, as well as a host of interesting insects.

You can't mix up a bowl of sap to offer butterflies, but you may have seeping sap on trees in your yard. Insect injuries, frost damage, even that place where the lawnmower nicked your precious weeping cherry tree may inadvertently offer an inviting reservoir or trickling path of sweet stuff.

I inherited an ancient chinquapin oak in the yard of my first home in Indiana. The electric company thoughtfully volunteered to cut the old dowager to the ground, but I declined. I didn't know how long the tree would live, but it was certainly worth keeping around as long as possible. The injuries it had accumulated with age made it an ideal draw for many of my favorite garden visitors.

Every year, a sap flow formed where someone had awkwardly lopped off a branch years before. At first glance, a passerby would notice nothing. If you stood beneath the tree for a few minutes, however, and looked up at the darker bark where sap had leaked, you could pick out the well-camouflaged wings of scores of feasting butterflies.

My current yard has its own special sap tree—a sugar maple that leaks sap every spring from a place about 5 feet up the trunk. Comma butterflies emerge early here, and we see them daily, clustered on the wet bark, probing the crevices with their unfurled proboscises to suck up the sweet stuff. Flies and myriad tiny insects often join the lovely commas.

After a few days of spring sunshine, the sugar maple sap ferments into an intoxicating brew, and the behavior of the insects changes along with the formula. Watching them is like watching a bar empty out at 3 A.M.—they literally stagger up and down the trunk, or fly off in a muzzy, unfocused flight, alighting on the first object they can to try and regain a sense of balance.

Oddball Foods

Fungi, manure, carrion—mmm! The complete list of butterfly foods would never show up on a human menu. Despite their loathsome appearance to human eyes (not to mention taste buds), you can still include such taste treats somewhere in your yard for the enjoyment of your winged visitors.

MANURE Don't worry; I'm not going to encourage you to set up a manure feeder to attract butterflies—although it would be very popular with the fluttery-winged set. Most gardeners are a bit too squeamish to purposely place a bowl of horse manure or other excreted

An Unusual Lunch Date

One of the most incongruous cases of mistaken identity I've witnessed was an interaction between a group of caterpillars and a hungry red admiral butterfly. The caterpillars were one of the many types whose appearance mimics the appearance of bird droppings to foil predators. (Unfortunately, the identity of those bird-dropping caterpillars remains a mystery. I haven't yet found a picture or description of them in any reference; field guides to caterpillars are necessarily less than comprehensive, because of the number of butterfly and moth species. But I'm still looking.) Some butterflies, however, including the red admiral butterfly, enjoy a sip of fresh bird excrement now and then. One afternoon I saw a lovely red admiral land directly on a caterpillar. The caterpillar thrashed about,

causing the butterfly to flutter off quickly, but it soon returned to try again. Over and over the scene was repeated until the caterpillar, apparently tuckered out, simply sat quietly when the admiral landed on top of it.

With delicate touch, the butterfly began to probe the plump "dropping" with its proboscis, apparently searching for a bit of accessible moisture. When it could find none, it flew to the next caterpillar in the group, and the scene started again. After two separate learning experiences, the red admiral gave up and flew off, probably shaking his little butterfly head in confusion.

That's the fun of observing the butterflies in your yard. When one alights or flutters about a particular spot, check it out. You may have the good fortune to be in the right place at the right time to see something intriguing.

delicacies near the patio. (If you don't care what the neighbors will think, feel free to give it a try. You'll get some fabulous customers!)

Even if you don't deliberately create a manure feeder, your yard no doubt already includes this tempting delicacy. Perhaps you can't sneak a horse or cow onto your suburban half-acre, but chances are good that you already have a smaller furry pet. The deposits of pet dogs and cats are a popular source of butterfly food in backyards.

If there is no Fido or Kitty at your home, don't despair. The fresh, wet droppings of songbirds fill the bill for many nutrient-seeking butterflies.

CARRION It might suit our sensibilities to think of carrion as meat juices, rather than lifeless creatures. Carrion-eating butterflies are simply seeking meat juices, albeit in a more pungent form, when they swarm on dead animals. As decomposition hastens the breakdown of animal tissues, butterflies flutter in to dine with gusto.

One of the best places to observe butterflies in the wild is at roadkill. Admirals, redspotted purples, hackberries, emperors, question marks, commas, and others alight in astonishing numbers upon the sad victims of our roadways.

You can offer meat scraps for butterflies in a tray-type bird feeder and protect them from marauding raccoons and cats by placing a wire or plastic grid over the food. Butterflies will perch on the grid to feed, extending their proboscises through the holes.

You won't want to keep carrion in the garden, of course, but if you'd really like the chance to observe carrion-eating butterflies in your yard, putting out meat scraps is a reasonable alternative. Fish is especially appealing, too.

A little goes a long way in such a feeder. Overgenerous servings—more than a drumstick or single fish tail at a time—quickly become odoriferous. Place such a feeder as far as possible from any area where family and friends regularly gather to avoid offensive aromas interfering with human activities. But don't forget to check the feeder frequently to see who's coming to dinner, and discard any leftovers in a day or two.

FUNGI There's a fungus among us, and it's a good thing—or the early-season butterflies would have a tough time of it. Few, if any, blossoms are in bloom when the mourning cloak emerges after a long winter's nap beneath a scrap of bark. Perhaps this butterfly doesn't frequent nectar flowers because of the timing of its life cycle, or it may be that its life cycle is timed so that it doesn't need to depend on nectar flowers. Either way, mourning cloaks manage to find food even if they emerge during an unseasonable warm spell in December. Although they depend largely upon last season's fruit and sap, they also eat fungi. Other butterflies may also occasionally visit fungi.

This doesn't mean you need to rush out and buy a mushroom-growing kit, but you can appreciate the variety of fungi that sprout naturally in your yard. The uniquely repulsive stinkhorn fungus, with its red-tipped phallic form and slimy coating, holds a certain allure to some species of butterflies. I have seen hackberry butterflies perched on the smelly growths. More aesthetically appealing fungi, including those that colonize dead wood and the slime molds that crop up on wood chip mulch, are also added to the menu on occasion. You can encourage the crop of fungi in your yard by importing a dead log or stump, or by not removing a dead tree (unless it's a hazard, of course, in which case go ahead and call in the chain saw). Fungi breed well in wood chip mulches and shade gardens with humus-rich soil as well.

CHAPTER 5

The Sheltering

GARDEN

Once you have nectar flowers, feeders, and water available in your yard, you're sure to have some butterfly and hummingbirds stop for a visit. The next step is to make your yard a year-round sheltering haven for these lovely winged creatures.

In Chapter 2, we covered the ins and outs of starting flowerbeds and planting nectar plants. There's lots more you can do to make your home landscape more attractive to butterflies and hummingbirds, and plants are the key to any plan. I recommend that you turn your attention to plants that do double- or triple-duty for butterflies and hummers—that is, plants that provide both food and shelter, or that produce both nectar for butterflies and tasty foliage for caterpillars.

The pretty native shrub called spicebush (*Lindera benzoin*) will feed the caterpillars of the appropriately named spicebush swallowtail, as well as serving as a windbreak or shade provider. The humble, easy-to-grow nectar flower common zinnia (*Zinnia elegans*) draws both butterflies and hummingbirds to its banquet.

In this chapter, I'll explain how you can design natural windbreaks that will protect butterflies and hummingbirds from strong gusts, as well as plantings to provide welcome areas of shade. I'll tell you about plants and constructions that provide roosting spots at night or during bad weather, and how to design areas that invite butterflies to hibernate.

EVEN DUMMIES CAN DESIGN!

Don't let the word "design" make you shake in your boots! When you're designing features or gardens for hummingbirds and butterflies, the only qualification you need is common sense.

I've learned four simple guidelines that lay the groundwork for creating a landscape to welcome both hummingbirds and butterflies to your garden.

1. Plant as many nectar flowers as you can shoehorn in—in beds, pots, and hanging baskets. If you've already read Chapter 2, you know all about planting nectar flowers. If you haven't, check it out! It starts on page 20.

2. Include open areas of flowers and grass or paving for unimpeded flight and access to sun.

3. Create islands, groups, and windrows of shade and shelter plants, including a few native shade trees, to act as havens from hot sun, heavy wind, and driving rain. These plants will also supply caterpillar food and hummingbird bathing and nesting sites.

4. Leave sites for overwintering. If you live in an area with cold winters, be sure there are plenty of sheltered spots where caterpillars or pupae can survive the cold safely.

WIDE OPEN SPACES

One thing all butterflies and hummingbirds need is room to fly. Although there are some butterflies and hummingbirds that frequent wooded areas, most species like to hang out where there's open space.

The spicebush swallowtail (*top*), once called the green cloud, will soon adopt any garden within its range that includes its host plant, spicebush (*above*).

Open space not only allows for free flight, it also creates a sunny area, the condition in which most nectar plants flourish best. So it makes sense to site your nectar flowerbeds in the open areas of your yard, where sunlight pours down for at least 6 hours a day. Hummingbirds and butterflies also particularly like sunny areas during spring and fall, when they need to warm up quickly after a chilly night.

Sunlight for Energy

Butterflies are cold-blooded—which means that the temperature of their body fluctuates with the temperature of the air around them. In spring, you'll rarely see butterflies on the wing before late morning because it takes them some time to warm up after a cool night. In summer, they may be busily at work in the garden as early as 7 A.M., thanks to the warmer nights and the increased strength of the morning sun.

Hummingbirds, too, have a metabolism that's sensitive to temperature fluctuations. Although they're warm-blooded, their bodies require the warming energy of sunshine to help fuel them in their activities. With their superfast metabolism—higher than any other animal on earth, with the possible exception of the notoriously hyper shrew (pictured at right)—they burn calories like lightning. The energy they would use up to keep their bodies warm is too precious to waste, so they wait until the sun warms the air before they venture out. During cold periods, they are apt to huddle in a state called torpor, in which their body processes slow down to conserve that precious energy.

Leave Some Lawn It may be fashionable to scoff at lawns these days, but a lawn area or meadow planting is an asset in the butterfly and hummingbird garden. The grassy spot provides an open flight corridor for winged visitors traveling from one patch of flowers to another. Open areas also provide a good place to situate sprinklers or misters (see Chapter 3), butterfly drinking stations, and basking areas (see Chapter 8 for more on basking). Patio areas serve the same function; just be sure that you position any attractors away from reflective doors or windows to prevent accidental collisions.

Your driveway and parking area—spaces you might not consider part of your actual garden "design"—can also be a flight corridor. Streets and sidewalks also function as open space in the total garden picture. Border these areas with beds of bright flowers, and you'll have a steady stream of nectar seekers.

Open space doesn't need to be free of obstructions all the way to ground level. Hummingbirds zip along at head height or above, while many butterflies flap through at waist-to neck-high (that's using my own 5-foot, 4-inch body as a yardstick). Thus, if you add a bed or border of plants—or even a 4-foot fence in some areas—it will still be useful open space for butterflies and hummingbirds.

(continued on page 84)

A BORDER OF PLANTS FOR OPEN SPACES

Adding a flowerbed or border along the edge of an open lawn area—or even along your driveway—creates a great combination for butterflies and hummingbirds: room to fly, and stuff to feed on. Here are some good plants for a sunny bed with average, well-drained soil. All are easy to grow.

ANNUALS

PLANT	DESCRIPTION	BEST FEATURES	COMMENTS
Dahlias (*Dahlia* spp.)	Dwarf to neck-high branching plants with abundant foliage and daisy-type flowers in a rainbow of hues. May survive winter in Zones 8 and south.	Nectar flowers for butterflies and hummers; shelter, perching	Grow in full sun. Stick to cultivars 2 feet tall or less for open areas to allow easy access. Plant simple daisy types to attract the most visitors.
Impatiens (*Impatiens* spp.)	Shade- and sun-loving species with a multitude of red, white, pink, salmon, and purple flowers.	Nectar flowers for hummingbirds	Grow in sun or shade. If you have lots of space (they self-sow), try moisture-loving orange jewelweed (*I. capensis*) or pale yellow jewelweed (*I. pallida*), a good choice for dry shade beneath maples.
Petunias (*Petunia* spp.)	Popular bedding plants with sprawling growth habit and many simple flared flowers in almost every color except true blue.	Nectar flowers for butterflies, hummingbirds, and sphinx moths	Petunias self-sow, producing plants the following year in soft pastel pink, lavender, white, and rich red-purple, with delicious fragrance.
Salvias (*Salvia* spp.)	Upright-growing plants with spikes of tubular flowers, usually in red or blue. Other colors also available. Most annual types reach about 2 feet tall or less.	Nectar flowers for hummingbirds and sometimes butterflies	Grow in full sun. A good free-flowering choice for window boxes as well as open spaces.
Verbenas (*Verbena* spp. and hybrids)	Usually low-growing plants, often with feathery foliage; clusters of many small tubular flowers in white, red, purple, salmon, pink, and other colors.	Nectar flowers for butterflies	Grow in full sun. Nestle verbenas along the edges of garden beds or plant them en masse.
Zinnias (*Zinnia* spp.)	Nothing-special looks until bloom—then a riot of vivid daisylike flowers. Susceptible to disfiguring whitish mildew.	Nectar flowers for butterflies; tall red zinnias (*Z. elegans*) attract hummingbirds	Grow in full sun. Experiment with low-growing, small-flowered zinnias, such as Mexican zinnia (*Z. haageana*), to attract smaller butterflies.

PLANT	DESCRIPTION	BEST FEATURES	COMMENTS
Coreopsis (*Coreopsis* spp.)	Golden daisies on relaxed or tidily compact plants; dwarf and tall varieties available. Zones 4–10, depending on species.	Nectar flowers for butterflies	Need full sun; may self-sow moderately. Plants tend to die out after a few years in the garden. Easy to grow from seed. Long-blooming.
Coneflowers (*Echinacea* spp.)	Drooping or flat fringe of purple or white petals surrounds raised tawny orange central disks. Many branched flower stems from a clump of coarse leaves. To about 3 feet tall. Zones 3–10.	Nectar flowers for butterflies	Grow in full sun. One of the best; no butterfly garden should be without it. Extra-long-blooming.
Blazing stars (*Liatris* spp.)	Spikes of fuzzy rose-purple flowers; narrow leaves in a clump at the base. Most about 2 feet tall. Zones 3–10, depending on species.	Nectar flowers for butterflies, especially swallowtails.	Plant in full sun. Long-blooming. Adds a visually appealing vertical accent to an open-space garden. Cheapest to grow from corms.
Bee balms (*Monarda* spp.)	Dense stand of aromatic foliage topped with fringed whorls of blossoms in red, pink, rose, muddy purple, or white. Zones 3–10, depending on species.	Irresistible nectar flowers for hummingbirds; perching, shelter	Grow in sun or shade, depending on species. Good for an open garden; keep in bounds by pulling up spreading rooted stems in early spring when leaves appear.
Salvias (*Salvia* spp.)	Plants of varying height and habit, but all with spikes of usually red or blue tubular flowers. Zones 5–10, depending on species.	Nectar flowers for hummingbirds; perching, shelter	Grow in sun or shade, depending on species. Stick to red salvias for guaranteed hummingbird appeal.
Goldenrods (*Solidago* spp.)	Familiar field flowers of North America, with arching sprays of sunny golden flowers in summer to fall. Spread rapidly by roots and self-sowing. Zones 3–10, depending on species.	Nectar flowers for butterflies. Hummingbirds will visit to dine on small insects.	Grow in sun or shade, depending on species. Unwanted plants are easy to pull up, and the flowers draw monarchs by the dozens.

(continued)

A BORDER OF PLANTS FOR OPEN SPACES—CONTINUED

GROUNDCOVERS

PLANT	DESCRIPTION	BEST FEATURES	COMMENTS
Bearberry (*Arctostaphylos uva-ursi*)	Ground-hugging mat of tidy, deep evergreen leaves, white flowers, and bright red berries. Zones 1–8.	Nectar plant for small butterflies; host plant for hoary elfin and Freya's fritillary	Grow in sun or shade. Pretty year-round.
Heathers (*Erica* spp.)	Large mounds of tiny foliage smothered by dainty flowers in pink, rose, and white. The foliage subtly changes color with the seasons. Zones 5–10, depending on species.	Nectar plants for small butterflies and occasionally hummingbirds	Must have acid soil and full sun. Excellent for seaside gardens; it grows wild in some places along the Atlantic coast.
Daylilies (*Hemerocallis* spp.)	Arching clumps of strappy foliage and bare stems topped by large, flared blooms in a variety of colors. Zones 4–10, depending on species.	Nectar flowers for butterflies, especially swallowtails	Spotting a freshly hatched velvety black swallowtail nectaring at a newly opened daylily blossom will take your breath away. Plant closely for groundcover effect.
Mints (*Mentha* spp.)	Deliciously scented foliage with spikes of tiny tubular flowers, usually white or pale pink. Zones 3–10, depending on species.	Nectar flowers for small butterflies	Grow in sun. Fast-spreading; plant them in a spot where they can have free rein, or confine their roots with a sunken metal barricade.
Thymes (*Thymus* spp.)	Fine-textured with diminutive leaves and spikes of tiny pink, rose, or white flowers. Most species spread into low, dense mats. Zones 5–10, depending on species.	Nectar flowers for small butterflies	Plant low-growing varieties between stepping-stones along the edge of your open garden.

GROUNDCOVERS—CONTINUED

PLANT	DESCRIPTION	BEST FEATURES	COMMENTS
Clovers (*Trifolium* spp.)	Familiar roadside and lawn weeds, but pretty plants in their own right, with rounded clusters of flowers in crimson, white, and purple. Zones 4–10, depending on species.	Excellent butterfly nectar plants. Host for at least a dozen species, including the common sulphur and the eastern tailed blue.	Grow in sun. Learn to appreciate clovers in your lawn, or transplant them to a garden. In the open garden, try eye-catching crimson clover (*T. incarnatum*) or the large-flowered purple clover (*T. pratense*).
Vincas (*Vinca* spp.)	Trailing or clump-forming plants with smooth leaves and simple flowers in bright colors. Zones 4–10, depending on species.	Nectar plants for butterflies; may be visited by hummingbirds	Perennials *V. major* and *V. minor* bloom early in spring, attracting cabbage whites; these plants can be invasive.

ORNAMENTAL GRASSES

PLANT	DESCRIPTION	BEST FEATURES	COMMENTS
Fescues (*Festuca* spp.)	Many species have fine-textured foliage, but fescues vary greatly in height, habit, and hardiness, depending on species and cultivar.	Host plants for various skippers; shelter for small butterflies	Grow in sun. Let your lawn grass grow, and you're likely to get a good specimen of a fescue, one of the most common types of turf grass.
Switch grasses and panic grasses (*Panicum* spp.)	Self-sowing perennial grasses, usually midheight at about 3 to 4 feet, with many airy flower- and seedheads. Zones 5–10.	Host plants for skippers; shelter for small butterflies	Grow in sun. With its arched foliage and erect flowers, switch grass (*Panicum virgatum*) makes a beautiful accent plant for a flower garden.
Feather grasses or needlegrasses (*Stipa* spp.)	Fine, arching foliage and beautiful seedheads with ultra-long hairlike extensions that catch the sun beautifully. Zones 7–10.	Western needlegrass (*S. occidentalis*) is the host plant for the Nevada skipper. The grass supplies shelter for small butterflies.	Grow in sun. Drought-tolerant. The hairlike "awns" on the seeds curl into a tight spiral when the seed drops in order to push it into the soil—or into your pants cuff!

CREATING SHADE

Hummingbirds seek the shelter of shade when they've had too much of a good thing—sun. They will perch briefly and even forage in the shade if they can find their favorite nectar sources there. Many species of butterflies, including most of the fruit eaters, spend much of their lives in shady places. Butterflies also like to use the trunks and leaves of shade trees as popular perching places.

Even if your yard has no shade trees, you still have several good options for providing a fast shade fix for hummingbirds and butterflies. Shrubs and trees will take a few years to grow to a useful size, but while you're waiting, you can depend on vines and extra-big annuals to create the pools of cool where your winged visitors can seek shelter from the hot summer sun.

Evaluating Shade
Slap that Sherlock Holmes cap on your head—it's time to do a little detective work around the yard. Before you begin adding new spots of shade, take stock of what's already there, and think about how you can add to it quickly and easily.

TRUE SHADE If you have a truly shady area in your yard, you probably already know where it is. It's the place where grass won't grow, and it's probably infiltrated by moss. It's the area where the only flowers that will flourish are impatiens. It's the spot where you lounge in the hammock on August afternoons. If you have a place like this, congratulations! Planting a shade garden will be an easy undertaking.

STUCK IN THE SUN If, on the other hand, your yard is almost entirely sun-baked in summer when Ol' Sol takes the high road overhead, you'll be starting from scratch. Yet you still have some areas that are more likely candidates for shade than other places. Start with the north side of your house or outbuildings. On all days but the summer solstice, the angle of the sun's rays are such that there will be a small shady space next to the structure for some part of the day.

DEGREES OF SHADE Most of us have yards that fall somewhere in the middle—a mix of sun and shade, or a yard that's dappled with what gardeners call "light shade." (Light shade is what's created by shifting leaves or moving shadows filtering some of the sun's light.) If your trees are bare of branches at the bottom, the sun can slip in for part of the day, creating "partial shade." Just to keep things interesting for us gardeners, the two terms are often used interchangeably.

Who's Counting?
In my garden I tend to push plants to the limit and beyond just to see what they can do. I've found that most plants touted as needing full sun will do quite nicely with a minimum of 6 hours of sun in summertime. It doesn't always need to be 6 hours in a row, either. You might have a spot that's sunny from 8 to 11 A.M., and again

from 3 to 6 P.M., for example. Any combination of direct exposure to the sun's rays that adds up to a total of 6 hours per day counts.

I've discovered that partial- or light-shade plants generally grow without complaint in areas that get either less than 6 hours of direct sun or an almost constant diet of filtered shade. Filtered shade is that lovely light found beneath birches, locusts, and other trees with cut leaves that dance in the breeze and allow the sun to penetrate in shifting glances.

Full-shade plants, in my opinion, thrive not only in total dimness but also in light shade of less than 4 hours of direct sun, or in all-day partial shade.

But forget the figures (unless you're the compulsive type), and use your noggin instead when selecting plants. Think of light requirements in terms of high, medium, and low, and your plant failures will be few and far between. High-light plants need lots of sun; low-light plants prefer to hide in the shadows; and medium plants can adapt to most combinations of direct light and shade. See? Easy, isn't it?

Cooling shade on a sunny day is just as welcome to hummingbirds as it is to their human hosts. Many species of hummers live in wooded areas and are adept at maneuvering through the branches and foliage. Butterflies also seek shade when summer sun is brutal, and they use trees for lookout posts and shelter in rain storms or at night.

Gardeners embrace hostas for their dramatic foliage and cast-iron disposition, but these shade-loving perennials also offer a bouquet of nectar flowers to hummingbirds.

Islands of Shade

It's best to restrict shade plantings to certain parts of your yard, rather than going for an all-over shade effect. This will leave areas open for easy flight. (Don't worry, though, if your yard is in shadow most of the time—by enticing butterflies and hummingbirds with food and water, you'll still have plenty of customers.)

Improve your yard with one shade grouping at a time. Start by choosing a flowering shrub for nectar or a shrub that serves as a host plant for caterpillars, and make a grouping of three of the same kind. Spread mulch around their bases to make them look like a single bed, and you have an instant shade garden!

Of course, if you shop for bargain-priced plants like I do, those shrubs may be just knee-high when you put them in the ground. The shade they offer is mostly of use to ants at first. Be patient and give them a year or two, and they'll soon be offering the shade your visitors crave.

Invest in a few shade trees right at the start, too, because they also take years to grow into their potential. Most people think of maples and oaks when they hear shade tree, but I also think fruit. Apples, pears, cherries, crabapples, and other fruits grow into respectable trees, often more quickly than the classic shade tree choices, and they do double duty by producing food for butterflies as well as shade for hummingbirds.

Shopping for Shade Plants

Annuals and perennials are easy to find at garden centers or nurseries, or by mail order—and you can always start from seed. Tracking down woody plants—trees, shrubs, and vines—can be more of a challenge. Most garden centers stock only a handful of different species or cultivars. Your best bet for getting a good-size, healthy woody plant is to pick it out in person from the grounds of a garden center or from a nursery. That way you can see what you're buying, and you can choose a plant whose shape most appeals to you.

The plants are nearly always potted in containers, which makes them easy to transplant to your selected site when you're ready. Locally owned nurseries are often amenable to ordering a few plants for an individual gardener. If you don't see what you're looking for, ask the manager if it's possible to order it. I've discovered that getting to know the staff at local nurseries pays off: They enjoy tracking down and learning about out-of-the-ordinary plants just as much as I do.

Mail-order sources offer a much wider selection of woody plants, but keep in mind that the plants will usually be much smaller than those sold in garden centers. They may arrive on your doorstep "bareroot"—dormant, without leaves, and with their root system protected by a bit of moist peat or simply wrapped in plastic or newspaper. This isn't a bad thing; the plants will begin to grow swiftly once you get them into the ground. But they will need immediate care when they arrive, unlike containerized plants, which you can park in a corner until you're ready to dig.

Don't be dismayed by the puny size of the woody plant that arrives on your doorstep. Younger "woodies" are quicker to get established than big specimens. I've learned that even twiglike trees and shrubs catch up to big, beautiful, and expensive store-bought specimens in just a few years.

SURPRISE FINDS Since many woody plants for hummingbirds and butterflies are native species, you may discover that you already have woody seedlings growing in your yard, perhaps sneaking into a flowerbed or an undisturbed corner along a fence or hedgerow. In my southern Indiana garden, for example, elm, wild cherry, and hackberry trees—three excellent host plants for caterpillars of my region—spring up each year all on their own, either from windblown seeds or "dropped" by birds. I yank out the extras and transplant others to more serendipitous sites. Within a year or two they've grown large enough to attract egg-laying butterflies.

Most woody plants are very adaptable characters that will thrive in ordinary

The yellow blossoms of oxeye sunflower (*Heliopsis helianthoides*) add lively interest to a shady spot and will attract a variety of butterflies.

One of my all-time favorite flowering shrubs for shade, red-flowering currant is a beauty, with graceful form and a profusion of fragrant blooms in early spring—just in time for the earliest hummingbirds arriving back from their winter vacation. It's a native of mossy green Northwest forests.

soil with minimal care. All they ask is a good start. "Right plant in the right place" is the mantra to keep in mind while you page through catalogs or stroll in garden centers. Read plant tags and catalog descriptions carefully to make sure the plant you're seeking is a good fit for your climate and growing conditions.

Planting Advice
Plant bareroot plants within a day or two of arrival. Set them in a shady place and keep the packing material moist until you're ready to plant. While you dig the planting hole, plunge the plants' roots into a bucket of water. (Don't leave the roots in water for longer than 24 hours, though, or they'll be likely to suffocate or decay.)

With potted plants, you can be as lazy as you want about planting. Plant them anytime during the growing season, up to within about 4 weeks of frost (so that their roots have time to grab hold before the ground freezes), or year-round in mild areas. If you plant them in summer or during a dry spell, supply extra water until the roots get established.

Dig a hole wide enough and deep enough to comfortably accommodate the roots of a bareroot plant or the rootball of a potted plant. Then widen the hole by several inches all the way around so that growing roots can stretch out luxuriously into loosened soil instead of fighting their way through compacted ground.

Fill the hole with water and let it drain, to saturate the surrounding soil and prevent it from wicking away moisture after planting. If the roots of a potted plant are wound in a tight mass, try to untangle them with your fingers, or slash through the mass with a sturdy knife to a depth of about ½ inch on three sides of the rootball.

Settle the plant in place, making sure to keep it at the same depth it was growing previously (to determine this, check the stem for a change in color or bark texture above the roots). Comb out any bare roots with your fingers and place them in various directions so they don't compete with each other, and so they make a solid anchor.

Hold off on amendments when you fill the planting hole. Research shows that too much kindness isn't healthy for a woody plant. If you fill the hole with "perfect" soil, the roots won't want to leave! They're likely to fill the area of amended soil instead of stretching out into surrounding unimproved soil. But if you fill the planting hole with "regular" soil, the roots will reach out for new territory to collect the moisture and nutrients they need, providing a much stronger foundation for the plant.

Fill the hole with soil and tamp it with your foot, but don't stomp too hard: Roots need some air spaces to thrive. Make a "dike," a low circular ridge of raised soil, around the new plant to form a reservoir that keeps water from running off too fast. Water the newly planted specimen generously.

CARE AFTER PLANTING Regular watering is the main care your new plant will need because its transplanted roots haven't yet sprouted the growth they require to serve

(continued on page 92)

At first glance, this shrub-and-perennial border seems to hold little appeal for hummingbirds. Guess again—among those branches are bound to be myriad spider webs, a source of food and nesting materials for hummers. A female bird may collect dozens of small webs on each trip at nest-building time.

SHRUBS FOR BUTTERFLIES AND HUMMINGBIRDS

Adding shrubs to sunny or shady spots in your yard will give you quick results for a small investment of time and money. Most shrubs are very reasonably priced—about $10. That's a real bargain for a plant that will contribute to your garden for decades to come. Look for flowering shrubs in bud and bloom at nurseries and garden centers. Take the potted plant home, pop it into the ground, and you have an instant addition to your nectar garden. Be sure to include butterfly bush (*Buddleia davidii*), which you'll find described elsewhere in this book.

SHRUBS FOR SHADE

SHRUB	DESCRIPTION	BEST FEATURES	COMMENTS
Spicebush (*Lindera benzoin*)	Graceful, open branches studded with little clusters of yellow flowers in spring before leaves appear. Bright yellow fall foliage and red berries. Spicy-scented foliage, flowers, and berries. Zones 5–9.	Host plant for spicebush swallowtails and the giant Promethea silk moth; provides good perching site for hummingbirds	Flourishes in humus-rich soil, but also grows well in clay or dry shade. In a dry site, provide extra water for the first 2 years. Check native plant specialty nurseries and catalogs, or ask your locally owned nursery to help you find this shrub.
Azaleas (*Rhododendron calendulaceum, R. bakeri, R. prunifolium, R. canescens* and other spp.)	Evergreen or deciduous shrubs with flared trumpet flowers in zingy bright colors and pastels. Height, form, and hardiness vary depending on species. Look for a regional native that will thrive in your conditions.	Nectar plants for hummingbirds. Some species are host plants for the brown elfin and some anglewings.	Stick to "unimproved" native species for best hummingbird appeal; many hybrids and cultivars don't seem to attract hummingbirds despite their bright blossoms.
Rhododendrons (*Rhododendron* spp.)	Usually evergreen shrubs of significant stature, with large, glossy leaves and fat, rounded clusters of tubular flowers in pink, red, white, and purple. Zones 4–9; but varies with species.	Nectar plants for hummingbirds; also attractive to hummingbirds because of spiders living among the branches	As with azaleas, native species of rhododendrons seem to attract more nectar seekers than improved varieties.
Currants (*Ribes* spp.)	Twiggy, sometimes prickly upright or globe-shaped shrubs, most to about 4 feet tall. Several native species from various regions. One of the best for hummingbirds is flowering currant (*R. sanguineum*), Zones 6–8.	Nectar plants for hummingbirds; host plants for several western butterflies, including the tailed copper and several anglewings	Grow well in average, unimproved soil; most species are drought-tolerant. Zones 3–10, depending on species. For host plants, seek out species native to your region and conditions.

SHRUBS FOR SUN

SHRUB	DESCRIPTION	BEST FEATURES	COMMENTS
Rose of Sharon (*Hibiscus syriacus*)	Shrubby when young, acquiring tree form as it matures. Reaches about 15 feet tall, but can be easily kept shorter by cutting back to desired size after bloom. Flaring flowers in white, pink, rose, red, and a near blue (cultivar 'Blue Bird'). Zones 5–9.	Nectar plant for hummingbirds; also supplies perches and spiders for extra appeal	An old-fashioned favorite worth rediscovering. Supremely easy to grow and inexpensive to buy.
Mock oranges (*Philadelphus* spp.)	Large deciduous shrub to about 10 feet tall, with sublimely fragrant white flowers in spring. Hardiness varies with species; most thrive to Zone 5.	Nectar flowers for some spring butterflies; perching places for hummingbirds, which also seek spiders among the branches	Buy a plant that you can sniff: The trademark scent of this plant has all but disappeared in some cultivars. Or ask a neighbor if you can dig up a young "sucker" from around the base of a sweet-smelling parent.
Arborvitae (*Thuja* spp.)	Evergreen, columnar shrub with fans of flat-needled foliage, highly popular for landscaping hedges. Hardiness varies with species.	No flowers mark this shrub, but it's a favorite of hummingbirds because it usually harbors a bounty of spiders (meaty hummingbird snacks) and spiderwebs (hummingbird nest material).	Other evergreens, including hemlocks (*Tsuga* spp.), spruces (*Picea* spp.), pines (*Pinus* spp.), and firs (*Abies* spp.), also get a good share of hummingbird visits. Good perching sites for shelter from summer sun or rain.
Chaste tree (*Vitex agnus-castus*)	An open shrub to small tree, reaching about 8 feet tall and 6 feet wide, with generous bloom of blue flower spikes in summer. Zones 6–9.	Nectar plant for multitudes of butterflies; also visited by hummingbirds; provides small insects for hummingbird snacks, as well as convenient perches	Thrives in average garden soil. Drought-tolerant. Excellent for coastal gardens. Cut back to near ground level in late winter to keep it bushy and vigorous. Or, leave it unpruned for greater height and a more treelike form.
Weigela (*Weigela florida*)	This large shrub, to about 6 feet tall, is upright when young, then arching into a dense mound. At early summer bloom time, the bush is covered with a multitude of small tubular flowers in red or pink. Zones 5–9.	Superb nectar shrub for hummingbirds	If you can grow weeds, you can grow weigela—it has a cast-iron disposition, thriving in average or poor soils as long as they are well-drained. Look for cheap bareroot dormant plants at garden centers in early spring and try a hedge of it.

the needs of the plant. If rain is lacking, water generously once a week. A transplanted woody plant needs extra attention paid to watering for at least the first 2 years after planting. The bigger the tree or shrub at the time of planting, the more water it will need. That's another reason why I like to start with small seedlings: Because there's not a lot of topgrowth to supply with water and nutrients, their young, vigorous roots don't need as much coddling as those of larger specimens.

The nutrients the plant needs will be taken up through the water, but you can also apply a half-inch layer of compost or aged manure around the plant to supply extra nutrients. I usually put down compost, then top it with about 2 inches of bark mulch over the root area to conserve moisture. Keep the mulch at least 2 inches away from the trunk to prevent decay and discourage bark-nibbling mice.

One more thing to keep in mind is that transplanted woodies take a while to put out a significant amount of new top growth. That's because their roots have to grow first before they can push out many new branches. For the first year or even two after planting, you'll think your new plants have stalled in their tracks. While you're waiting for your new plant investment to take off, reassure yourself with this old gardeners' saying: "The first year it sleeps, the second year it creeps, the third year it leaps."

To lure hummingbirds almost all summer long, rely on the gorgeous red-and-yellow blossoms of coral honeysuckle (*Lonicera sempervirens*).

Vines for Swift Shade

While you're waiting for your shrubs and trees to grow up, make or buy a trellis—and an arbor, if you like, or even a pergola or gazebo—and plant the structures in your yard. These additions instantly create small spots of shade. Fast-growing annual vines will cover all these supports in a hurry. If you plant scarlet runner beans (*Phaseolus coccineus*) or hyacinth beans (*Lablab purpurea*) in spring, you'll have 10-foot vines by early or midsummer.

Perennial and woody vines also grow swiftly, though nowhere near as fast as the

LONG-LIVED VINES FOR
HUMMINGBIRDS AND BUTTERFLIES

Snuggle a few of these permanent vines wherever you can find some room for them to grow up: a trellis against the house, a bower over a bench, or a windbreak on a sturdy support. Vines are also great for camouflaging an unphotogenic fence.

PLANT	DESCRIPTION AND HARDINESS	APPEALING FEATURES	COMMENTS
Trumpet vine (*Campsis radicans*)	Vigorous, high-climbing woody vine with glossy, deep green foliage and clusters of orange-red tubular flowers. Zones 4–10.	Nectar flowers for hummingbirds	This rampant-growing, heavy vine can infiltrate the boards of house siding or window frames; supply strong support away from structures or cut back yearly in late winter to keep in bounds.
Blood-red trumpetvine (*Distictis buccinatoria*)	Evergreen vine with spectular trumpet-shaped flowers that open bright orange-red and age to a purplish red hue. Well-drained soil; sun to light shade. Zones 9–10.	Nectar flowers for hummingbirds	To keep in bounds, prune yearly by cutting back errant stems.
Coral honeysuckle (*Lonicera sempervirens*)	Deep green foliage; lovely red tubular flowers with yellow interiors are produced freely over a long period of bloom. Average, well-drained soil; sun to shade (flowering is reduced in full shade). Zones 3–10.	Nectar flowers for hummingbirds	A much better-behaved honeysuckle than the white-and-yellow flowered Japanese species (*L. japonica*) that has invaded American wild places. Good choice for a north-facing wall.
Passionflowers (*Passiflora* spp.)	Conversation-piece flowers of unusual, intricate structure, with the stamens making a "crown of thorns" laid upon the petals, which may be purple, blue, red, greenish, or yellow, depending on species. Hardiness varies with species.	Host plants for Gulf fritillary and other fritillaries, as well as the Julia, zebra longwing, crimson-patch longwing, and other warm-region butterflies	Excellent choice for covering a chain-link fence. Suckers may spring up from spreading roots; mow or cut them off if undesired.
Cape honeysuckle (*Tecomaria capensis*)	A South African honeysuckle with dark green foliage and clusters of skinny, vivid orange-red blossoms. Well-drained soil; sun to light shade. Zones 9–10.	Nectar flowers for hummingbirds	Good vine for coastal gardens. Tie to trellis to support stems and promote twining. Also good for groundcover, or prune it into a shrub shape.

Red morning glory, also known as cardinal creeper (*Ipomoea coccinea*), has little red trumpets that might as well be neon when it comes to hummingbird appeal. The similar cypress vine (*I. quamoclit*) has look-alike flowers but delicate feathery leaves, making it ideal for rambling at will over perennials in the border.

annuals that must mature in a single season. I like to mix it up when planting a new vine support. First I plant a perennial vine in front of the trellis, then I poke seeds of an annual vine on both sides of the perennial.

One of my trellises—which is nothing more than a piece of wire fencing stapled to a wooden frame—holds a climbing coral honeysuckle (*Lonicera sempervirens*), a native vine with knock-your-socks-off red flowers. I knew that this species of honeysuckle would take a year or two to really begin to stretch, so I partnered it with feathery-leaved cypress vine (*Ipomoea quamoclit*), a delicate-looking annual climber that also has fire-engine red flowers. The combo was an instant hit with my hummingbirds, who fight over the flowers of both plants all season long. Cypress vine, which is also called star glory, self-sows moderately, and I let it do so, even after the honeysuckle grew into its promise. The star glory's delicate stems and fine foliage don't hinder the honeysuckle, and the combined firepower of two red-blooming vines boosts the hummingbird magnetism of the planting.

Although my trellises are simply vertical walls, they provide shade on the side away from the sun. I added a few shrubs in this shady area to give hot hummingbirds a place to perch. The trellises also break the force of the winds that come ripping through my backyard on summer afternoons. These windbreaks keep my butterflies fluttering happily in the protected flowerbeds that they frequent.

Annuals for Instant Shade
Annuals equal almost instant shade. These plants have their work cut out for them. In a single season they must sprout, flower, and set seed because their demise follows quickly. That makes them ideal as a high-speed hedge or barrier for shade and windbreaks.

Some annuals are actually tender perennials, which can stay in the soil for a repeat performance if you're blessed with a mild climate. In colder areas, you'll need to lift the tubers of cannas and dahlias, or say "sayonara" at frost time.

SUPER-SIZE ANNUALS Amaranth, tall cultivars (*Amaranthus* spp.). This terrific plant offers dramatic upright plumes in rich burgundy and other colors, plenty of big leaves, and stout stems that don't keel over in windy weather.

Tickseed sunflower (*Bidens aristosa*), **shepherd's needle** (*B. pilosa*). Buttery yellow daisies atop 5-foot stems appeal to butterflies. In fall and winter, the seedheads will draw songbirds, too.

Cannas (*Canna* spp.). Tropical glamour is a bonus of the huge, unfurling leaves and straight posture of these plants, which provide shelter from breezes and spikes of hummingbird nectar flowers.

Dahlias, tall cultivars (*Dahlia* spp.). Multiple branches help balance the height of these leafy plants, but you may need to offer additional support, like a fence. Flowers attract butterflies and hummers.

Sunflower (*Helianthus annuus*). Plant the seeds of these big, happy daisies just

Canna flowers are hummingbird favorites, whether they are either the usual red or orange, yellow, coral, or pink. Clip off old blooms for another round of flowers.

4 inches apart. This way, the big-leaved plants can stand shoulder to shoulder in the garden to break the force of the wind as it blows through your yard.

Castor bean (*Ricinus communis*). One caveat to planting castor beans: This plant is toxic, and its intriguing seedpods could be a hazardous temptation to children.

Mexican sunflower (*Tithonia rotundifolia*). These flowers are big and bold, with towering height and screaming-for-attention orange-red flowers. This is an excellent nectar plant for both hummers and butterflies.

Corn (*Zea mays*). Corn seems to grow a foot as soon as you turn your back. It's knee-high by the 4th of July; shoulder height 2 weeks later. Try planting the kernels of last fall's Indian corn decoration as this year's crop.

SOFTENING THE WIND

Gardeners on the American plains and prairies and those who dwell along the coast know that strong winds can be a constant in the garden even in summer. Persistent winds are not conducive to a butterfly-welcoming yard because these insects are highly vulnerable to the vagaries of wind, which can batter their wings and blow them hither and yon.

No matter where you garden, it makes sense to erect a windbreak along the side of your yard from which strong breezes typically blow. For many of us, that means a windbreak on the western side of the garden. In the Gulf states, your gales may come from the south. In the northern tier, look out for those Canadian clippers.

Trees and shrubs are the best choices for windbreaks because their tough trunks and branches will stand up to stronger forces than even the most statuesque annuals. Trellises and fences also are a great help in modifying the strength of the wind, and they can be a fast fix that allows you to entice butterflies while your slower-growing trees and shrubs are filling in.

SHELTER FROM THE STORM

Where do butterflies go when it rains? They usually slip under an overhanging leaf, the same shelter they often seek for sleeping. Hummingbirds retreat to the protection of trees, shrubs, and vines in inclement weather, where they can huddle among the abundant foliage without getting wet and chilled.

Select shelter plants with relatively large leaves for butterflies—a minimum of about 2 inches long and 1½ inches wide. That will afford plenty of space for most sizes of butterflies. For hummingbirds, almost any plant that's weatherproof has shelter potential. You might think they require an open branching habit with room for flight, but I have watched many a hummingbird take shelter in the dim interior of a densely branched blue spruce in my neighbor's yard.

A Place to Perch

It's a myth that hummingbirds never sit still. They stop to rest frequently, perhaps as often as every 15 minutes. By supplying a comfortable spot for them to sit a spell, you can save hummingbirds the trouble (and energy) of leaving your garden between rounds of feeding. Hummingbirds are adept at finding a perching site—the top curve of a shepherd's crook nectar hanger is a popular spot—but you can also plant trees and shrubs to give them more options.

Openly branched trees and shrubs such as spicebush (*Lindera benzoin*), hawthorns (*Crataegus* spp.), willows (*Salix* spp.), and eastern redbud (*Cercis canadensis*) work well as perching places for hummingbirds because the gaps among the branches allow the birds to easily navigate. (Of course, this means they're not good choices for shelter plantings because rain and wind can easily infiltrate the interior of the plant.) Trees and shrubs with small leaves or delicate foliage, such as wattle (*Acacia* spp.), birches (*Betula* spp.), butterfly bush (*Buddleia davidii*), and honey-locusts (*Gleditsia* spp.), are also best reserved for perch sites.

You don't need to include evergreens for butterfly and hummingbird shelters because these visitors disappear in the cold months except in very mild Florida, the Gulf states, the Southwest, and California. In the warm areas where butterflies and hummingbirds are present in winter, many of your plants will be in full leaf even though the calendar says it's winter. Of course, if you like evergreens, by all means add a few!

Plants with overlapping branches and leaves that create a water-shedding shingle effect are perfect for shelter. Among trees and shrubs, there is a huge variety of possibilities, from lowly privets (*Ligustrum* spp.) and ubiquitous forsythia (*Forsythia* × *intermedia*) to elegant Japanese maples (*Acer palmatum*) and giant live oaks (*Quercus* spp.).

A HAVEN FOR WINTER

Gardeners in warm-winter areas—and you know who you are—have the delightful task of hosting hummingbirds and butterflies year-round. While the rest of the country is locked in the deep freeze and making do with chickadees and suet, you can enjoy beautiful wings and bright blossoms. For you lucky folks, winter hummingbird and butterfly

STORM-SHELTER PLANTS

Keep the multifunction rule in mind when you select plants for shelter. It's likely that the plants you pick first for nectar or host opportunities will be perfectly satisfactory as shelter, too. The plants described below are all double-duty plants.

PLANT	TYPE OF PLANT	DESCRIPTION AND HARDINESS	OTHER TEMPTATIONS
Maples (*Acer* spp.)	Medium to large trees	Deciduous trees with large leaves. Height, fall foliage color, and hardiness vary with species.	Hummingbirds may bathe on the wet surfaces of leaves. Interestingly, no American butterflies are known to use maples as a host plant, although caterpillars of several moth species eat the foliage.
Red buckeye (*Aesculus pavia*)	Small tree	Deciduous, attractively shaped tree. To 15 feet. Average, well-drained soil; sun to shade. Thrives beneath larger shade trees. Zones 5–8.	Nectar flowers for hummingbirds.
Spruces (*Picea* spp.)	Evergreen trees	Short, stiff needles cover the branches of these common landscape and forest trees. Height, hardiness vary with species.	Hummingbirds seek spiders and their prey among the branches. Black spruce (*P. nigra*) is a host plant for the bog elfin, a butterfly of northern regions.
Douglas fir (*Pseudotsuga menziesii*)	Evergreen tree	Tall, stately, short-needled conifer; for very large yards. Zones 5–7.	The branches conceal small spiderwebs, which hummingbirds visit for nesting material and insect food. Sometimes used as nest site by hummingbirds. Host plant for pine white butterfly.
Oaks (*Quercus* spp.)	Large trees	Grand, graceful trees with evergreen or deciduous leaves, depending on species. Most southern and western oaks are evergreen; most in cold-winter climates are deciduous. Height, hardiness vary with species.	Various species are host plants for elfins, hairstreaks, and skippers. Fuzz on the undersides of leaves used by some hummingbirds in nest building. Bountiful acorns attract songbirds and other wildlife.
Hemlocks (*Tsuga* spp.)	Evergreen trees	Lovely, fine-textured drooping branches with short, soft needles. Height and hardiness vary with species and cultivar.	Watch for hummingbirds making darting movements among the branches as they seek spiders and other small insects.

gardening is no different than the summer season. Keep the flowers blooming and the feeders filled, and your yard will be alive with life and color.

Meanwhile, in snow-and-ice land, the hummingbirds flee to the southern lands sometime around Labor Day. Flowers, too, disappear for the winter months and butterflies no longer flutter about, except for the occasional stray when the weather warms for a few days. But except for monarchs, butterflies don't migrate—they wait out the winter as adults, eggs, caterpillars, or chrysalises. Protecting those butterflies-to-be is a simple matter of adapting your garden practices.

Don't Be Too Quick to Clean
Butterfly eggs, caterpillars, and chrysalises are often hidden in and around the remains of your garden plants. Many immature forms of moths and butterflies winter over in the soil, so they are safely tucked out of reach. But others spend the cold months on the plants themselves or among fallen leaves, and that's where you come in.

If you follow the usual tradition of cutting back plants for winter and generally tidying up the garden, you're probably carting a lot of potential next-season visitors to the compost heap along with the leaves and branches.

This is a case when tidiness just does not pay. Let your fallen leaves nestle around the bases of plants to shelter chrysalises or larvae. Instead of cutting back perennials and annuals to ground level in the fall, let the plants stand until spring. It's easy to get used to that messy look when you think of all the butterflies that may spring forth from the clutter in the spring. If you simply must tidy up your garden, examine the remains of plants carefully for chrysalises, but be warned: They are bound to be so well camouflaged they look like part of the plant. Caterpillars may overwinter within seedpods or other plant parts, and hopefully will emerge even though you've piled their homes on the compost heap. If you wait until late winter or early spring to remove old growth and add it to the compost pile, any potential butterflies in the

Some butterflies, such as this question mark, have a drab brown chrysalis that blends into fall foliage. Be careful not to disturb camouflaged chrysalises when you clean up your garden.

A big hit in catalogs and nature stores, butterfly houses aren't nearly as popular with butterflies themselves. Don't be too disappointed if you get no takers for your sheltering structure.

debris will have a chance to emerge before the materials become too compacted or they are deeply buried in the pile.

Hibernation Homes

Adult butterflies of some species seek the shelter of cracks, crannies, and other hiding places to survive the winter. Their main consideration is protecting their wings from damage. Once settled safely, their cold-blooded bodies will slow with winter temperatures and revive in spring. Not being eaten is also important, so butterflies search for winter homes that keep them out of sight of hungry birds. Mourning cloaks, question marks, red admirals, and other species often slip into the small space beneath a flap of loose bark for their long winter's nap.

Butterfly houses have become a standard offering in garden-supply catalogs and stores. Made of wood, with slits cut in the front, they are designed to be used as shelter by over-wintering butterflies that creep in through the narrow entrances. I have found that providing these houses is quite unnecessary. In most cases, the natural places in your garden provide plenty of shelter for your guests.

Early Arrivals, Late Departures

Seasonal weather—or rather, unseasonal weather—can wreak havoc on vulnerable butterflies and hummingbirds. Don't despair! You can help them cope with these seasonal emergencies.

- A warm spell that settles in for 2 or 3 days in winter may draw hibernating adult butterflies from their niches at a time when food is probably extremely scarce. When you see the first flutterer, put out overripe bananas or other fruits. Fill saucers with a very thin layer of pear nectar, apple juice, or grape juice and place them on the ground around the garden.
- Immature hummingbirds are the most likely to get their travel schedule confused. These rookies sometimes linger long after the rest of their kind have departed. If a latecomer shows up, get that feeder filled fast. Offer another feeder filled with a very

weak solution of unsalted beef bouillon to substitute for the protein the bird would normally consume in the form of small insects. Be sparing when you add the bouillon: ¼ teaspoon of liquid bouillon per 2 cups of water will supply these little guys with an adequate protein boost.

- Occasionally, a hummingbird fails to move on even after its energy has been restored by abundant food. People have gone to enormous lengths to keep such birds alive, including, believe it or not, specially chartered airplanes; but the best bet is to call a rehabilitator for help. These experienced people have the proper licenses to keep the bird under their care indoors, something that is a federal offense for the rest of us. Call a nearby nature center, state park, or veterinarian to locate a licensed rehabilitator.

HOMEMADE HIBERNATING BOX

My most successful butterfly hibernating box happened entirely by accident—or perhaps poor housekeeping! Try making your own "intentional accident" and see how many and what kinds of butterflies will choose your snug creation for hibernation.

MATERIALS

Rectangular birdhouse with front removed
Pieces of corrugated cardboard or thin wood slices, ⅛ to ¼ inch thick
Handful of small pebbles

1. Collect as many cardboard or wood "partitions" as will fit loosely in the box when stacked vertically.

2. Cut or break partitions to fit the box height. Don't worry if wood partitions extend a bit past the front of the box, but cut cardboard so that the front edge is not exposed to wet weather.

3. Mount the box on the side of a building or a tree, about 6 feet above ground, with the open front facing away from winter winds (south or east, in most areas of North America).

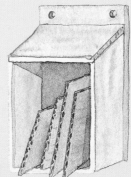

4. Fill the box with the partitions, allowing them to lean at whatever angles they naturally fall into.

5. Insert a pebble or two wherever there is a small crevice between the partitions to prevent the partitions from shifting during the winter.

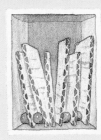

CHAPTER 6

The Next

GENERATION

Beautiful flying creatures will fill your yard as you offer butterflies and hummingbirds a bounty of food, bolstered by water features and sheltered spaces. As your visitors come to depend on the resources you supply so abundantly, it's natural for them to start checking out the neighborhood as a place to settle down and raise a family.

Getting butterflies to raise a family in your yard is as easy as getting them to feed there. Plant the right things and they will come: It's that simple. Specific plants tempt specific butterflies—not with nectar, but by holding the promise of essential food for a new brood. Filling your yard with flowers increases the number of fluttering wings you will see day by day, but adding even a few plants to host caterpillars can boost the numbers of butterflies in your yard by unbelievable numbers. The following pages will help you understand the stages of butterfly life and give you lots of ideas for adding the attractions that will pay off with more of your favorite butterflies.

Hummingbirds are trickier to tempt into becoming residents because, unlike butterflies, their nesting needs aren't tied to specific plants. The key is to supply as many of their needs as possible so that your garden looks like a good neighborhood to raise a family. Hummingbird territories are much larger than those of butterflies, but with a few tricks, you can at least improve the chances of having your yard taken under consideration at nesting time.

BUTTERFLY LIFE CYCLE

The butterfly life cycle is a miracle that happens right under your nose. The process that transforms a creeping, wormlike creature into a winged adult of grace and beauty is one of the most amazing everyday wonders of the entire natural world.

Metamorphosis—literally, "great change"—is the perfect label for a butterfly's life cycle. The timing of the cycle is different for various species, but all follow the same four stages: egg, larva (caterpillar), pupa (chrysalis), and adult.

The Egg
All butterflies begin life as an egg. Butterfly eggs are quite beautiful, with variations in color, size, and shape from one species to the next. Treat yourself to a 5-dollar hand lens or magnifying glass from a discount store to see the eggs in all their glory. They

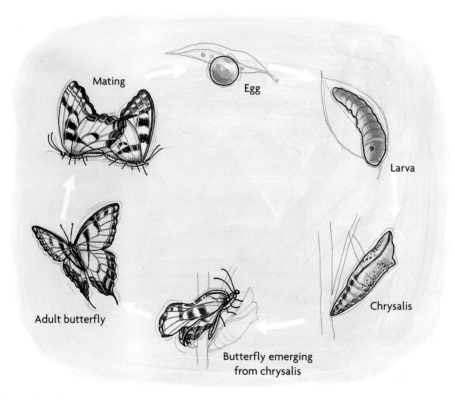

The wonder of butterfly life begins with the egg, a tiny work of art. The caterpillar that hatches is the larva. It may change color as it grows and sheds its skin. In the pupal stage, the chrysalis is formed, protecting the insect as it finishes its body changes. Finally, the adult emerges, finds a mate, and the whole process begins again.

are nature's version of the exquisite jeweled eggs that Faberge created for the Russian czars. These tiny jewels—round, rain-barrel–shaped, or ribbed; green, orange, or opalescent like beautiful pearls—may all be hiding on the leaves of your garden plants.

A BUTTERFLY EGG HUNT To find butterfly eggs, spy on the parents. You probably won't be able to distinguish the males from the females just by looking because in many species, the sexes look almost exactly alike. Noting the behavior of the adults is a much better clue to the sex of a butterfly.

A quick touch with the hind end, and a female black swallowtail deposits her precious pearl-like egg on Queen Anne's lace, a favorite host plant.

Watch the butterflies in your garden on a midsummer day, and you're sure to spot one that seems to be a little restless. Instead of finding a satisfying flower and stopping to drink deeply, it will float from one plant to another, sometimes alighting for a brief instant before moving on to the next. It seems to have lost all interest in flowers or feeding. If the butterfly you're watching is a cabbage white, chances are it's nervously flitting about your broccoli plants; if it's a pipevine swallowtail, it may be examining the Dutchman's pipes (*Aristolochia* spp.) you planted to shade the porch.

That single-minded butterfly is probably a female looking for a suitable home to start the next generation. Although butterflies don't parent their progeny like birds or animals do, they do make sure the young get a good start in life. When a female is ready to lay eggs, she will fly until she finds the kind of plant that will nourish her youngsters. Then she will deposit the eggs, either one by one or in a group of varying size, on or near this particular plant.

The actual process of egg laying is incredibly swift, especially if the butterfly is a species that lays its eggs singly: one here, one there. The butterfly may not even alight on the plant. A quick dab with the hind end is all it takes.

When you suspect you're seeing egg-laying, move in close to get a look. Most butterflies don't seem to mind being observed at intimate range. I've watched common blue females lay their eggs with my nose just 3 inches away from the butterfly. If you feel more comfortable giving the busy female some privacy, make a mental note of where she's laying the eggs and come back later (be sure to bring your hand lens!).

Scent of a Host Plant

Butterflies are experts at sniffing out the plants they need at egg-laying time, and "sniffing" may indeed be the right word. Fritillaries, whose larvae eat the leaves of violets, appear to use scent to detect the roots of violets whose leaves are dormant at egg-laying time. They lay their precious bundle at the roots of the plant, where the eggs overwinter. In spring, when the foliage emerges, the eggs hatch and the young'uns have a ready feast.

Most butterflies lay their eggs on a stem or leaf of the host plant, but a few, like the common blues I watched, lay their eggs on the flowers of plants. The caterpillars of these species actually dine on the flowers that served as their nurseries. The well-named harvester butterfly lays its eggs near colonies of woolly aphids on its host plants. When the caterpillars emerge, they munch on the aphids instead of the plants.

The Wonders of Caterpillars

A butterfly egg hatches into a larva, or caterpillar, which is so tiny at first that it's difficult to see with the naked eye. The caterpillar immediately begins its only job—eating. It munches practically nonstop and soon outgrows its first skin, which conveniently splits so the caterpillar can shed it and show off the new, bigger body it's been growing beneath. This molting process happens several times as the caterpillar continues growing. Each step along the way of this molting is called an "instar." The caterpillar's skin is often different colors in its different instars.

When it comes to food preferences, butterfly caterpillars are selective to an even greater extreme than that 4-year-old you know who eats only peanut-butter-and-jelly sandwiches (or strawberry yogurt or Cheerios) for weeks on end. Unlike the young human who is simply going through a finicky stage, biology determines a caterpillar's eating preferences as part of the instinctual code that's hard-wired into its cells.

Many of us know that monarch caterpillars eat milkweeds (*Asclepias* spp.), and indeed they do, plus a few other plants in the milkweed family. What that means, however, is that if you offer a monarch caterpillar a banquet of a thousand other yummy plants—but no milkweeds—it will starve to death before it takes a single nibble. A caterpillar's preferred food is called its "host plant."

Of course, what comes in must go out, so the other thing caterpillars do to perfection is excrete. Lepidoptera enthusiasts call caterpillar excrement "frass." Sometimes, when caterpillars are abundant or large, their falling droppings sound like rain. When gypsy moths grew to plague proportions around our Pennsylvania house several years ago, I'd often close my eyes and imagine I was hearing a gentle spring shower instead of the sound of thousands of pests defoliating the oaks and maples.

Nature's Artistry

When I begin enthusing about a particular caterpillar I've found, my friends often remark that I seem to like caterpillars better than butterflies. That may be true. I think they're beautiful, and they hold such potential. To me, a "new" caterpillar—one I've never seen, and particularly one unknown to me—brings me a great sense of anticipation as I wait to see what kind of chrysalis and butterfly it will become.

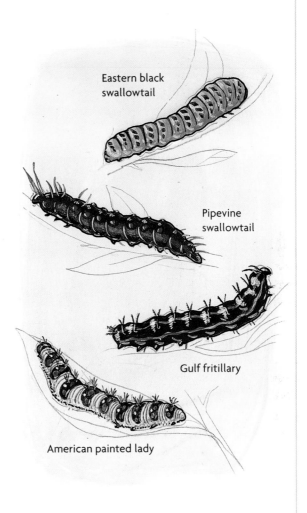

Eastern black swallowtail

Pipevine swallowtail

Gulf fritillary

American painted lady

Some people feel a slight revulsion when looking at a caterpillar, but if you examine one closely from an aesthetic viewpoint, I think you'll understand why I call them beautiful. Caterpillar skin is a canvas of bright and subtle markings, often slashed with bold stripes or dotted with perfectly spaced punctuation marks. It's still hard to find good pictures of many American caterpillars, so I like to make colored sketches of the caterpillars I find—for my own future reference and for my own enjoyment. It's a lot easier than trying to draw a butterfly—caterpillars don't move very fast, if at all, when feeding.

CATERPILLAR CLUES Finding caterpillars around your yard is easy once you know what to look for. Keep an eye out for leaves with chunks eaten from the outside inward (holes within a leaf are often beetle damage), or with only veins or a bare stem attachment remaining. Frass is also a good indicator of caterpillar occupation. It collects on leaves and in the junctions of leaves and stems below where the caterpillar feeds. When caterpillars are small, frass looks like fine-ground pepper. As they grow in size, it gradually becomes a coarser grind, until eventually, in the largest caterpillars, the droppings look like pepper-

A familiar caterpillar to gardeners, the black swallowtail is known as the "parsley worm" because of its predilection for that tasty green. You may also spot it on dill, fennel, cultivated carrots, or wild Queen Anne's lace. Put a couple in a jar along with their food and try your hand at raising butterflies.

corns. It's not easy to see the caterpillars that feed high above our heads in mature shade trees, but I always know they're up there when I find frass on the ground below.

Mortality is high in the caterpillar world. Caterpillar populations are at their peak during bird migration and nesting seasons, thanks to Mother Nature's impeccable sense of timing. To avoid becoming lunch for hungry birds, caterpillar species have developed some tricky defenses. Some, including the comma and question mark, show off formidable spiny projections, which discourage birds and other predators from dining on their succulent bodies.

Other caterpillars, such as the spicebush swallowtail, sport scary-looking eyespots to deter potential diners. In some species the entire bodies are camouflaged. Caterpillars may look like a bit of leaf or a bird dropping, which most predators ignore. I inadvertently and unhappily discovered the superior camouflage of the bright green cabbage white caterpillar when munching on fresh broccoli from my garden. I am more careful now to inspect my veggies to avoid ingesting any unexpected protein.

The Great Change

The Great Change The next stage of a butterfly's metamorphosis—the pupa—is a mysterious one, with great bodily transformations taking place out of view. The pupa of a butterfly is called a chrysalis.

When a butterfly caterpillar has eaten all it can hold and achieved maturity, it attaches itself to a support, rests a while, then molts a final time to reveal the chrysalis. Incredibly, the chrysalis itself is just another change of skin for the transforming butterfly. It separates from the body within so that it becomes an outer shell that the butterfly can cast off when the time is right.

Butterfly chrysalises are works of art as diverse as caterpillars and butterflies. All of the many types of chrysalises, however, share a general resemblance. Each one looks like a tiny Chinese lantern, anchored at the tip. Some dangle freely, while others are held more tightly to their support.

Looking more like a fresh bird dropping than a plump and tasty tidbit, a giant swallowtail caterpillar is safe from the sharp eyes and sharp beaks of hungry birds.

This variegated fritillary caterpillar is beginning its miraculous transformation to a butterfly by surrounding itself with a protective chrysalis.

A soon-to-emerge monarch butterfly (*left*) is cramped and squished inside its chrysalis. Once it breaks free (*right*), getting those damp, furled wings to work requires patience. It may take hours for a butterfly to pump fluid through the veins of its wings to stiffen them for flight.

Each family of butterflies has its own unique chrysalis. All swallowtails, for example, rest in a bumpy, angular chrysalis, with a sharply pointed bottom tip; a loop of silk holds the chrysalis to a stem, with the top end tilting outward. The checkerspots transform into a chrysalis that looks like a bird dropping, with a lumpy white exterior blotched with brown.

Amazing changes take place within the chrysalis, as wings develop and other body parts change to the equipment the adult butterfly will need when it emerges. The covering of the chrysalis—which was once the actual skin of the caterpillar-turned-pupa—becomes only a protective cover that shields the work going on inside.

Back to the Beginning
Butterflies emerge easily from the chrysalis when their metamorphosis is complete. A section of the chrysalis opens like a trapdoor to let the butterfly crawl out into the world, leaving its empty chrysalis behind.

Despite the fact that the caterpillar has turned into a butterfly while hidden away in the pupa, its work is not yet complete. The critter that makes its debut doesn't look much like the final product. Newly emerged butterflies have a fat, large body and very small, softly wrinkled wings that hang damp and limp. As the butterfly pumps fluids through the veins of its new wings, they expand and stiffen. As it expels these fluids from its body, its abdomen shrinks until eventually a brand-new, fully transformed butterfly finally takes to the air.

In many species, the entire process takes about a month—about 2 weeks in caterpillar life, 2 weeks in pupa, then presto! Butterfly! Actually, "p . . . r . . . e . . . s . . . t . . . o" is more like it, as the butterfly takes a few hours to pump up its wings and slim down its body.

DESIGNING GARDENS TO HOST BUTTERFLIES

If you'd enjoy watching the unfolding of butterfly life cycles in your yard, the most important thing you can do is plant host plants. They're an even better invitation to butterflies than nectar flowers! While butterflies can usually find their food in many places, finding host plants that will nourish their young is a different story. These essential plants become scarcer and scarcer as we tame wild areas, mow along roadsides, and spread asphalt in place of wild plants.

Some butterflies-to-be are so fussy about their food that they eat only one species of an entire genus, or related group, of plants! The Chinati checkerspot, a species of west Texas, dines exclusively on Big Bend silver leaf (*Leucophyllum minus*), a plant native to the butterfly's limited habitat in shrubby desert. As you might imagine, butterflies with such restrictive appetites can get in trouble quickly as a species when development or unusual weather patterns threaten their host plants. Luckily, these picky eaters are the exception. Most species have wider tastes and will dine on a number of related plants. The eastern black swallowtail, for instance, lays its eggs on many members of the parsley family, as well as some members of the citrus family. You may find the distinctive green-and-black-striped caterpillars on plants as varied in size and shape as dill plants and citrus trees!

The list of host plants that will attract butterflies is as varied as the butterflies themselves, and the plants differ from one part of the country to the next, just as butterflies do. You can simply add your favorite native plants to your garden. Or you can consult "Annuals and Perennials for Caterpillars" on page 114 and "Trees, Shrubs, and Vines for Caterpillars" on page 118, and choose host plants according to the butterflies you want to attract. I prefer the first course of action because with all the thousands of butterflies in America, no list will ever be complete. Besides, I love surprises!

Depend on Natives
Nature links plants and butterflies together, just like all other living things. So it makes sense that southern California butterflies

With wings a striking combo of gold and black, the regal fritillary is a crowning touch for any garden. Here it nectars on wild bergamot (*Monarda fistulosa*).

What's Native, What's Not?

How can you tell whether a plant is native to your area? Sad to say, most of the plants for sale at your local garden center probably aren't natives—many of them originated across the oceans or thousands of miles away. Zinnias, for example, are a fine native if you live in Mexico, but not if you garden in Connecticut. In general, the aisles of shade trees and shrubs are often a better place to find natives than the tables and shelves of perennials and annuals. When in doubt, ask a knowledgeable staff person for guidance at your local garden center.

To learn for yourself what natives grow in your area, find a field guide to wild plants and take a walk through the wild places near your house. Most field guides to wild plants include a word or two about the plants' origins. If the plant isn't a native, it's usually noted as a European weed, a garden escapee, or by another description that tells you that it wasn't growing here before the Europeans arrived.

Another approach is to send for catalogs from native plant specialty nurseries for your area (see "Resources and Recommended Reading" on page 287). Thanks to the spreading interest in our heritage of wild plants, you can find catalogs that cover just about every area. Consult the offerings to find native plants suited—both geographically and culturally—to your garden.

depend on southern California plants, Appalachian butterflies seek out Appalachian plants, prairie butterflies look for prairie plants, and so on in every ecological niche across the country.

American plants evolved right along with American butterflies. Although a few species have also adapted to plants from other countries, it's the time-tested native species that get the most attention from egg-laying females. Over the years, I've learned that nearly every native plant, from grasses to trees, has a butterfly (or moth) that depends upon it for fodder in the caterpillar stage. I enjoy the fun of discovering the first signs of chomping, then searching out the caterpillars and watching them grow. If they're unfamiliar to me, or if I can't find them in a field guide, I put a few in a container with their plant food of choice. Only when I've raised them to maturity can I be sure what species they are. (You'll find complete directions for rearing butterflies later in this chapter.)

Unless you've let your yard go wild, you may have only a few mature shade trees to represent the natives that once graced the place you call home. Even my naturalistic gardens aren't purely native (who could live without the fragrance of bearded irises in June?), but over the years I've added more and more native plants to my gardens. I chose the plants because I liked their flowers or form, or for sentimental reasons, and the butterflies they support have been a delightful bonus.

One of my latest discoveries happened just a few years ago in my backyard, on a warm, late spring day. I was trimming back some wayward branches of an eastern red cedar

(*Juniperus virginiana*), when I noticed some well-camouflaged, dark-green-striped caterpillars among the foliage. Amazed to find something dining on this eastern native tree, I snipped a few short pieces of branches with larvae and popped them into a spacious jar. In less than 2 weeks, the mystery caterpillars had made dark brown chrysalises, which hatched into one of my favorite butterflies, the lovely olive hairstreak. This small butterfly is a beauty, typically sitting with wings closed, showing off the bright green undersides of its wings and delicate hairlike wing "tails."

Keep It Local I found the hairstreak caterpillars when I was living in Indiana, where red cedars are common. Had I been living in Oregon, all the eastern red cedars in the world wouldn't have brought me a single olive hairstreak because this butterfly lives only

(continued on page 116)

Butterfly or Moth?

It can be as difficult to distinguish between moths and butterflies in the early stages of life as when they are adults. Though each unknown larva or pupa offers a mystery, there are some simple clues to help you determine whether your new guest will be a moth or a butterfly.

Each of the stages, except the egg, offers a hint. Moth larvae frequently have hairs covering their bodies, and in some species, these hairs are actually modified spines that pack a painful sting at the slightest touch. The larvae of the Io moth, for instance, which looks as temptingly fuzzy as a new kitten, can leave your skin red and painful for hours, should you brush against it even lightly. I give fuzzy caterpillars even more respect than I give stinging nettles.

If you find a pupa tightly bound along its full length to a twig, the final product will be a moth, not a butterfly. We even label the pupas differently. In moths we call the pupa a cocoon instead of a chrysalis. And if you note a creature struggling to free itself from a strong-walled cocoon, chances are you're looking at an emerging moth. The moth cocoon doesn't have the built in trapdoor that makes a butterfly's emergence relatively easy.

ANNUALS AND PERENNIALS
FOR CATERPILLARS

If you can put up with the look of ragged or rolled-up leaves, or if you don't mind sacrificing a few blossoms, you can increase butterfly populations in your yard by including flowers that serve as host plants for hungry caterpillars. Some of the same annuals and perennials that serve as food for caterpillars will also serve as food for adult butterflies, which will visit to sip nectar from the blooms.

PLANT	DESCRIPTION	BUTTERFLIES ATTRACTED	COMMENTS
Mallows (*Abutilon*, *Malva*, *Sidalcea*, and *Sphaeralcea* spp., and other genera of the family Malvaceae)	Annuals, perennials, and weeds with often colorful flowers. Start with biennial or perennial hollyhocks (*Alcea rosea*) to bring the widespread painted lady butterfly to your garden. Plant in full sun in well-drained ordinary soil; hardy to Zone 3.	Columnella hair-streak, gray hairstreak, reddish hairstreak, painted lady, West Coast lady, several species of skippers	Both native and imported mallows are used as host plants. Plant nectar flowers in front of the hollyhocks so that the spikes of hollyhock flowers can still be seen while their leaves are hidden from view.
Dill (*Anethum graveolens*)	Annual herb with filmy, aromatic leaves and showy heads of chartreuse flowers. Foolproof from seed; just scatter the seeds onto cultivated soil in a sunny spot and let them grow. All zones.	Eastern black swallowtail	Dill is a magnet for egg-laying females of the beautiful eastern black swallowtail. Bring a few caterpillars and dill stems indoors and enjoy the metamorphosis from chrsyalis to butterfly.
Swamp milkweed (*Asclepias incarnata*)	Multistemmed perennial with willowlike leaves and stems topped by packed clusters of rose-pink flowers. Grows well in average garden soil, in sun, as well as in wet places such as along streams and ponds. Hardy to Zone 3.	Monarch	Like other milkweeds, this perennial is sought for nectar by many butterfly species. It is a host plant for monarchs. A white-flowered variety is also available, though aphids may have an affinity for it, which reduces its appeal as a host plant.
Asters (*Aster* spp.)	Experiment with your area's native asters. In the East, plant flat-topped aster (*A. umbellatus*) or blue wood aster (*A. undulatus*). In the West, try showy aster (*A. conspicuus*).	Aster checkerspot and other checkerspots, field crescentspot and other crescentspots	Crescentspot caterpillars metamorphose in aster foliage. Once they emerge from their chrysalises, the adult butterflies will also revisit the plants.

PLANT	DESCRIPTION	BUTTERFLIES ATTRACTED	COMMENTS
Broccoli (*Brassica oleracea*, Botrytis group)	Broccoli florets are bunched flower buds that eventually open into billowy clusters of small yellow flowers. Plant it in sun, in average to fertile well-drained soil, in any zone.	Many species of whites and sulphurs	If you don't appreciate cabbage whites visiting your broccoli, keep a floating row cover of lightweight spun fiber over your plants.
Alfalfa (*Medicago sativa*)	A trailing perennial with long stems of paired leaves and pointed clusters of rich blue to deep purple flowers that are sought by nectaring butterflies. Smells like new-mown clover. Grow it in sun to part shade in any ordinary soil.	Marine blue, orange-bordered blue, and especially the vividly colored orange sulphur (the "alfalfa butterfly")	Train this sprawling plant to lean against a fence or upright neighbors, such as Joe-Pye weed (*Eupatorium purpureum*). Caterpillars eat its flowers and leaves, but don't worry—you'll still have some of the pretty flowers to enjoy yourself.
Scarlet runner bean (*Phaseolus coccineus*)	A downsized, bush-type version of the scarlet runner bean vine. Popular with nectaring hummingbirds, this annual is a great plant to add to flower gardens (as is its vining relative). Grow it in full sun, in average to fertile well-drained soil, in any zone.	Gray hairstreak	Take advantage of the bean-eating appetite of the caterpillars of this delicately colored butterfly. Farmers call them pests when they burrow into developing bean pods, but you'll enjoy the bounty of adult butterflies that hatch in early spring.
Nasturtium (*Tropaeolum majus*)	Trailing annual with bright, spurred flowers in yellow, orange, red, apricot, rose, and cream. Easy to grow in all zones. Plant seed in early spring in sunny, well-drained, ordinary soil. Also nice in window boxes and containers.	Cabbage white, other whites	Nasturtium leaves have a peppery tang that is similar to mustards. Hummingbirds adore the blossoms.
Violets (*Viola* spp.)	Common, low-growing perennials with a cluster of leaves holding a nosegay of blue to purple flowers; may also have white or yellow blooms, depending on species. Easy to grow in any ordinary soil, in sun or shade. Cultivate native violets for butterflies; you can find the plants in native plant specialty catalogs.	Most species of the beautiful golden orange and black fritillaries; also the atypical Diana, a fritillary species in which the female is black and blue instead of orange	As with most host plants, native species are usually the egg site of choice for butterflies. The Atlantis fritillary has been known to prefer a few native white-flowered Canada violets (*V. canadensis*) over a multitude of common sweet violets (*V. odorata*), plants that originally hailed from Europe.

Like other swallowtails, the pipevine is marked with spots on its underside. Wide open, its large wings are dramatic black with a blue sheen.

in the eastern half of the country. Host plants can attract butterflies from only a relatively short distance, usually less than a mile. You'll wait in vain if you plant sweet bay (*Magnolia virginiana*) in New York hoping to attract the Palamedes swallowtail because this butterfly rarely travels beyond the great swamps of the South.

In a very few cases, butterfly experts believe that gardeners adding host plants to our gardens may have contributed to the expanding ranges of butterflies. Pipevine swallowtails, for instance, have moved northward from their usual more southerly haunts, burgeoning with the garden popularity of their host plants, the four native American species of Dutchman's pipes (*Aristolochia* spp.), a genus of vines that also includes plants native to other countries. The increased ornamental use of maypops (*Passiflora incarnata*) seems to be having a similar effect on the Gulf fritillary, whose caterpillars munch the vines. But the expansion of these ranges didn't happen in leaps and bounds of hundreds of miles. It has been very gradual, from one garden to another.

Host Plants for Favorite Butterflies

Many butterflies are limited in their range; their favored host plants are usually native plants that thrive in the areas where the butterflies do. Many butterflies that have become endangered or threatened by extinction are species that depend on a native plant that grows only in a small area. When those areas are destroyed by development or population pressure, the availability of those host plants declines, and so do the butterflies.

It's highly worthwhile for butterfly enthusiasts to include regionally native plants in the garden, both to counteract the effects of development and to increase the delight in our own backyards. In the tables in this chapter, I've included many native plants as well as some nonnatives. All of the plants I recommend have wide appeal as host plants to butterfly species that range across nearly the entire continent and sometimes to butterflies of more limited range as well. No matter where you live, you can add some of these plants to your garden and enjoy the likely prospect of more butterflies season after season.

ADD SOME NONNATIVES, TOO Even nonnative plants can host a good crop of caterpillars when butterflies select host plants within a family or genus of plants. Giant swallowtails and eastern black swallowtails feed on native members of the citrus family, which include the small trees prickly ash (*Zanthoxylum americanum*) and hop tree (*Ptelea trifoliata*). They will also readily adopt another member of the citrus family, the lovely gray-foliaged herb called rue (*Ruta graveolens*), which hails from the Balkans and southeastern Europe. A vivid turquoise-blue Texas butterfly called the flashing astraptes uses species of chaste trees (*Vitex* spp.) as a host plant, even though they're not native to North America.

You'll find some great exotic plants on the host plant charts in this chapter, some of which may already be growing in your garden. Other nonnatives are common weeds that grow in your lawn or flowerbeds, such as plantain, a favorite host plant of the buckeye butterfly.

To identify additional nonnative plants that butterflies like, keep your eyes open for signs of caterpillars. Discovering feeding holes in the foliage or the collected pepperlike droppings of frass on the leaves will tell you that someone has adopted your nonnative plant as its home.

Adopt Imperfections

When you plant gardens with host plants, keep in mind that caterpillars eat a *lot.* Your plants are likely to acquire a certain moth-eaten look as the caterpillars feed and may even be entirely stripped of foliage. When I snuggled in some bronze fennel next to my red dahlias in the border, I intended its smoldering dark foliage to counteract the zing of the flowers. I never got to see whether it worked. A discerning eastern black swallowtail laid her eggs on this plant (which belongs to the same family as dill and parsley). By the time they were full grown, the swallowtail caterpillars had chewed that feathery stalk down to a nub.

Bare stems topped by flowers look bad in the garden, but leafy stems with no flowers are even worse. In my garden, yellow ironweed, also known as wingstem (*Verbesina alternifolia*), once added a nice splash of yellow

(continued on page 120)

Common milkweed has deliciously fragrant flowers that draw nectaring butterflies, and its stout leaves are the dinner for monarch caterpillars.

TREES, SHRUBS, AND VINES
FOR CATERPILLARS

Try some of these permanent plants to bring more butterflies to your neighborhood. Because the caterpillars that eat tree foliage will be high out of view, you won't get the up-close-and-personal look at their lives that you would have if the larvae were at lower levels. Watch for frass (black pepperlike caterpillar droppings) below the trees, or look upward for chewed leaves, to find out whether your efforts are paying off. Of course, a freshly hatched batch of viceroys or hackberries at your flowers and fruit feeders will also give you a good clue that your butterfly habitat is happening.

PLANT	DESCRIPTION	BUTTERFLIES ATTRACTED	COMMENTS
Dutchman's pipes (*Aristolochia* spp.)	Vigorous perennial vines with high-climbing stems, heart-shaped leaves, and strange brown flowers. More than 300 species of pipevine exist in the world, but only 4 species are known to be used by butterflies: American natives *A. californica*, *A. longiflora*, *A. macrophylla*, and *A. serpentaria*. Plant in sun to shade, in average soil; provide a sturdy trellis, arbor, wall, or fence for the vine to climb. Hardiness varies with species.	Pipevine swallowtail	Only one butterfly is attracted to the host plant pipevine, but what a beauty! Huge and black with a cobalt sheen on its hindwings, the pipevine swallowtail was once restricted to those areas where the native species of the vine naturally grew. As the vine spread outside its former range, thanks to gardeners who adopted its use, the butterfly has also expanded its range.
Ceanothus, California lilacs (*Ceanothus* spp.)	Shrubs bear usually blue but also white, pink, or lilac flowers. Hardiness varies with species; most are hardy to Zone 8 and several to Zone 7; Oregon tea (*C. sanguineus*) thrives through Zone 5 and New Jersey tea (*C. americanus*) to Zone 4.	Spring azure, mottled duskywing, brown elfin, western elfin, California hairstreak, hedgerow hairstreak, Nais metalmark, pale tiger swallowtail, California tortoiseshell	Many of the species that use ceanothus as a host plant are butterflies of the western United States, where most of these shrubs are native. The spring azure ranges throughout the continent, so try its host plant, New Jersey tea (*C. americanus*), in any region.
Hackberry (*Celtis occidentalis*, *C. laevigata*, *C. pallida*)	Large, deciduous, and native American shade trees; best for large yards. Odd, warty gray bark and yellow-green fall color; bears bountiful small fruits cherished by songbirds. Plant in sun to shade, in average soil. Hardiness varies with species; *C. occidentalis* is hardy to Zone 2.	Empress Antonia, Empress Flora, Empress Leilia, hackberry butterfly, mourning cloak, question mark, pavon, red-bordered metalmark, snout butterfly, tawny emperor	In areas where hackberries (and the related sugarberry, *C. laevigata*) are native, you'll see common hackberry, mourning cloak, and question mark butterflies, among others. Some butterflies are more particular; Empress Leilia seeks only the desert or spiny hackberry (*C. pallida*), which grows in the Southwest.

PLANT	DESCRIPTION	BUTTERFLIES ATTRACTED	COMMENTS
Hops (*Humulus lupulus*)	Perennial vine with delicate leaves and papery clusters of conelike bracts surrounding the flower spike. Grow in full sun in average to fertile well-drained soil, and provide the vine with a trellis, arbor, or fence to climb. Hardy to Zone 5.	Comma, question mark, red admiral	Hops are native to America as well as to Europe and Asia.
Passionflowers (*Passiflora* spp.)	Perennial vines, mostly frost-tender, with complex flowers. Plant in sun to part shade, in average to fertile well-drained soil. Try *P. incarnata*, hardy to Zone 6, or try tropical types in milder climates.	Gulf fritillary, Mexican fritillary, variegated fritillary, Julia, crimson-patched longwing, zebra longwing	Passionflowers are native mostly to the American tropics. The caterpillars that feed on the plants are also southern species. The fruit of *P. incarnata* is edible.
Oaks (*Quercus* spp.)	Usually large trees with leathery, glossy, often lobed leaves, which may be deciduous or evergreen. Those retaining green leaves year-round are called live oaks. Plant in soil and site appropriate for the species you select; purchase seedlings at local nurseries or from specialty catalogs. Or, plant acorns, which yield trees several feet high in 2 or 3 years.	Several species of duskywings and hairstreaks, as well as California sister, Araxes skipper, and short-tailed Arizona skipper	Plant oaks that are native to your region. Any butterflies whose caterpillars eat oak leaves are likely to be attracted. If you plant a native canyon live oak (*Q. chrysolepis*) in the Southwest or a coast live oak (*Q. agrifolia*) in the Pacific Northwest, either tree will be apt to receive the attentions of the California sister's caterpillars.
Willows (*Salix* spp.)	These plants have slender leaves and flexible young branches. Native and imported willow species will attract customers. Willows vary in habit (tree to shrub), form (weeping to upright), and hardiness, depending on the species. Plant willows far from any pipes that carry water (or sewage); their water-seeking roots can travel great distances and wrap around pipes or even break through them! Hardiness varies with species.	Admirals and fritillaries, faunus anglewing, dreamy duskywing, Acadian hairstreak, sylvan hairstreak, striped hairstreak, mourning cloak, red-spotted purple, great northern sulphur, Scudder's willow sulphur, western tiger swallowtail, Compton tortoiseshell, viceroy	Choose your favorite willow seedlings at a local nursery or from a native plant specialty catalog. To start your own seedling, try snipping a few 12-inch stems from a willow in early spring. Strip off the stem's lower leaves, and place the stem in moist soil to root. To avoid pipe-infiltration problems, stick to dwarf or shrubby species rather than tree types, and know what's underneath your planting site.
Elms (*Ulmus* spp.)	Small-leaved shade trees found nationwide. Some native species, including slippery elm (*U. rubra*) and rock elm (*U. thomasii*), are hardy to at least Zone 4. Imported Siberian elm (*U. pumila*) may go uneaten.	Zephyr anglewing, European large tortoiseshell, comma, question mark, mourning cloak	Elm seeds are a favorite of some songbirds, so seedling trees may spring up in your garden.

near the end of summer to partner the late-season purples. But the common blue butterflies claimed their rights to this native perennial, and now I've sacrificed the clusters of blooms as larvae food.

Many host plants will be targets the same season you plant them, although it may take a year or longer for butterflies to discover some plants. If you don't like the look of shabby foliage or sparse flowers, keep your host plants in a more discreet part of the garden—the back row or a far corner.

I let my chomped-on plants stand proudly throughout the garden. My gardens are never "perfect" as far as design anyway, and the pleasure of watching caterpillars up close is worth the sacrifice of some degree of plant perfection. Besides, the feeding caterpillars are great fun to show off to friends and family that come to visit.

BEST PLACES FOR HOST PLANTS Many butterfly host plants are pretty things that look good in the garden—at least until the caterpillars devour them. In most cases, your plants won't disappear wholesale, so you'll still benefit from some foliage and flowers. Use them just as you would if they weren't butterfly plants.

- Add annuals and perennials to flowerbeds, or start a new patch just for caterpillars.
- Plant trees to shade your yard, or create a layer of midheight plants under mature shade trees.
- Use host-plant shrubs as hedges or in groups for the most eye appeal.
- Slip flowering shrubs into mixed borders or along a fence.
- Grow vines up your porch posts, along your deck railing, or over an arbor or trellis.
- Even if you have no yard at all, you can offer butterflies a fine feast. Plant annuals, perennials, and vines in containers on a balcony or in a window box to get more butterfly gardening out of your space.

For designs for creating gardens of host plants and incorporating host plants with other garden areas, see Chapter 7.

PICKERS BEWARE Almost every time I bring a big bunch of cut flowers into the house from the garden, I end up importing a caterpillar or two. I usually notice the hitchhiker when I spot a sprinkling of the caterpillar frass, looking like spilled pepper on the table beneath the bouquet. When I find the caterpillar, I carefully transfer it to another plant of the same kind in the garden. I like to find these mystery guests because it adds to my knowledge of who's eating what. When I visited a friend in southern California a few years ago, I was surprised to find that her pretty bouquet of marigolds on the dining room table was crawling with small purple-striped green caterpillars. They turned out to be the larvae of the dainty dwarf yellow butterfly, the smallest member of the sulphur family.

CABBAGE-WHITE WINDOW BOX

Enjoy a close-up view of the entire miracle of metamorphosis from your favorite easy chair by filling a window box with simple-to-grow nasturtiums and broccoli to attract egg-laying cabbage white butterflies.

MATERIALS

*Window box, about
32 inches long
Window-box liner
Mounting hardware
Potting soil mix for containers,
with a few scoops of compost and aged manure
added for extra fertility and
improved water retention
8 broccoli plants
Nasturtium seeds*

---

1. Soak the nasturtium seeds in a saucer of water overnight so that they germinate more quickly.

2. Empty the potting mix into a heavy-duty trash bag, being careful not to inhale the dust.

3. Add compost and warm water and squeeze the bag until mix is moistened throughout.

4. Mount the window box at a window where you will be able to see it closely from inside.

5. Insert the liner and fill it with potting soil.

6. Scoop aside the soil to plant the young broccoli plants, spacing them roughly equidistantly. Firm the soil around each plant.

7. Poke the nasturtium seeds 1 inch deep and 1 to 2 inches apart into the soil along the front edge of the box.

8. Water as often as needed to keep the soil moist.

9. Enjoy the view!

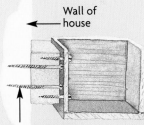

Wall of house

Mounting screw

WEEDS TO TOLERATE FOR CATERPILLARS' SAKE

Tolerating weeds is a lesson that's hard for many gardeners to learn, but lots of these scorned plants are favored by butterflies as hosts for the succeeding generation. These common and widespread weeds also attract many widespread (and limited-range) butterflies.

PLANT	DESCRIPTION	BUTTERFLIES ATTRACTED	COMMENTS
Queen Anne's lace (*Daucus carota*)	Tall, lacy-leaved plants with flat-topped clusters of tiny white flowers. The garden carrot was bred for size and taste from this perennial species.	Anise swallowtail, desert swallowtail, eastern black swallowtail, short-tailed black swallowtail	Make a habit of giving a quick once-over to every Queen-Anne's lace plant you pass; surprisingly often, you'll spot swallowtail caterpillars.
Plantains (*Plantago* spp.)	Rosettes either of long, narrow leaves with bare-stemmed flowerheads, or wide, simple leaves with small flowering stems. Produces many small seeds. Perennial.	Buckeye, Baltimore checkerspot, chalcedon checkerspot, colon checkerspot, Edith's checkerspot, variegated fritillary	Except for the cosmopolitan buckeye, most butterflies that use plantain as a host live in the western United States.
Knotweeds, smartweeds, bistorts (*Polygonum* spp.)	Usually sprawling plants with jointed stems, simple leaves, and spikes of pink, white, or reddish flowers and seeds. Both annuals and perennials.	Acmon blue, bog fritillary, bronze copper, purplish copper, Napaea fritillary, Titania's fritillary	The widespread bronze and purplish coppers make use of various species of *Polygonum,* while the other butterflies stick to a single species. Butterflies also visit knotweeds for the nectar in their tiny flowers.
Docks, sheep sorrels, sorrels (*Rumex* spp.)	Coarse, big perennial weeds with deep taproots. Large bannerlike or arrow-shaped leaves will grow in a clump, from which arises an attention-getting stalk decorated with many brown seeds. Favored by birds in winter.	Buckeye, American copper, bronze copper, Edith's copper, great gray copper, lustrous copper, purplish copper, ruddy copper	Sorrel—an herb prized by the French for flavoring soups—is just a tamer version of these common garden weeds!
Clovers (*Trifolium* spp.)	Three leaflets make up the distinctive clover leaf, the hallmark of these widespread perennial weeds. Some grow to knee-high or better, while others, including the lawn weed white clover (*T. repens*), spread into patches by their rooting stems. Sweet-scented flowers may be white, pink, or purple.	California dogface, dogface butterfly, eastern tailed blue, greenish blue, Shasta blue, Mexican cloudywing, sleepy orange, little yellow, and several species of sulphurs	Sulphurs love their clovers, just as whites go for mustards and fritillaries depend on violets. The ultra-common lawn weed, white clover (*T. repens*), is valuable both for its lure as a host plant and for being a nectar plant for blues, sulphurs, whites, and other butterflies.

Larvae on edibles are not quite so charming. I use floating row covers for complete protection of all my cole crops, just to make sure we don't inadvertently eat any cabbage-white caterpillars. Because parsley, fennel, and dill are so popular with my beloved black swallowtails, these herbs always get a careful going-over before I snip them for cooking or salads. My most surprising caterpillar find was a lovely, tiny, deep blue character that was happily feeding on blueberries I'd bought at the supermarket. I blessed the grower for not using pesticides, removed the caterpillar, and ate the rest of the berries with my eyes closed.

Raise Your Own Butterflies Caterpillars are so single-minded, focused only on eating, that it's a simple process to raise them in captivity. All you need is something to hold a handful of leaves. A washed glass or plastic jar from peanut butter or mayonnaise is perfect, or you can use a circle of wire screening with a paper plate for a top and bottom (see page 124). As long as you supply fresh quantities of their chosen food plant, they won't have any interest in leaving the jar. Only when it's time to pupate will they want to venture outside their little world. At that point, supply a stick as prime real estate for pupating, and just slip a cover over the container. If you use the original jar lid, poke a profusion of air holes in it.

Raising caterpillars to butterflies is an ideal project for adults of any age and for older children. Little ones may get impatient because of the "long" wait between developments. You know your kids best, so decide up front whether you want to get them excited about anticipating a butterfly from the start of the project or only when the chrysalis is near hatching.

HUMMINGBIRD FAMILY LIFE

Hummingbirds are just as full of surprises as butterflies. One of the biggest surprises (dare I say disappointments?) for me was to discover that—unlike nearly every other bird I was familiar with, in which pair bonds and shared duties are part of the game—hummingbirds go it alone when it comes to family life. In this clan, it's the female that does all the work: building the fabulous nest, sitting on the eggs, and feeding the babies, while the male acts like a 20-something guy out for a night on the town. She's not complaining, though—in fact, she vigorously drives the male away should he get anywhere near the nest.

Males and females of a species may stake out separate territories when mating is on their minds, often far apart: females in the bottom of a canyon, for instance, with males hanging out on the higher, drier slopes. Females begin work on their nest even before they find a mate. Only when the undeniable urge to start a family strikes do the two get together. Males show off with fancy, high-flying aerial stunts until eventually the female acquiesces and the seed is planted. Then the mom-to-be goes her own way, finishes the nest, and raises the kids, while Romeo hangs out waiting for the next available partner to come along.

HOMEMADE BUTTERFLY FARM

There's no need to send away for a kit to raise butterflies. You can do it yourself for free, using a recycled container and caterpillars you find in the garden. Check the parsley, dill, and fennel first for likely candidates—black swallowtails are very easy to raise.

MATERIALS

*Strip of stiff wire screening or
   fine-mesh hardware cloth,
   about 10 inches wide by 20
   inches long*
Twist-ties
Caterpillar
*Handful of host plant foliage
   (one short stem with leaves)*
2 paper plates
*Stick of about pencil thickness,
   about 8 inches long*

---

1. Bend the wire mesh into a circle, overlap the ends, and secure in place with twist-ties.

2. Set the wire container on a paper plate.

3. Find a feeding butterfly caterpillar in your garden. Try to identify it so that you are sure it is not a moth caterpillar; moths often pupate underground and overwinter, so they are usually harder to raise to adulthood.

4. Put the caterpillar and host plant into the container.

5. Place the stick at an angle inside the container for the caterpillar to use when pupating. (It may also use the screen walls or the host plant).

6. Cover the container with a second paper plate.

7. Every day, lift the top and carefully remove any wilted or dried leaves and replace with fresh greens. Do not bump or drop the caterpillar. If necessary, hold fresh foliage at the caterpillar's head to transfer the caterpillar from the old foliage to the new.

8. If many droppings accumulate, lift the container, holding the plates in place. Slide the bottom plate aside about 1/2 inch and allow the droppings to fall out. (Frass is a great fertilizer for houseplants; just dump it on the soil surface.)

9. When the caterpillar transforms to a chrysalis, remove everything but the chrysalis (and whatever it is attached to) from the container.

10. Check the chrysalis daily. When the butterfly is about to emerge, the color of the chrysalis will change.

11. When the adult emerges, do *not* touch its wings. Remove the top plate. Allow the butterfly to make its own way up the stick or the wall of the container toward the open top.

12. When the butterfly fully expands its wings, carry the container outside and let the new flyer go free.

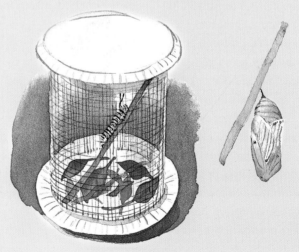

NESTING PLACES FOR HUMMINGBIRDS

Like all birds, hummingbirds have their favorite haunts when it comes time to build a nest. These tiny, complex constructions, with an outside diameter no bigger than a golf ball, may be saddled to a branch, stuck to a porch light, or hung in a curve of a vine or a coil of rope.

The average gardener is lucky to find even a single hummingbird nest in a lifetime. The homes are so well camouflaged and so tiny that they look like nothing more than a bump on a log. Even in winter, when branches are bare, the nests are practically invisible.

Some hummingbird researchers have made a career out of tracking down nests. Thanks to their observations, we can plan additions to our yard that may tempt the tiny birds to make it their home base, too. (If you'd like to read some of their accounts, check the books listed in "Resources and Recommended Reading" on page 287.)

Plants for Nest Sites

As you might expect, hummingbirds work with what's naturally available in the areas where they breed. The parent bird's goal is to keep the nest hidden and the young protected from the vagaries of weather. The same species may nest from just above waist-height to 80 feet up, which makes finding nests a challenge.

In the dry West, hummingbirds may seek the shelter of cottonwoods along a stream or build in a prickly clump of cactus. In the rainy Northwest, they build in dense conifers that provide a roof to keep the nestlings dry. Palm trees are popular nesting sites in southern California. In high-altitude areas where temperatures fluctuate widely between night and day, they may choose a sheltering tree on the eastern side of a forest, where the sun's rays will shine early in the morning to warm the nest after the cold night.

Willows, alders, aspens, cottonwoods, oaks, sycamores, pines, spruces, and firs support hummingbird nests in the West, where these trees and shrubs are native. Not surprisingly, in the high mountains, the typical alpine fir (*Abies lasiocarpa*) is often the tree of choice. These tiny birds frequently use blackberry vines in the Pacific Northwest. In the East, the list of nest sites

A black-chinned hummingbird's nest, like the similar homes of its relatives, is built to blend in. Watch the female bird for clues to the location.

If it's soft and fuzzy, a hummingbird may want it for nest material. This broad-tailed hummer is checking out the possibilities of cattail fluff.

for the ruby-throated hummingbird is practically endless—oaks, hickories, sweet gum, sour gum, tuliptree, and other hardwoods, plus junipers, hemlocks, and pines.

What's the lesson here? Well, if you're choosing plants with hummingbird nest sites in mind, go for the most common native trees and shrubs in your area. One interesting theory suggests that hummingbirds may be more likely to nest in a tree that has a healthy growth of lichens on its bark and branches. The birds use this material when they build their nests, and perhaps they prefer not to travel too far with construction materials.

Birds with an idiosyncratic bent may use very unnatural nesting sites, too. Sharp-eyed observers have spotted nests on utility wires, pathway lights, and old tire chains hanging on a shed wall. I even detected one on a loop of a forgotten plastic extension cord dangling from the roof of a mobile home.

Finding and Observing the Nest
If you go out looking for a hummingbird nest, your chances of finding one are slim. But if you pay attention to hummingbird behavior in your yard, you may have the rare delight of pinpointing a home site.

It's practically impossible to overlook hummingbird courtship flights and mating (you'll find descriptions in Chapter 9) because they're loud, high-motion activities. When you notice such goings-on, you can be sure that an occupied nest will soon follow.

Even if you miss the first stages of the romance, you may still see the female bird working on construction duties. It takes a lot of trips to collect enough spider silk to build a substantial cup—even one that's only a couple of inches across. Get in the habit of sitting quietly and scanning your yard for a female hummingbird. When you spot one, watch where she goes and what she does.

It takes some practice to be able to follow the flight of a hummingbird. Try it for a few days to improve your skill. If you're lucky, you may spot her repeatedly entering a particular tree or shrub, narrowing your search. Keep in mind that many people who find nests do so accidentally, while gazing out a window, doing the dishes, or daydreaming as they sweep the porch.

When you've determined the general area of a hummingbird nest, stand motionless nearby, far enough away to avoid causing distress to the bird (15 feet should be fine).

Wait for the female to arrive, and try to pinpoint where she goes. Then follow up with a slow scan through binoculars.

Should you find a nest site, give the young family some privacy. You don't want the female to abandon the site once you've discovered it! If the parent threatens you with a buzzing attack, back off and watch from a little farther away.

Nesting Materials Disguise is the name of the game when it comes to hummingbird nest construction. These ingenious birds use strands of sticky spiderweb to bind their small, stout cup together, adding various other materials according to their species or their whim. They stud the outside of the nest with fragments of lichen, cupped pieces of bud scales fallen from leafing-out trees, and tiny bits of bark to make the nest blend into the surroundings. They line the inner cup with softest plant down, spider silk, or animal hair.

While all species build marvels of construction, I'd give the top prize to the calliope hummingbird, which decorates its nest with bits of bark so that it looks just like a pinecone, and hangs it from a group of cones dangling from a branch.

HELPING HAND FOR NESTING HUMMINGBIRDS

Hummingbirds resent observers at the nest, but they welcome handouts of nesting material. They will find their own spider silk, bark fragments, and lichen, but you can help by offering soft, fine-textured materials for the nest lining.

MATERIALS

Wire-basket–type suet feeder
Combings from a dog's soft
  undercoat
Cotton (not spun polyester)
  balls or sheets
Small, soft feathers from an
  old down pillow
Cottonwood fluff

1. Pull cotton into pieces, allowing long fibers to extend.

2. Hang suet feeder about 6 feet from ground, away from all seed, suet, and nectar feeders and away from nectar flowers, to allow female hummingbird unchallenged access.

3. Fill the wire basket loosely with collected nesting materials. Let some protrude through openings in the wire grid.

If you enjoy watching songbirds and other birds gather nesting materials, add a second wire suet feeder filled with the soft stuff. Nail this suet basket to a board and attach it securely to its support so it doesn't swing under the bird's weight—the motion of the hanging suet feeder tends to deter bigger birds.

CHAPTER 7

Butterfly and Hummingbird

GARDEN DESIGNS

Planting a garden designed especially for butterflies and hummingbirds is the finishing touch for your backyard habitat. The gardens shown in this chapter are easy to care for and bloom abundantly, filled with nectar plants to tempt hummingbirds and butterflies to your yard.

At the beginning of the chapter, you'll find some easy designs using only annual flowers. These are gardens you can start from seed or bedding plants, and the only care required is some watering and weeding until the plants are established. I've followed up these easy annual gardens with more complex designs that include perennials, shrubs, and even a tree or two. For adventurous gardeners, I finish out the chapter with "idea gardens." I provide a list of plants for a particular color scheme, with descriptions and care information, and leave it to you to choose the size, shape, and arrangement of the garden.

No matter where you live, you'll find that butterflies will certainly visit these gardens, and in many places hummingbirds will find the flowers, too. Watch the gardens closely, and you'll also spot many other beautiful nectar drinkers, like wasps, bees, and interesting beetles. These visitors needn't alarm you—as long as you don't disturb them while they're feeding, you can enjoy their company while they enjoy the flowers.

Pot of Fire

A container garden is perfect for a beginning gardener or for anyone who wants a quick and easy gardening project. Because the color red is so attractive to hummingbirds, this container group will attract them even in a courtyard or other area where there are no flower gardens nearby. It will hum with activity all summer and into fall, especially during migration season, when you're likely to see territorial squabbles erupt over sipping rights to your bright flowers.

Use the largest container you can afford—and carry. A wooden half-barrel or extra-large plastic pot is perfect. Fill the bottom third of the container with packing peanuts to save on soil mix; plant roots will go no deeper than about 12 inches. Use a soilless planting mix and add some compost to improve soil fertility and water retention. You can supply a trellis for the climbing cypress vine (*Ipomoea quamoclit*), also called star glory, or let it wend its way among the arrangement. It's a delicate vine, with light, lacy foliage, and will not overpower the other plants. The plants need full sun.

For even more drawing power, plant one or two other pots with some of the same plants, and group the pots together. Or, echo your pot of fire by setting the containers elsewhere in your yard. Coral gem, also called parrot's beak (*Lotus berthelotti*), for instance, makes a beautiful hanging basket; red nasturtiums are striking in a window box; and 'Fiesta del Sol' Mexican sunflower (*Tithonia rotundifolia*) can brighten a patio party all by itself.

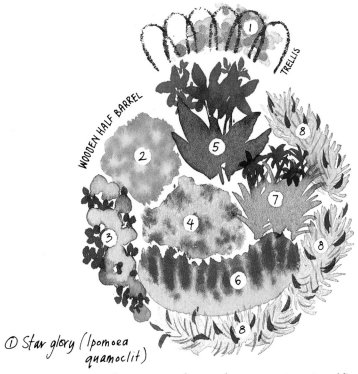

① Star glory (Ipomoea quamoclit)

② 'Fiesta del Sol' Mexican sunflower (Tithonia rotundifolia 'Fiesta del Sol')

③ 'Empress of India' nasturtium (Tropaeolum 'Empress of India')

④ Maltese cross (Lychnis chalcedonica)

⑤ Red-flowered canna (Canna 'The President' or other red flowered cultivar)

⑥ Scarlet sage (Salvia splendens)

⑦ 'Viva' hybrid lily (Lilium 'Viva')

⑧ Coral gem (Lotus berthelotti)

Butterfly-Shaped Garden

Here's a great garden for kids to plant and watch—the idea of "coloring in" a butterfly shape with flowers will charm them. The ideal spot for this garden is on a sloping area of lawn or in a spot where you'll be able to see the butterfly silhouette from an upstairs window. This garden needs full sun and average to fertile well-drained soil.

The design relies on long-blooming annuals to fill in the wings and body of the butterfly. Most are inexpensive and readily available as bedding plants, already in bud and bloom, at garden centers. You can also grow the zinnias and cosmos from seed easily and quickly.

As a bonus, this garden radiates delightful scents, thanks to the lightly scented cosmos, the alyssum (which smells like honey), and the heliotrope (which carries the fragrance of vanilla).

Feel free to exercise your own creativity and make a butterfly-shaped bed of other colors. Just pick flowers of bright colors that contrast sharply with each other to define the various sections of the wings and the body of your creation. For a good view of your artwork, plant this design where you can see it from an elevated vantage point—your deck or upstairs window, perhaps.

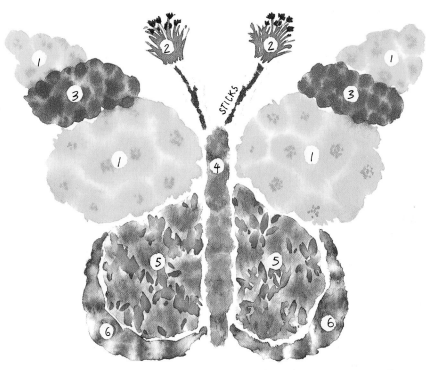

1 Yellow cosmos (Cosmos sulfureus)

2 Deep pink or red-flowered dianthus (Dianthus cvs.)

3 Red-flowered dwarf-type common zinnia (Zinnia elegans)

4 Purple-flowered sweet alyssum (Lobularia maritima)

5 Purple-flowered heliotrope (Heliotropium arborescens)

6 White-flowered sweet alyssum (Lobularia maritima)

10-Dollar Butterfly Garden

Planting a garden from seed is a great bargain, and it can be an even better deal if you manage to hit the 10-for-a-buck seed sales held by many discount stores early in the season. I always stock up on as many packs as the store will let me buy. I find that outdated seeds still germinate well enough to make the price a bargain, even 5 years down the line.

This is another great garden for children to plant. It features flowers that are among the easiest of all annuals to grow from seed. They flower in several weeks after planting in spring. Even better, they self-sow in moderate to liberal amounts, so the garden renews itself. Plant in full sun, in lean to good well-drained garden soil. Keep the garden weeded until the flowers fill in thickly. Then stand back, and let the butterflies have at it.

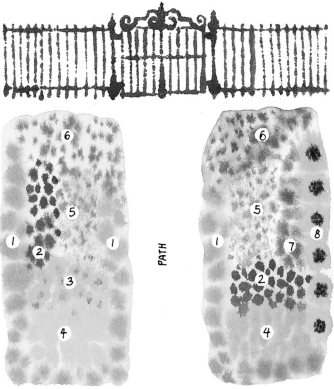

① Marigolds (Tagetes 'Golden Gem' or other cvs.)

② Zinnias (Zinnia, any spp. or cv.)

③ Calliopsis (Coreopsis tinctoria)

④ Yellow cosmos (Cosmos sulfureus or C. bipinnatus)

⑤ Bachelor's buttons (Centaurea cyanus)

⑥ Garden balsam (Impatiens balsamina)

⑦ Cosmos (Cosmos bipinnatus)

⑧ Sunflowers (Helianthus debilis or H. annuus, any cv. — or a handful of bird sunflower seeds)

Summer Garden of Easy Annuals

If you like a riot of color, this garden of bright lights will shine for you. Even from a distance, it will catch the eye of your human garden visitors, as well as butterflies and hummingbirds. All of these plants will thrive in full sun and in average garden soil.

Perfect for gardeners on a budget, this design uses annuals that are easy to grow from seed. You can also buy most of the plants as bedding plants at garden centers if you're impatient for the color. Expect to begin enjoying flowers in early summer, with blooms continuing until frost—or into late fall in mild areas. Many of the flowers will self-sow to give you a start on next year's garden for free. Four o'clocks (known as Marvel of Peru for their different-colored flowers on the same plant) often spring back from their tuberous roots, even in cold climates. Some of the plants will attract butterflies, while others signal to hummingbirds. A few garner the attentions of both.

① Star glory (Ipomoea quamoclit)

② Four o'clock (Mirabilis jalapa)

③ Red-flowered common zinnia (Zinnia elegans)

④ Snow on the mountain (Euphorbia marginata)

⑤ Garden balsam (Impatiens balsamina)

⑥ China aster (Callistephus chinensis)

⑦ Cleome or spider flower (Cleome hassleriana)

⑧ Globe amaranth 'Strawberry fields' (Gomphrena 'Strawberry fields')

⑨ Calendula (Calendula officinalis)

⑩ Blanket flower (Gaillardia pulchella)

⑪ 'Fiesta del Sol' Mexican sunflower (Tithonia rotundifolia 'Fiesta del Sol')

⑫ Annual phlox (Phlox drummondi)

⑬ Signet marigold (Tagetes tenuifolia)

Herb Garden for Butterflies

Flowering herbs are a great nectar source for butterflies. Larger swallowtails and monarchs generally prefer large flat flowers like zinnias that give them a more stable perch. Many smaller butterflies, however, visit the smaller flowers of flowering herbs, clinging to the stems or spikes while extracting the sweet stuff. This garden will invite tiny butterflies known as blues, coppers, and metalmarks, as well as hairstreaks, whites and sulphurs, and many others.

Plant your herb garden in full sun, in well-drained soil, where the plants will thrive on minimal care. Fertilizing or amending the soil isn't necessary. As the plants grow, those that tend to spread will weave throughout the clumps and more upright growers, creating a tapestry of muted grays and greens. All of these herbs are perennials, except the dill and parsley. They're easy to buy as potted plants at garden centers. Dill, an annual, is simple to grow from seed, but buy young plants of parsley, which takes forever to sprout from seed. A biennial that will bloom in its second year, parsley will attract egg-laying black swallowtails to its foliage as well as butterflies to its Queen Anne's lace–like flowers.

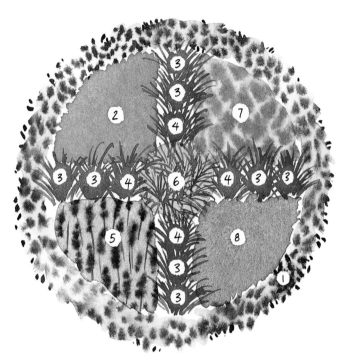

① Creeping thyme (Thymus serpyllum)
② Parsley (Petroselinum crispum)
③ Chives (Allium schoenoprasum)
④ Garlic chives (Allium tunersosum)
⑤ Lavender (Lavandula spp.)
⑥ Dill (Anethum graveolens)
⑦ Oregano (Origanum spp.)
⑧ Rosemary (Rosmarinus spp.)

All-in-One Garden for Butterflies

Butterfly host plants can look ratty in a garden setting, thanks to the caterpillars that chomp their leaves. When you work them in among other plants, however, the foliage damage is hardly noticeable, and the garden is doubly attractive to butterflies. This design includes many plants that serve as both host plants to caterpillars and as nectar plants for butterflies. Expect to spend exciting hours playing detective as you hunt for caterpillars among the flowers! The garden will also satisfy fruit-eating butterflies—they will appreciate the overripe fruits of the crabapple and tomatoes. The egg-laying adult butterflies will find plenty of plants to lavish attention on—the parsley, dill, broccoli, butterflyweed, swamp milkweed, and clover all serve as host plants.

Plant this design in full sun, in average, well-drained garden soil. Replant parsley and broccoli each year from young plants. The dill, clover, cosmos, tomatoes, and zinnias will sow themselves for following years. The other plants are perennials or shrubs that will reappear to greet the next crop of caterpillars and the next generation of nectar-seeking butterflies. The plants in this garden will grow well in Zones 3 to 10.

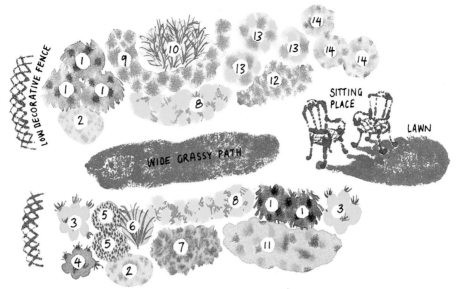

① Purple coneflower (Echinacea purpurea)

② Butterfly weed (Asclepias tuberosa)

③ Yellow pear tomato ④ Cherry tomato ⑤ Broccoli

⑥ Chives (Allium schoenoprasum)

⑦ Parsley (Petroselinum crispum)

⑧ Lanceleaf coreopsis (Coreopsis lanceolata)

⑨ Pink flowered common zinnia (Zinnia elegans)

⑩ Dill (Anethum graveolens)

⑪ Ornamental crabapple, any fruiting cultivar (Malus spp.)

⑫ Crimson clover (Trifolium incarnatum)

⑬ Orange and yellow cosmos (Cosmos sulfurens)

⑭ Swamp milkweed (Asclepias incarnata)

Streetside Planting for Butterflies

So many good nectar plants, so little space—even if you have an acre of garden, it seems it's never enough! This design includes 13 of the best butterfly nectar plants in one concentrated area, perfect for lining a fence or planting in that unloved strip of grass between the street and sidewalk.

It's easy to expand this garden, depending on the space you have available, just by increasing the number of plants you plant. The plan shown here includes three of each of the perennials, plus a packet's worth of seed for the easy-to-grow annuals. It covers an area about 4 × 20 feet with closely spaced plants that make an almost solid mass of bloom.

Plant this design in full sun, in lean to good well-drained garden soil. The mix of perennials and self-sowing annuals will create an ever-changing but always-pleasing arrangement as the annual flowers plant themselves among the permanent perennials. They bloom from early summer through fall, during the height of butterfly season.

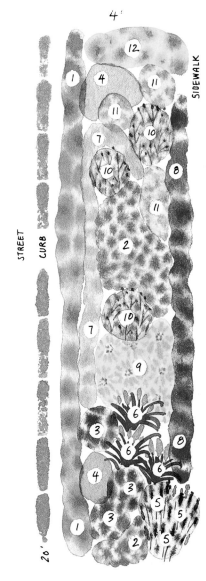

1. Mexican zinnia
   (*Zinnia haageana*)

2. Crimson clover
   (*Trifolium incarnatum*)

3. Pincushion flower
   (*Scabiosa atropurpurea*)

4. Brazilian vervain
   (*Verbena bonariensis*)

5. Lavender
   (*Lavandula* spp.)

6. Blazing stars
   (*Liatris* spp.)

7. Sensation Series cosmos
   (*Cosmos bipinnatus* Sensation
   Series)

8. Dahlia (*Dahlia* cvs.)

9. Tickseed sunflower
   (*Bidens aristosa*)

10. Russian sage
    (*Perovskia atriplicifolia*)

11. Butterfly weed
    (*Asclepias tuberosa*)

12. 'Fiesta del Sol' Mexican sunflower
    (*Tithonia rotundifolia* 'Fiesta del Sol)

A Walk on
the Shady Side

Designed mostly for hummingbirds, this garden for full or partial shade includes just a few splashy flowers. The rest of the plants display understated blooms, but hummingbirds will be quick to notice their appeal. A few early bloomers will tempt the spring butterflies that brighten the garden before hummingbirds return from their winter vacation. The Dutchman's pipe and spicebush will nourish the caterpillars of a couple of spectacular swallowtail species.

This is a layered design, with shrubs topping lower-growing perennials, shaded by small trees. The garden will also appeal to songbirds seeking shelter and nest sites. Choose a place that gets at least 6 hours of shade, whether it's filtered shade from trees or solid, even shade from a house or other building. Dig in compost, humus, and aged manure to make the soil fluffy and well drained. Mulch with chopped leaves to add even more humus as the leaves decompose, and to keep the soil moist. All plants are permanent. Supply a trellis or arbor for the Dutchman's pipe to keep this lusty grower from overpowering less-vigorous plants.

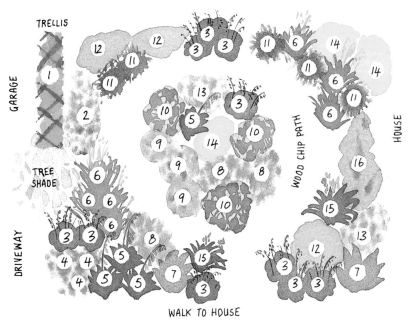

TRELLIS

GARAGE

HOUSE

TREE SHADE

DRIVEWAY

WOOD CHIP PATH

WALK TO HOUSE

① Dutchman's pipe (Aristolochia spp.)

② Columbines (Aquilegia spp. and hybrids)

③ Coral bells (Heuchera spp. and hybrids)

④ Cut-leaf toothwort (Cardamine diphylla)

⑤ Foxglove (Digitalis spp. and hybrids)

⑥ Giant yellow hyssop (Agastache nepetoides)

⑦ Hostas (Hosta cultivars)

⑧ Lyre-leaved sage (Salvia lyrata)

⑨ Hardy fuchsia (Fuchsia magellanica)

⑩ Violets (Viola spp.)

⑪ Red bee balm (Monarda didyma 'Jacob Cline')

⑫ Flowering currant (Ribes sanguineum)

⑬ Eastern redbud (Cercis canadensis)

⑭ Spicebush (Lindera benzoin)

⑮ Virginia bluebells (Mertensia virginica)

⑯ Western bleeding heart (Dicentra formosa)

PLANTS FOR A SHADY SPOT

Hummers and butterflies frequently crave a spot of shade as well as sunshine. If you have a shady area in your yard that you'd love to turn into a garden, try some of these shade-loving plants.

PLANT NAME	PLANT TYPE AND HARDINESS	DESCRIPTION	COMMENTS
Giant yellow hyssop (*Agastache nepetoides*)	Perennial. Zones 3–10.	Candelabra-form plant with a single stem and side branches topped by spikes of close-packed yellow-green flowers from summer through fall.	Nectar plant for humming-birds. Occasionally visited by butterflies.
Columbines (*Aquilegia* spp. and hybrids)	Perennials. Zones 3–10, depending on species.	Clump of rounded leaflets forms a tidy mound, from which several bare stems topped by spurred flowers arise in spring through summer. Height varies from about 6 inches to 3 feet.	Superb hummingbird nectar plant. *A. canadensis* and *A. vulgaris* are used as host plants by the well-named columbine duskywing.
Dutchman's pipes (*Aristolochia* spp.)	Perennial vine. Zones 3–10, depending on species.	Rampant, leafy vine gives quick coverage, although it may take a year for a transplanted plant to become established. Brown, pipe-shaped flowers hidden beneath foliage.	*A. macrophylla* is widely accepted in all areas as a host plant and adapts easily to cultivation.
Cut-leaf toothwort (*Cardamine diphylla*)	Perennial. Zones 5–8.	A pair of divided leaves that look like a bird's three-toed foot arise on a single stem and bear a loose cluster of small white flowers. Spreads slowly into a larger colony. Dies back after flowering in early to mid-spring.	Nectar plant for small butterflies. Host plant for falcate orange tip.
Eastern redbud (*Cercis canadensis*)	Small deciduous tree. Zones 4–9.	Heart-shaped leaves and open branching habit. Pink flowers are borne in spring, before leaves, studded tightly along bare branches.	Hummingbird nectar plant. Host plant for Henry's elfin, a small brown butterfly found from southeast Canada to Florida and Texas.

PLANT NAME	PLANT TYPE AND HARDINESS	DESCRIPTION	COMMENTS
Western bleeding heart (*Dicentra formosa*)	Perennial. Zones 3–9.	Lacy leaves grow in a spreading clump. Pink "inflated" flowers dangle from bare stems above the foliage. Blooms spring through summer.	Nectar plant for hummingbirds. Host plant for Clodius parnassian, a mostly white butterfly of the West.
Foxgloves (*Digitalis* spp. and hybrids)	Biennial, annual, or perennial, depending on species. Hardiness varies; annuals, all zones.	Stout, long oval leaves grow in a neat clump, from which emerges a tall spike of tubular flowers from spring to summer.	Nectar plant for hummingbirds. Snip off stalk when seedpods form to encourage later rebloom.
Hardy fuchsia (*Fuchsia magellanica*)	Deciduous shrub. Zones 6–10.	Multistemmed shrub decorated with red and purple bicolored dangling blooms from late winter (in mild areas) through fall.	May die back in cold winters; cut back to the ground and it is likely to regrow from its roots. Favored nectar plant for hummingbirds.
Coral bells (*Heuchera* spp. and hybrids)	Perennial. Zones 4–10.	Neat clump of rounded leaves, above which rises zingy red or red-pink blossoms on bare, wiry stalks. Often reblooms until fall.	Nectar plant for hummingbirds.
Hostas (*Hosta* cultivars)	Perennial. Hardiness varies with cultivar.	Elegant, large leaves in a tidy clump. Cultivars with smooth or puckered leaves in green, chartreuse, blue-gray, or variegated colors. Bare stems topped with tubular, often sweet-smelling flowers from summer to fall, depending on cultivar.	Nectar plant for hummingbirds.
Canada lily (*Lilium canadense*)	Perennial. Zones 3–7.	Tall, leafy stalks topped by clusters of yellow, red, or orange bell-shaped flowers in midsummer. Flourishes in moist soil.	Nectar plant for hummingbirds and large swallowtail butterflies.

(continued)

PLANTS FOR A SHADY SPOT—CONTINUED

PLANT NAME	PLANT TYPE AND HARDINESS	DESCRIPTION	COMMENTS
Spicebush (*Lindera benzoin*)	Deciduous shrub or small tree. Zones 5–9.	Aromatic in every part, this native shrub bears small bumbles of yellow flowers on bare branches early in spring. Red berries, sought by songbirds, ripen in fall.	Host plant for spicebush swallowtail.
Virginia bluebells (*Mertensia virginica*)	Perennial. Zones 3–7.	Loose clumps of spoon-shaped leaves, which emerge purple in very early spring, then turn apple green. Stems of lovely sky blue bells, opening from pink buds, dangle about 18 inches high.	Nectar plant for spring butterflies; occasionally visited by hummingbirds.
Bee balm (*Monarda didyma*)	Perennial. Zones 4–10.	Fast-spreading member of the mint family, to about 3 feet tall, with odd shaggy flowers in red, pink, purple, or white, depending on cultivar.	'Jacob Cline' has bright red flowers and is less susceptible to powdery mildew than many other bee balms. Excellent hummingbird nectar plant.
Flowering currant (*Ribes sanguineum*)	Deciduous shrub. Zones 6–10.	A graceful, multistemmed shrub with dangling clusters of pink, red, or white flowers in very early spring.	Hummingbird nectar plant. Choose pink or red cultivars; white is less appealing to hummingbirds.
Lyre-leaved sage (*Salvia lyrata*)	Perennial. Zones 5–9.	Leaves are held at the base, close to the ground, and are easy to overlook until the plant comes into bloom with beautiful spikes of blue flowers. Spreads by creeping roots at a moderately slow pace.	Hummingbird nectar flower; also occasionally visited by nectaring butterflies. Oddly, our native salvias are not used as host plants by any species of butterfly.

Self-Serve Garden Design

Using preplanned garden designs, like the ones on the previous pages, is a great way to plant your first garden to attract butterflies or hummingbirds. Experienced wildlife garden designers (or just experienced gardeners!) have a lot of helpful ideas and useful advice about choosing, planning, and planting a variety of flowers in a pleasing arrangement.

That said, you also have the option of ignoring all those carefully planned designs, turning your back on the plant-by-number gardens, and designing your own groupings and beds of flowers to attract the winged visitors in your area to your own yard.

Let your creative juices flow, and be your own garden designer. To help you along the way, the next several pages contain tables of flowering plants that are sure-fire winners when it comes to luring butterflies and hummingbirds into the garden for a visit.

Need another small push in the right direction? Keep in mind these basic garden design principles. Follow them and you won't go wrong; disregard them and you probably won't go terribly wrong, either.

• **Choose plants for microclimates.** Sure, your yard is sunny. But if you're planning a garden for a spot by your house, garage, or a tree that's shaded all afternoon, choose plants that love the shade. Check out "Plants for a Shady Spot" on page 146 for choices.

• **Plant groups of flowers.** Including more than one of each kind of plant you choose is never a bad idea. Also, plant quick-spreading, clumping plants like daisies—just a few plants in the spring will fill your garden with blooms by the end of summer.

• **Group similar colors together.** Selecting a few different plants that bloom in the same color gives your garden a built-in unifying theme, and it will be easy for hummers to spot the large areas of color. Check out the tables "Red-Hot Winners," "True Blue Garden," and "The Color Purple" beginning on page 150.

• **Make sure the plants can "see."** Pretend as you plan your garden that your plants will be looking at you when they flower. Will they all have a good view? To make sure they do, put the tallest ones in the back, and the shortest ones toward the front. This way, you'll have a good view of them, too—and so will butterflies and hummers flying by.

• **Put host plants on the outer edges of the garden.** Position plants that caterpillars like to munch at the edges of your garden so you get a front-row seat to watch the fascinating behavior of the caterpillars and egg-laying adults. While you're there, try raising some yourself! See page 123 for details.

• **Leave space for you.** Don't forget to plan or leave a place where you can sit and watch all the activity. Sometimes, positioning a new garden near where you already spend a lot of time works well. A foundation planting around your deck, a garden outside a large bay window (for butterflies, please—let's not cause hummingbird concussions), or a window box within sight of the breakfast table are all options that include you in your new garden. And isn't that the point, after all?

RED-HOT WINNERS

A garden that's chock-full of tubular red flowers is bound to attract hummingbirds because to hummers, red is as irresistible as a siren's song. My listing of red flowers for hummers includes a mix of annuals and perennials in shades of red ranging from fire engine to orange-red. They bloom from spring through fall, longer in mild winter areas. In cold-winter areas, replant annuals from seed or plants in subsequent years. All of these plants will grow well in full sun, in average garden soil.

PLANT NAME	PLANT TYPE AND HARDINESS	DESCRIPTION	COMMENTS
Red-flowered canna (*Canna* 'The President' or other red cultivar)	Perennial. Zones 6–10; grow as annual elsewhere.	Grow from rhizomes sold at garden centers. Architectural presence, with huge, furling leaves and commanding height, often to 8 feet. Spikes of bright blooms atop stem.	Hummingbird nectar flower. Try leaving rhizomes in ground instead of digging them up as usually recommended; they survive even in my Zone 6 winters.
Coral bells (*Heuchera* cultivars)	Perennial. Hardiness varies.	Neat clump of foliage surmounted by wiry, graceful stems of tiny red or pink flowers from early summer through fall.	Hummingbird nectar flower. Gratifyingly long bloom period for a perennial often in flower for months.
Cypress vine (*Ipomoea quamoclit*)	Annual vine. All zones.	Delicate, feathery foliage (like that of the dawn cypress tree) starred with small, bright red tubular flowers.	Hummingbird nectar flower. Grow on trellis, in window boxes, or let it clamber among garden plants.
'Viva' hybrid lily (*Lilium* 'Viva')	Bulb; Zones 6–10.	Big, flaring flowers crown the 2- to 3-foot-tall plants.	Hummingbird nectar flower. Swallowtails may also visit.
Coral gem or parrot's beak (*Lotus berthelotti*)	Perennial in Zones 9–10; grow as annual in all other zones.	Cascading gray foliage of the finest texture, with pea-shaped red flowers.	Hummingbird nectar flower. Use it as an edging plant in containers to attract hummingbirds.
Maltese cross (*Lychnis chalcedonica*)	Perennial. Zones 4–9.	Leafy plant to about 3 feet tall topped by rounded, brilliant orange-red flower clusters.	Irresistible to hummingbirds. Give it extra aged manure to encourage a bigger clump to form.

PLANT NAME	PLANT TYPE AND HARDINESS	DESCRIPTION	COMMENTS
Texas sage (*Salvia coccinea*)	Annual or perennial, in mild climates. All zones.	Airy, open-branching plant with abundant spikes of small, bright red tubular flowers.	Hummingbird nectar flower. Self-sows moderately; learn to recognize the seedlings so you don't accidentally weed them out.
Scarlet sage (*Salvia splendens*)	Annual. All zones.	Leafy, single-stemmed plant of varying height, depending on cultivar, from 1 to 2 feet tall. Grows in clumps, and sports spikes of bright red flowers from summer through fall.	Hummingbird nectar flower. A lot of drawing power from an inexpensive bedding annual.
Fire pink (*Silene virginica*)	Perennial. Zones 4–8.	Loose clusters of fire-engine red flowers on a leafy plant about 2 feet tall. Flowers have notched petals.	Hummingbird nectar magnet.
'Torch' tithonia (*Tithonia rotundifolia* 'Torch')	Annual; all zones.	Big, branching plant to 6 feet tall and 4 feet wide, with vivid orange-red daisy flowers from late summer through fall.	A favored nectar plant of many hummingbirds, as well as monarchs and many other butterflies. Stems are velvety soft to the touch. A good choice for creating a quick hedge.
'Empress of India' nasturtium (*Tropaeolum* 'Empress of India')	Annual; all zones.	Trailing plant with round leaves and deep red, spurred flowers from early summer to fall.	Hummingbird nectar plant. Host plant for cabbage whites and other whites.
Common zinnia (*Zinnia elegans*)	Annual. All zones.	Daisylike flowers, also available in shaggy "cactus flowers" or double flowers, in all colors of the rainbow but blue.	Choose a tall, red-flowered cultivar such as 'Scarlet King'.

TRUE BLUE GARDEN

Red isn't the only way to a hummingbird's heart—they also flock to many blue flowers. This list includes plants with a variety of flower shapes, including tubular or spurred types for hummingbirds, and disks and spikes for butterflies, so you'll attract both kinds of customers.

These plants are all true blue—not what I think of as "catalog blue," which can be anything from deep purple to pale lilac, even though the catalog calls it blue. For a bit of contrast, I include both deep shades and paler sky hues.

Look for the plants at garden centers, nurseries, and in catalogs. Plant in full sun, in lean to good well-drained garden soil. Then let the wave of blue begin to sweep across your yard.

PLANT NAME	PLANT TYPE AND HARDINESS	DESCRIPTION	COMMENTS
'Blue Bird' rose-of-Sharon (*Hibiscus syriacus* 'Blue Bird')	Deciduous shrub or small tree. Zones 3–10.	Leafy, undistinguished tree or shrub except when it blooms in summer, with occasional hollyhock-like blossoms into early fall.	Hummingbird nectar flower. Great for a quick-growing hedge.
'Blue Horizon' ageratum (*Ageratum houstonianum* 'Blue Horizon')	Perennial in mild-winter areas; grow as annual in all zones.	Powder-puff clusters of fuzzy blue flowers from summer through fall.	Butterfly nectar flower. May self-sow, yielding a crop of seedlings that may not resemble the parent except in their flowers.
Blue spirea (*Caryopteris incana*)	Deciduous shrub. Zones 6–10.	Gray-green foliage is almost overwhelmed by the billow of fuzzy, soft light blue flowers from summer through fall.	Excellent butterfly nectar plant.
Larkspur (*Consolida ambigua*)	Annual. All zones.	Tall, fine-textured plants with lacy leaves and many spikes of blue, purple, pink, or white flowers from early summer through fall.	Choose a blue-flowered cultivar.
Delphiniums (*Delphinium* spp. and hybrids)	Perennial. Hardiness varies.	Usually tall, erect plants with cut foliage and spikes of often blue flowers.	Choose any blue cultivar; 'Blue Mirror', a lower-growing, bushy plant, is extra-long-blooming.
Edging lobelia (*Lobelia erinus*)	Perennial in mild winter areas; grow as annual elsewhere.	Low, dainty plant with tiny leaves and masses of blue flowers.	Choose a blue-flowered cultivar such as 'Crystal Palace'.

PLANT NAME	PLANT TYPE AND HARDINESS	DESCRIPTION	COMMENTS
Blue cardinal flower (*Lobelia siphilitica*)	Perennial. Zones 5–10.	Leafy clump with spikes of blue tubular flowers from summer to late summer.	Hummingbird nectar plant. Snip off faded flower spikes to encourage rebloom.
Blue sage (*Salvia azurea*)	Perennial. Zones 4–10.	Tall, somewhat gangly plant, to 4½ feet, with flowers that redeem its less-than-stellar growth habit: they're rich, true blue. Blooms summer through fall.	Hummingbird nectar plant, especially welcomed during fall migration when it is at the peak of bloom.
'Victoria' salvia (*Salvia farinacea* 'Victoria')	Perennial in mild winter areas. Grow as annual in all other zones.	Branching plant about 18 inches to 2 feet tall, with many spires of small blue flowers.	Hummingbird nectar plant; may also be visited by butterflies.
Argentine sage (*Salvia guaranitica*)	Perennial. Zones 6–10.	Tall plant, to 5 feet, topped with deep blue tubular flower spikes in fall.	Hummingbird nectar flower, especially during fall migration. Blooms very late in the season, but worth the wait.
Blue anise sage (*Salvia hispanica*)	Annual. All zones.	Branching plant, to about 3 feet tall, with spikes of blue flowers in summer.	Hummingbird nectar plant. A native of Mexico. Often self-sows.
'May Night' salvia (*Salvia* 'May Night' or 'Mai Nacht')	Perennial. Zones 5–10.	Low mound of compact foliage topped by deepest blue flowering spikes from late spring through fall.	Butterfly and hummingbird nectar plant. An extra-long-blooming perennial.
Culinary sage (*Salvia officinalis*)	Perennial. Zones 5–10.	Gray-green foliage and spikes of true-blue flowers from late spring through summer.	Hummingbird and butterfly nectar plant. Cut off faded flowers to encourage rebloom.
Pincushion flower (*Scabiosa caucasica* 'Fama' or *S.* 'Butterfly Blue')	Perennial. Zones 4–10.	Tidy mound of foliage, decorated by bare-stemmed blossoms that sport a fuzzy pincushion look.	Execllent butterfly nectar flower. Long-blooming, from early summer through fall.
Chaste tree (*Vitex agnus-castus*)	Deciduous small tree. Zones 6–10.	Attractively branched small tree, to about 12 feet tall, with spikes of blue flowers tipping each branch from early summer through late summer or early fall.	Butterfly and hummingbird nectar plant. Good in coastal conditions.

THE COLOR PURPLE

Purple is just one step removed from blue on the arc of the rainbow, and butterflies flock to it. Hummingbirds may also visit a garden featuring these multi-tones of purple, but butterflies will be your number-one customers. Because the dark shades of purple are hard to see from a distance, plant your purple garden in a full-sun location near a path or sitting spot, where you can admire the flowers and their fluttery visitors up close.

The annuals and perennials in this list thrive in average, well-drained garden soil. Their hues vary from the richest deep violet to purple-tinged pinks that liven up the color scheme. All plants are readily available at garden centers and nurseries.

PLANT NAME	PLANT TYPE AND HARDINESS	DESCRIPTION	COMMENTS
Adenophora (*Adenophora confusa*)	Perennial. Zones 3–10.	2-foot-tall spires of bell-shaped purple-blue blossoms, similar in appearance to a bellflower. Easy to grow; spreads at a moderate rate.	Hummingbird nectar flower; may also be visited by butterflies.
Anise hyssop (*Agastache foeniculum*)	Perennial. Zones 6–10.	Single-stemmed but abundantly branching, with many close-packed spikes of tiny blue-purple flowers.	Butterfly nectar flower. Spreads by roots and self-sows at a moderate pace.
Bachelor's buttons (*Centaurea cyanus*)	Annual. All zones.	Bushy plant with abundant flowers in blue, purple, pink, or white. Cut back when blooms begin fading to keep plant vigorous longer.	Choose purple-flowered cultivars. Self-sows abundantly; seedlings may be a different color than their parent.
Persian cornflower (*Centaurea dealbata*)	Perennial. Zones 4–8.	Large mound of pretty grayish foliage, decorated with rich rose-purple flowers from summer through fall.	Butterfly nectar plant. May self-sow.
Sensation Series cosmos (*Cosmos bipinnatus* Sensation Series)	Annual. All zones.	Tall, feathery-leaved plants to 5 feet, with simple, silken blossoms in pink, rose, purple-pink, and white. Blooms summer through fall.	Butterfly nectar flower. Will self-sow from year to year.

PLANT NAME	PLANT TYPE AND HARDINESS	DESCRIPTION	COMMENTS
Heliotrope (*Heliotropium arborescens*)	Perennial in mild winter areas. Grow as annual in all other zones.	Flat clusters of intense, deep purple flowers with a scent like vanilla. Usually about 2 feet tall.	Excellent butterfly nectar flower. Sniff plants in bloom before buying; some seed-grown plants may smell more like ammonia than the usual vanilla scent.
Blazing stars (*Liatris* spp.)	Perennial. Hardiness varies with species.	Tough, trouble-free plant with needle-like foliage lining stems topped with fuzzy spikes of pink-purple flowers from summer through fall.	Excellent butterfly nectar plant. To save money, buy bulbs instead of potted plants; they'll bloom the same year you plant them.
Wild bee balm (*Monarda fistulosa*)	Perennial. Zones 3–9.	Fast-spreading perennial with shaggy, soft pastel purple flowers atop 3- to 5-foot stems.	Nectar plant for humming-birds. Keep in bounds by pulling up errant roots as the plants spread.
Petunias (*Petunia* hybrids)	Perennial in mild winter areas. Grow as annual in all other zones.	Popular garden plant with large tubular blossoms in many colors, including purple, blue tones (but not true blue), red, pink, yellow, and white. Trails or sprawls.	Butterfly and hummingbird nectar flower. Choose purple-flowered cultivars such as 'Purple Wave' or 'Misty Lilac Wave'.
Garden phlox (*Phlox paniculata*) and **meadow phlox** (*P. maculata*)	Perennial. Zones 4–10.	Sturdy upright stems to 3 feet, with flowers in a wide variety of colors, many with darker centers or "eyes." Usually fragrant.	Butterfly nectar flower. Choose purple or pink-purple cultivars, including 'Franz Schubert'.
'Homestead Purple' verbena (*Verbena* 'Homestead Purple')	Perennial. Zones 6–10. Enjoy as annual in colder areas.	Mat-forming, fast-spreading plant is well-covered in vivid purple flowers from early summer through fall.	Butterfly nectar flower. May survive Zone 5 winters under a deep, loose mulch of fall leaves.
Garden verbena (*Verbena* × *hybrida*)	Tender perennial grown as a tender annual.	Trailing, ground-covering plants with lacy foliage and large clusters of many small flowers in purples, reds, pink, white, and apricot.	Butterfly nectar flower. Choose purple-flowered cultivars. Covers ground fast for a gratifying display.

CHAPTER 8

Butterfly and Hummingbird

BEHAVIOR

Once you've created a welcoming garden for winged visitors, you'll have a front-row seat for a three-ring circus of fascinating fun. You'll be in the thick of things as butterflies and hummingbirds eat, drink, take flight, and nest right outside your back door. You'll witness courtship and mating rituals that may be either wonderfully beautiful or bordering on the bizarre.

You'll also see the dramatic side of hummingbird and butterfly life. These little winged creatures engage in spats over territory and mates, duels with other creatures, and life-and-death encounters with spiders and cats.

The behaviors of these beautiful winged creatures are as varied as their colors when it comes to the details of daily life. In general, however, their lives focus on three main activities: finding food, avoiding danger, and passing their genes along to the next generation—the same necessities that motivate every animal on earth, including humans.

At first, your butterfly and hummingbird observations will center on figuring out who's who and learning what flowers or feeders each species like best. It's fun to attach names to your guests and, as you identify individuals, you'll become a better observer. The descriptions and illustrations of many of the most common garden visitors in Chapters 9 and 10 will help you get to know your new friends.

THE BACKYARD NATURE SHOW

As you spend time watching butterflies and hummingbirds, you'll notice behaviors that make you wonder why, what, and how. Why does a red admiral ride on your bare shoulder on a hot day? What are the hummingbirds saying with those squeaks and twitters? How do butterflies know when it's going to rain?

This curiosity is the start of a lifelong learning experience. Even scientists don't know all the answers to the questions, but the behavior is always fascinating to watch and fun to try to understand. As you watch the daily lives of your garden friends unfold, you'll observe all kinds of goings-on—from tender family care to vicious fights.

WATCHING BUTTERFLIES DAY TO DAY

The more time you spend observing butterflies, the more fascinating they become. Even the most ordinary activities are fun to watch and puzzle over. Once you've learned to recognize the meanings behind their postures or movements, you'll have an inside understanding of the butterflies that frequent your yard.

It's a red-letter day when you spot a hummingbird *and* a butterfly at a single flower! Both hummers and butterflies are drawn to red zinnias like this one.

This zebra swallowtail is basking in a patch of sunlight to warm its body for takeoff.

Basking Because they're cold-blooded, butterflies must wait for the sun to warm their bodies before they can take to the air. A butterfly sitting still in a patch of sunlight is probably basking—soaking up solar energy. Basking takes place on chilly mornings and in the coolness of spring and fall.

Look closely at a butterfly as it basks. Like a sunbather getting the perfect tan, the butterfly slowly moves to keep the sun at precisely the right angle to its body to take best advantage of the heat. The basking butterflies I've observed position their heads away from the sun and point their hind ends directly toward Ol' Sol. Some species bask with wings open, while others hold them closed. I like to watch as the butterfly first does a little shimmy when it alights, then quickly positions itself.

Place rocks throughout your garden where the morning sun hits early in the day to give your butterflies prime basking spots. They may also use the paving of patios or pathways, or a deck railing—any surface that soaks up the heat. Tree trunks are popular, too.

A patch of light will draw woodland species so strongly that they'll alight upon a white cloth dropped on the forest floor. Sometimes butterflies will even spar over sitting rights to a good patch of sunlight. If you have a shade garden, you can experiment with this attraction by setting out a sheet of white paper towel and watching who visits.

Perching Butterflies aren't always on the wing. They often stop to rest. The larger species, like swallowtails and monarchs, seem to meet their resting needs while nectaring. They linger at a flower far longer than many of the smaller species that flit about more. Erratically flying butterflies called skippers, for example, zip about with as much nervous energy as they like, pausing between darting flights to restore their energies on a handy perch. Still other species—especially those that don't seek nectar—sit still or nearly still for long periods. They often adopt a favorite perch, just as you have your own well-worn easy chair.

Look for butterflies on practically any kind of perch. Anglewings, hackberries, and red admirals may choose a particular leaf as their lookout post. These perching species may also select your shoulder, gardening hat, or head as a good sitting spot!

Many male butterflies perch in an opportune location to wait for a passing female. When the male detects an approaching female, he abandons his waiting place and flies after her.

Exotic in both form and color, the zebra longwing adds a dash of tropical splendor to gardens in the Deep South. Look for these elegant beauties when you're vacationing in Florida: They're a common sight in carefully groomed gardens at Disney World as well as in wild places like Sanibel Island.

Some butterflies seem to be territorial about their perching areas, chasing away anything that dares to trespass, no matter its size.

One summer, from my own favorite sitting spot on my side porch, I had a clear view of a small brown hackberry butterfly's regular perch—a leaf of a sugar maple near the fence. I spent many hours watching the hackberry dart after bumblebees, butterflies, starlings, robins, and even my dogs when they wandered into what seemed to be its claimed territory. A red admiral butterfly seemed to arouse particular ire. At least once a day, the hackberry would chase the larger admiral 10 feet away before returning to its perch.

When you do find a butterfly that's attached to a particular perch, watch when it alights. I've noticed that after they settle in place, these fascinating creatures often engage in grooming. They rub their "hands" over their face, antennae, and body like a cat taking a bath. (Binoculars make spying on perching butterflies a lot easier on the eyes!)

As you get to know the "regulars" in your garden, you may notice that some individuals patrol your yard rather than staying put on a perch. Usually it's the male of the species who does the patrolling, and it's female butterflies he's looking for on these forays. The top of a hill or even the area above tall flowers is often favored by patrolling males.

Butterfly Barometers Here in the lower Midwest, where summer temperatures can climb into the high 90s for weeks at a time, I can always tell whether the day will be a scorcher by checking what time butterflies arrive in my garden. If they are few and far between at 8:00 A.M., I know I'll have at least a couple of hours of good gardening conditions before the heat drives me to the iced-tea jug. But if I open my door at 7:30 A.M. and discover that butterflies are already on the wing, I pull on the lightest-weight clothing I own and prepare for a steamy day.

In spring and fall, it's a different story. The sun takes longer to heat the cooled earth, and the butterflies are as lazy as I am in the morning. They don't arrive in force until midday.

Sunny, warm, calm to slightly breezy weather is the best for butterflies. Those are the perfect conditions for cold-blooded winged insects to take to the air for a full day of feeding. When the afternoon shadows lengthen toward evening, butterflies sail off to find shelter for the night under leaves or other roosts.

Wind and rain discourage butterflies. Their wings aren't strong enough to withstand the force of the wind, and they'll go into hiding on a briskly windy day. They may come to the

Butterflies will perch on flowers, branches, rocks, and many other places to rest and survey the scene. Some, like this red admiral, will use a perch as a home base from which to chase off other butterflies, insect, birds, and even large animals.

garden on a gray day that threatens showers, but they'll vanish before the first drops begin. Rain can cause serious harm to fragile butterfly wings, both by damaging the tiny scales that cover their surface and by battering and breaking the wings themselves.

SOME LIKE IT (VERY) HOT Extreme heat can send butterflies to seek shelter, too. When the thermometer climbs above 100°F, the only butterflies in my garden are at the fruit feeders in the shade. Larger butterflies retreat from extreme heat first. The smaller species—metalmarks, skippers—hang on longer, but eventually they, too, seek cool shelter. Butterflies will return to your flowers when the sun's angle changes in the late afternoon.

Tropical and subtropical species are better adapted to heat. On trips to Florida, I've watched long-tailed skippers and zebras flit about unconcernedly long after I wilted with unladylike perspiration.

WEATHER AND CATERPILLARS Like adult butterflies, caterpillars have periods of activity tied to weather conditions. Some species avoid the sun (and day-flying birds) altogether by feeding at night. Others pause in their munching when the summer sun

Like hummingbirds, the color of many butterflies shifts with the light, as sun ignites the flash of iridescence. On a gray day, the vivid color of the pipevine swallowtail all but disappears, leaving only dull black wings. On a sunny afternoon, this big butterfly is a beauty queen, luminous in glowing blues.

reaches the zenith, then go back to eating when the temperature has moderated a bit. Caterpillars appear to be less sensitive to light and heat than their parents. I've successfully raised many species on a shady side porch that never gets the direct rays of the sun, and they contentedly feed even on dark, rainy days.

Flying and Flight Patterns

You can use flight patterns to help identify butterflies just as you would birds. If you're a birdwatcher, you probably recognize the up-and-down dips of a goldfinch or the flap-flap-glide of an accipiter hawk. Butterfly flight patterns can be just as distinctive. Swallowtails have a slow, steady, deliberate flight. Red admirals are fast and jerky. Skippers are, well, skippy.

Pretty as a piece of jewelry, the malachite butterfly is about the size of a monarch. Look for its lovely wings in the warmest parts of Texas and Florida.

Some butterflies fly low, some fly higher. Monarchs often glide along above head height, while blues tend to hug the ground or fly just above the tops of the plants in the garden.

After a few seasons of watching butterflies, you should be able to recognize which family group a butterfly belongs to by seeing it in flight. Because there are so many species in each butterfly family, however, it's unlikely you'll be able to spot a butterfly in your neighbor's yard and know which species it is. With butterflies, visual color clues are usually necessary to pinpoint an individual any further than "fritillary," "swallowtail," "skipper," or other general designations. Luckily, butterflies are generally abroad in good light that lets us make out colors as well as size and wingbeats. With practice, you'll learn to spot the quick flash of red on a red admiral, or the eyespots on a buckeye, even when the butterfly is 50 feet away.

Fighting Researchers are overhauling the "official" interpretation of feisty butterfly behavior. Many of the actions that experts once thought indicated fighting and friction may hint of mating behavior instead.

Part of the problem when trying to determine what butterflies are doing is that it's almost impossible to tell males from females in many species. Two butterflies flying upward in close proximity, wings beating at each other, may look like sparring partners. Yet many researchers now think that these aerial performances may be courtship dances. Butterflies recognize other members of their species, approach each other, and the dance begins. If the pair happens to be a male and a female, mating may take place. But if the two butterflies involved are both males, they will eventually split up and one will return to his perch to await a better prospect.

I have definitely hosted a number of rowdy fighters over the years. The swallowtail matches I've seen may have been a prelude to egg-laying, but the behavior of the hackberries, red-spotted purples, and red admirals in my yard certainly seemed antagonistic. Surely these combative creatures couldn't have mistaken my cat and dogs as potential mates!

My feisty butterflies seem to favor the sneak attack. They perch in an unobtrusive place, then come charging out at passersby, whether two-, four-, or six-legged. Usually the feint is enough to cause the intruder to divert its course. I've even seen hummingbirds alter their path to avoid a territorial hackberry butterfly on their approach route to the feeder.

Mating monarchs are a fairly common sight in summer. They may stay coupled for quite a while, and often fly about while still "engaged." Take a closer look whenever you see a monarch on the wing that seems to be flying with effort instead of its usual weightless flight; it may be a double-decker ride.

Only once did I see such a joust end in tragedy: A hackberry butterfly made the mistake of harassing a kingbird one day. In midflight, the kingbird whirled and snatched the hapless butterfly from over its shoulder, putting a very final end to such tomfoolery.

Puddling

The need for moisture and minerals, particularly salts, draws butterflies to mud puddles. Tiny blues, midsize sulphurs, and big swallowtails will gather by the dozens. The occasional admiral, red-spotted purple, and other varieties will also stop and sip for a while. These puddle groups are boys' clubs. For reasons that we can only guess, only male butterflies generally engage in the activity, and usually only recently hatched males. The attractive puddle can be on a dirt country lane, along the edge of a lake or creek, or a homemade construction in your backyard, like the ones described in Chapter 3.

A little dab'll do ya: This swallowtail and other butterflies spend just an instant depositing their precious progeny-to-be on suitable plants.

Roosting

Where do butterflies sleep? Good question! The answer seems to vary. During nasty weather I've discovered them roosting under large leaves—sunflowers are a favorite in my garden. They will also hide under strips of bark or beneath the eaves of a roof.

During their long migration flights, monarchs sleep in trees. The first arrivals cling beneath a leaf, and later guests pile up onto their bodies. This living chain of butterflies can look like heavy theater drapery by the time thousands are clustered together.

If mature shade trees fill your yard or line your street, look up at the treetops in the early morning to spot butterflies leaving the foliage as the sun warms them. I have often spotted tiger swallowtails this way. Along mountainous roads, where lower elevations drop away sharply on either side, I've seen the same behavior by looking down at the trees from the car traveling above. I've also seen butterflies flying into the sheltering branches of maples, oaks, beeches, and catalpas in early evening, perhaps to find a room for the night.

BUTTERFLY LOVE LIFE

If you watch butterflies around your yard regularly, you'll probably see some of their mating and egg-laying behavior. Butterflies mate on a catch-as-catch-can basis. The first male astute enough to recognize a willing female and strong enough to beat out other suitors will prevail.

Mating Maneuvers Texas two-step dancers may be terrific at line dancing, but butterflies are just as good at group synchronization—and they don't need any lessons to stay in line. On a sunny summer day, watch for the common butterflies called cabbage whites arrayed in a vertical line, moving over flowers and lawns in aerial group maneuvers.

It's a delight to watch the dance, and even more interesting when you know the reason behind it. These lines are made up of several males jockeying for the attention of a female in the line. Those with the quickest and most agile flight—admirable traits to pass along to the next generation—win the prize of a receptive partner.

When you see two or more butterflies spending time within inches of each other, take a closer look. You may be watching males jockeying for position, or awaiting the attention of a female who's almost, but not quite, ready to submit.

A freshly hatched Gulf fritillary shows off splendid wings that, like those of other butterflies, will become faded and tattered in the daily pursuits of a butterfly's life.

Butterfly mating often requires persistence and patience. I once watched a male pipevine swallowtail spar with other males until his wings were rather battered. Then, as the lone remaining suitor, he positioned himself above a female nectaring at ground level. She continued sipping at clover for over an hour while he stayed hovering over her, looking exhausted but still determined. He must have expended an enormous amount of energy before she consented and the two joined their abdomen tips together.

Many species mate on the wing, flying together in an awkward dance, with one partner hanging upside down. Watch for conjoined monarchs from early through late summer, then look for eggs and caterpillars on milkweed near the mating spot.

A Fresh Brood

Mortality is high in insects, butterflies included. That's why Nature's plan builds in plenty of extras. Butterflies reproduce in such abundance that even with many fatalities, there will always be new butterflies to delight us next year. A single butterfly may lay hundreds of eggs, dotting them in neat rows on the undersides of leaves or placing them one by one, like pearls scattered over the host plants.

Each butterfly species has its own schedule for reproduction. Some lay eggs in early spring and again in summer, or throughout the year in mild areas. Others lay eggs only in fall.

Butterfly egg laying is timed to the host plants that provide food for the emerging caterpillars. You'll spot the falcate orange tip butterfly in the eastern woods in early spring, when its host plant, the spring wildflower called toothwort (*Dentaria* spp.), is evident.

Mourning cloak butterflies may be out and about in late winter, but they reproduce only in spring. When the leaves of elms, willows, and other host trees are turning from tender spring green to deeper summer hues, the female butterfly starts her next generation. She moves her body around a twig of the host tree to deposit clusters of 20 or more eggs around the twig. When the eggs hatch about 2 weeks later, the itty-bitty caterpillars crawl to a nearby leaf and start chowing down on tasty greenery.

The egg-laying of fritillary butterflies is truly remarkable. The fritillary uses violets as host plants, but the plants are often dormant when the butterflies are ready to lay eggs in fall. Recent research suggests that the adult butterfly can actually smell the violet roots. Locating the dormant violet, she lays her eggs near the crown of the plant. Some of the eggs hatch and begin feeding, then overwinter as larvae. The other eggs stick tight until the following spring when

Variations in color are common in butterflies, including these giant swallowtails. Climate and season of hatching, as well as genetics, may have an effect.

the violets leaf out again. The butterflies that hatch in May or June lay a second generation of eggs upon violets, portulaca, sedum, and other plants. Those eggs then hatch and lay their eggs in the fall, continuing the cycle.

SEASONAL VARIATIONS

You may have already noticed that butterflies appear on a seasonal timetable. Summer is the high point, with big, gorgeous swallowtails and monarchs mingling with smaller species at flowers and feeders. Some species, however, are abroad in very early spring, and others linger well into autumn or even hang on into winter in the Sunbelt.

As you watch the butterflies in your yard, you'll soon notice when a new brood emerges. Suddenly your flower gardens will fill with fresh wings, their colors bright, their edges intact. Make a note on your calendar so you can watch for them next year at about the same time.

Some butterflies of the same species may vary greatly in size as the seasons pass. In my area, members of the early brood of red-spotted purples are nearly as big as monarchs. The late summer hatchlings are significantly smaller. Among red admirals, on the other hand, individuals of summer broods are bigger than those of the spring batch.

Color may also vary depending on when butterflies hatch. The spring brood of the common blue is darker than the sky blue summer form. Red admirals that hatch in summer are deep brown, while the spring representatives are lighter colored.

Your first look at monarchs on winter grounds is likely to surprise you. The clustered butterflies look like brown rags hanging from the trees.

Migration and Emigration

In the butterfly world, emigration is an occasional one-way trip, while true migration is a regular round-trip ticket. No one knows for sure the reasons behind these long-distance treks. They are most likely an adaptive behavior from eons ago, when climate was much different than it is today.

The Mystery of Monarch Migration

Monarchs are the only North American butterfly that follow a yearly migration. The most astounding thing about monarch migration is that no single butterfly ever makes the entire trip! It's an ancestral roadmap that steers these creatures on their way from south to north and back again.

THE JOURNEY SOUTH In late summer, monarchs in North America begin to congregate. By August, they are on the move southward, winging along some of the same migratory routes used by birds. Midwestern and eastern monarchs flow southward to Mexico, many of them following the Atlantic Coast and the Blue Ridge mountains. Western monarchs head for the central and southern California coast.

In late summer and early fall, monarch butterflies traverse huge distances to reach their overwintering grounds in California evergreen groves and in the Sierra Madre of Mexico.

Expect to be delighted by the late summer sight of buckeye butterflies. These intricately patterned emigrants stream far from their breeding areas, spreading out across much of the country to finish the season feasting at flowers. Look for the travelers en route, flying just a few feet above the ground.

THE DESTINATION Monarchs winter in just two places: the Sierra Madre of Mexico, and the evergreen groves of coastal California. Here the butterflies converge by the millions, gathering in hanging clusters that hardly move.

THE JOURNEY NORTH When spring comes, the adult monarchs begin the journey north. They have nearly reached the end of their lives, so most never make it back to the starting point of the summer before. The adults breed along the way, lay their eggs, and most die. Their eggs hatch, caterpillars grow and pupate, and the freshly emerged generation takes up the final leg of the trip, heading north unerringly for unseen ancestral summering grounds.

THE CYCLE BEGINS AGAIN The new progeny breed on their summer grounds and their offspring (yes, the third generation!) undertake the return flight to wintering grounds—two generations removed from the monarchs that started the trip!

Emigration Compared to the feat of monarch migration, the one-way trip of emigration seems like a snap. Yet this, too, is an extraordinary journey. Each tiny, emigrating creature beats its way on fragile wings hundreds or even thousands of miles to find a new home.

Buckeyes, painted ladies, and cloudless sulphurs are the big three of emigrants. They will sometimes erupt into motion, with millions of butterflies taking to the air. Emigrators go in various directions. Cloudless sulphurs and painted ladies move north. West Coast ladies head eastward. Buckeyes travel south in fall.

Emigration is an unpredictable, irregular phenomenon. Not all butterflies of a species move on, nor do they end up in the same place. Even the direction of the mass movement varies. Some members of the species may go north, while others move south or east. The number of emigrants varies from year to year. Here in southern Indiana, I'm always delighted to see the unmistakable big, light yellow wings of a cloudless sulphur, a species that visits only in late summer, and in unpredictable numbers. In my eight summers here, I've had four years when the garden was filled with dozens of these butterflies; other summers, only one or two show up to brighten the day.

When I lived on the coast of Oregon, I was lucky enough to spot a massive flight of painted ladies that were heading north. For 3 days, the butterflies streamed up the coast. My son and I did rough calculations as we stood on a cliff along the ocean, figuring that we were seeing 30 butterflies a minute moving past us. Then we drove inland to gauge the width of the stream. The cloud of butterflies was roughly 30 miles wide. Our minds boggled at the numbers. Uncountable millions of painted ladies were on the move.

One of the best spots in the country to see both migrating and emigrating butterflies is at Cape May, New Jersey, also famed as a hot spot for songbird and hawk migration. Winged travelers stop to rest before attempting the next step of the journey, a 30-mile flight across the Delaware Bay. From September through October, you can see thousands of beautiful monarchs and buckeyes drifting over wildflowers near the coast and among the cultivated flowers around the historic Victorian homes. (Look up now and then to see peregrine falcons and eagles.)

Hibernation

Since few butterflies migrate, you may be wondering, what do butterflies do in the winter? The answer is—they hibernate. The adult butterflies either snuggle safely into hibernation roosts, or they pass the torch to the next generation, which usually slumbers through the cold as a chrysalis or egg, or even as a caterpillar in some species.

Hibernating caterpillars, chrysalises, and adults can turn up just about anywhere. Many

If you find a curled-up caterpillar around your yard in winter, don't disturb it. It's not dead, it's hibernating.

times in early spring I've lifted a stack of flowerpots stored outside over winter, only to discover a caterpillar nestled between the pots. Friends who have stacks of firewood in their yard have found mourning cloak butterflies when they lifted a log to bring into the house.

When I take winter walks, I make it a habit to peek beneath any large flap of bark I spy. Every once in a while I find a sleeping butterfly tucked away. Many caterpillars hibernate in loose leaves or the mulch beneath your plants, a good reason not to tidy up your garden completely in the fall.

Species that suspend their chrysalis within a loop of silk thread seem to overwinter in the snug domicile of loose tree bark more than other types of chrysalis-makers. Perhaps the silk thread holds the chrysalis more securely in place than one that hangs from its top, like the monarch's.

PREDATORS AND HAZARDS

As you become more aware of butterflies, you'll learn that they have a tough existence. Delicate butterflies are no match for a bird, which can dart at much higher speeds. Nor can they outwit the grille of a speeding car. Cats, bullfrogs, fish, and even owls may make a meal of that winged body.

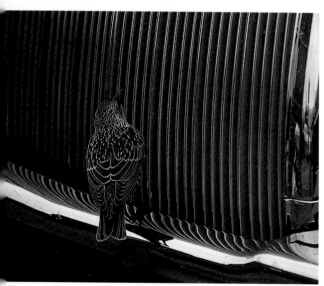

Many butterflies and other insects meet their demise on the grille of a fast-moving automobile. This clever starling has learned where to find easy pickings.

Wheels of Doom Automobiles take an enormous toll on butterflies. Dozens of framed specimens decorate my kitchen wall, but I've never killed a single butterfly for my collection. I found every single one along the shoulder of a highway near my house.

On a single summer day, when swallowtails are at their peak and obliviously flying from one side of the road to the other, I've counted more than a hundred dead butterflies in a quarter-mile stretch. Others may survive the hit-and-run encounter, but their wings are too damaged to fly. I lift those unfortunate victims off the pavement onto flowers along the roadside, where at least they can feed until they meet their eventual fate.

Rest-stop parking areas and fast-food restaurants along interstates yield remarkable specimens of formerly fluttering butterflies. The winged beauties meet their sad fate at 60 mph, then drop off when the cars come to a halt in the parking area. My son and I travel each summer, and we habitually do a butterfly check wherever we pause along the way. It's sad but true that we can tell where a car has been by the battered insects on its grille. In one rest stop in Missouri, we came upon a Florida car. On its grille, we identified the remains of long-tailed skippers, zebra heliconians, and Gulf fritillaries. Mixed among them were bodies of sulphurs, admirals, and swallowtails of the Midwest.

Butterfly Eaters

Birds, other insects, mice and other small rodents, spiders, and just about any creature that needs a quick meal of protein will prey on butterflies. A butterfly is fair game to predators at any stage of its life: egg, caterpillar, chrysalis, or adult. A chickadee has as sharp an eye for an overwintering butterfly pupa as it does for sunflower seeds, and its little black beak is adept at pecking into the chrysalis to get at the meat inside.

One summer, I watched several steps in the food chain play themselves out in my garden. An adult pearl crescent butterfly laid its eggs on a plant of oxeye sunflower (*Heliopsis helianthoides*). The spiny black caterpillars fed in colonies, stripping the leaves bare. They had a quick and effective defense when birds investigated them. When a branch of the plant was disturbed, the caterpillars immediately loosed their holds and dropped to the ground to hide under leaf litter. When the coast was clear, they crawled back up. When the caterpillars pupated and hatched, however, it was a different story. As the brand-new butterflies visited the flowers of the very same plant that had nurtured them earlier in their metamorphosis, they became fast-food tidbits to a small flycatcher that moved in. For 2 days, I heard the bird's beak clicking like castanets in my garden as it snapped up the small orange-and-black butterflies one by one. A few also fell victim to a praying mantis that moved in for the feast, and still more were devoured by a golden crab spider.

The great crested flycatcher also snaps up moths and butterflies with relish. Birds depend on the hordes of insects to fuel their own survival.

This crab spider has nabbed a silver-spotted skipper for lunch. Crab spiders wait in ambush at the center of a flower for an unsuspecting butterfly. When the butterfly alights to dine, it ends up being the featured item on the menu instead.

Crab spiders are fascinating to watch, if you steel yourself not to stop their feasting. These medium-size spiders, often goldenrod-yellow in color, hide motionless near the center of a flower, waiting to pounce on any nectar seeker that comes near. If you notice a butterfly in an odd position on a flower, or one that seems to be staying much longer than usual, take a closer look and you may find a crab spider enjoying its dinner. Usually I spot discarded butterfly wings beneath the plant before I see the spider itself.

I rarely interfere with Nature's plan, but one year, the crab spiders were decimating my butterfly visitors badly. Every afternoon, I would find the wings of at least a dozen swallowtails beneath a clump of phlox. When I investigated, I found 14 crab spiders in residence on the phlox. That didn't seem fair, so I moved some of the spiders to the mint patch. They spent the rest of the summer there, grabbing small wasps and beetles.

Parasitic Predators

Parasitic insects are one of the biggest threats to butterflies. These insects use butterfly eggs or caterpillars as a host for their own young.

You've probably encountered the huge caterpillars called tomato hornworms in your garden. They're the larvae of a large sphinx moth, one of the hummingbird-like dusk fliers that visit your petunias and moonflowers. Tiny wasps often prey upon these caterpillars, eating the living caterpillar from the inside out. If you spot a hornworm caterpillar bedecked with what look like white grains of rice on its back, you're actually looking at the cocoons of the immature wasps that have emerged from the doomed caterpillar's body.

Should you decide to try your hand at raising butterflies from eggs or caterpillars you collect in the garden (see page 124 for instructions), you may see the results of a parasitic invasion up close. Many times, I have collected what looked like a healthy caterpillar, only to have it decline as tiny wasp or fly larvae devoured it. If you see your caterpillar shriveling or failing to thrive, cover the container with a lid that has very small air holes, such as a piece of fabric cut from an old T-shirt. If your caterpillar is indeed infected with parasites, they will eventually hatch from the body of their host.

Colors with Meaning

When it comes to most predators, butterflies have at least a fighting chance. Over time, they have evolved the protection of an incredible system of camouflage to ensure the species' survival. Color is the key to butterfly protection. Those fragile flapping wings will never outfly a determined pursuer that has wings of its own, but if Mr. Chickadee never spots the butterfly, the insect will stay safe.

Protective coloration works at all stages of butterfly life. Green eggs are hard to see against green leaves, and so are green caterpillars. Mottled brown or gray butterflies are tricky to distinguish from tree bark.

Butterfly Baiting

Once used by butterfly enthusiasts looking for new specimens to add to their collections, "baiting" butterflies is a harmless technique that will allow you to observe many beautiful butterflies and moths and beetles up close. Try it in summer, when butterfly populations are at their peak.

The bait recipe is simple: Just mash 3 or 4 overripe bananas in a small bowl, slide them into a bucket, and add the contents of a bottle of molasses and a 1-pound box of brown sugar. For the finishing touch, pour in a bottle of beer and stir the whole gloppy mess together. Proportions and ingredients don't need to be exact; the objective is to have a sweet, smelly, fruit-scented fermented mixture. I've substituted peaches or cantaloupe for bananas, and corn syrup for molasses. An old book in my collection recommends adding a dead snake, but that's a step I gladly forgo.

Park the bucket in an out-of-the-way place in the shade and let it sit to ferment for a day or two. Then dip a big paintbrush into the bucket and slap some of the mixture onto tree trunks, fenceposts, or other inconspicuous spots, near eye level. Make a "trail" by applying bait at various places around your yard.

Check your bait trail daily for butterflies, and nightly for moths (whose eyes shine red in the glow of a flashlight beam). Renew the bait whenever it dries up or stops attracting butterflies.

Once you start looking at caterpillars—their presence betrayed by chewed leaves or droppings—you'll notice that many of them look like something else. Some have points that mimic thorns or leaf edges, others have splotches of brown that look like dead vegetation, and some even adopt the color or shape of bird droppings.

Chrysalises employ the same range of disguises. Because they don't move, they're practically impossible to discern among the plants in your garden.

Now You See Me, Now You Don't

Adult butterflies use a few different methods to lessen their vulnerability. Try watching a red admiral flutter across the yard and you'll see it's a lot harder to track than a yellow tiger swallowtail. That's because its undersides are patterned in nondescript browns. As the butterfly flaps, it's a now-you-see-it, now-you-don't effect.

Some butterflies, including the subtly beautiful anglewings, have wings that fold up to look just like a jagged leaf. The hackberry simply disappears when resting on a tree trunk

The most famous mimic is the viceroy (*top*), which has adopted the coloring of a monarch (*above*). Viceroys feed on harmless willows, apples, and poplars, but birds don't know that and steer clear of the monarch coloring. Were you fooled, too? The viceroy has a thin, curved black line drawn across its hindwings.

or the forest floor, thanks to a wing pattern of browns and grays dappled with lighter colors, which look like spots of sunlight.

Many of the best-camouflaged butterflies are not nectar eaters. You can get a good look at them by painting a surface with butterfly bait, as described on page 175.

Advertising Bad Taste
Caterpillars that devour plants that contain toxic compounds, like milkweed, are unfazed by the chemicals in their food. As they chomp, they collect, or sequester, the toxin in their bodies, and it remains even after they emerge as butterflies. Birds suffer ill effects from even a taste of such a caterpillar or the adult it becomes.

Butterflies that devour such plants proclaim their unpalatability with bold advertising: They flash bright orange, like the monarch, or blue, like the pipevine swallowtail. Some species that dine on perfectly harmless plants mimic this coloration so well that birds avoid them too.

WATCHING HUMMINGBIRDS DAY TO DAY

Hummingbirds seem like such miraculous creatures, with their tiny bodies, faster-than-the-eye-can-see wings, and aerobatic flight. But like any other birds, hummingbirds court, nest, lay eggs, and raise young. Only the details are different—and often in fascinating ways.

Considering that hummingbirds can cruise at speeds up to 50 miles per hour, it's no wonder that it takes a little practice to train your eyes to follow hummingbirds on their daily rounds. But the time spent practicing is well worth it!

Eating All Day Long
You'll get your first good look at how hummingbirds live by watching them at feeder and flower. The first thing you may notice is that hummingbirds eat a lot! They visit the feeder or the garden from sunup to sundown, and seem to be constantly snacking.

That's no illusion. On average, hummingbirds feed every 10 minutes. Hummingbirds have the fastest metabolism of any creature on this continent—with, as the books always say, the possible exception of the shrew.

A typical hummingbird weighs about 4 grams. That's less than half the weight of a teeny-tiny house wren, and about $\frac{1}{25}$ of the weight of a robin. You might think that flyweight body wouldn't need a lot of fuel to keep it stoked, but just the opposite is true. Hummingbirds burn calories three times faster than a wren, and ten times faster than a mourning dove!

These tiny creatures have such enormous needs because of their habit of fast and frequent motion. It's fun to consider the diet you'd need if your body processes worked as fast as a hummingbird's. First of all, you'd have to boost your 98.6°F temperature to more than

Eating is an almost constant occupation of high-energy hummingbirds, which burn calories faster than just about any other living creature on earth. Supplying sustenance in the form of nectar flowers and feeders sustains birds like this blue-throated hummer and delights our human sensibilities at the same time.

750°F to match the heat of a hummingbird's body. Then you'd have to chow down on enough ice cream and prime rib to boost your typical 2,000-calories-a-day diet by almost 80 times that much—by hummingbird standards, 155,000 calories a day would be just about right for your human body size!

To someone like me, who gains 5 pounds every time I look at a chocolate bar, hummingbird metabolism seems enviable—at first. Then I realize how much I appreciate being able to push back from the dinner table long enough to read, walk, and watch birds and butterflies in the garden!

CARBOHYDRATES FOR HUMMERS Flower nectar is no different nutritionally than the sugar water you use to stock your feeders, although the sweetness content varies considerably depending on the individual flower and the weather. Nectar, whether nature makes it or you cook it up, is carbohydrate. That means the hummingbird can easily use it for fast fuel.

If you could slow down a feeding hummingbird, you'd see that its tongue actually licks up nectar. It doesn't suck it up as you might imagine because the tongue is not a hollow tube. Slow down the view even further, and you might be able to see that a hummingbird licks nectar faster than a kid with a melting ice pop—no matter what the species (or how large the tongue), a hummingbird drinks nectar at about 13 licks a second.

Nectar is a main food source for all species of hummingbirds, but exactly what proportion of it they consume compared to other foods is hard to calculate. It's easiest to count the trips hummingbirds make for nectar and compare them to foraging trips for insects, their other main food. My own observations match those of ornithologists, who estimate that more than 80 percent of food-gathering is for nectar; only 14 to 16 percent of foraging trips are for insects. That means for every eight visits to a nectar flower, a hummingbird nabs just one or two bites of insect.

Sugar-laden sap pooling at woodpeckers' holes is also a carbohydrate source for some North American hummingbirds. Although only four species have been recorded as drinking sap, chances are other species do it too—they just haven't been caught in the act. Hummers have also been seen drinking juice from fruit, although this also seems to be a rare occurrence.

If you have a sweet tooth yourself, you know that an excess of sugar leads to body fat. Scientists have discovered that hummingbirds actually weigh more in the afternoon than in the morning—sometimes by as much as 16 percent. Presumably, the extra weight is the fuel the bird needs to maintain itself during the night. (See the section on torpor on page 184.) Hummingbirds overindulge in sugar to the extreme when they need to store calories as fat for long trips, such as across the Gulf of Mexico on migration. Then they stuff thousands of extra calories into their tiny bodies, increasing their body weight by 50 percent or more. Some of the excess is held in their crops, a storage organ in the throat.

CREATURES OF HABIT Hummingbirds are definitely creatures of habit. They will return to the same feeder or the same plant year after year, trusting fully that it will be there.

I discovered how true this was when I transplanted a tree in my yard. It's a red buckeye (*Aesculus pavia*), and when it blooms in early spring, its candelabras of skinny red-orange flowers pull hummingbirds into the yard as if the flowers were sending some kind of electromagnetic signal.

One spring I decided to lever the tree out of the ground and move it to a better location around the corner of the

Perhaps licking her chops after settling in the nest, this female broad-tailed hummingbird is caught by the camera with her incredible tongue extended.

Lines of sapsucker drillings attract a ruby-throated hummingbird to dab up sweet sap and perhaps the tiny insects that collect at the holes.

house, where I could watch the feeding hummingbirds from my office window. Being a procrastinator, I didn't move the tree until it was already in flower. I did wait for a rainy day to do the job, crossing my fingers that with minimal root disturbance and cool, damp weather, it would resettle easily into the new spot.

No hummingbirds were about when I dug up the buckeye, thanks to the weather. It seems that none watched me lug the thing around the corner either—because to my surprise, the tree suddenly lost its magical powers. A day went by, then two, without a single hummingbird visit.

I then discovered that the hummers were still hovering around the tree's original location, looking dumbfounded.

Not wanting good flowers to go to waste, or hungry hummingbirds to go without lunch, I laid a trail of red herrings—okay, red hankies—in a path from the former planting site to the tree. Like a pack of well-trained field hounds, the birds followed along, almost at my shoulder, until one of them spotted the tree and made a beeline for the blossoms.

You've probably seen this same behavior if you've been tardy hanging up your nectar feeder once springtime rolls around. The hummers will congregate where the feeder hung the previous season, making scolding noises until they shame you into quickly putting it in place and filling it.

PROTEIN-PACKED INSECTS To get the protein they also need for a balanced diet, hummingbirds turn to insects. That hummingbird at your flowers may not be drinking nectar at all—if you look closely through binoculars, you may be privileged to see that it is actually snatching up tiny insects.

Thanks to the superfast hummingbird metabolism, even insects don't hang around long in the digestive system. It may take only 10 minutes from the time an insect goes down the hatch until it's fully digested.

A lot of insect eating takes place away from the flowerbeds. Keep your eyes open and you may see a hummingbird patrolling along your porch railing, the wall of your house (especially near an outdoor light), or among shrubbery. The bird may be a female gathering spider silk for nesting material, but it's even more likely to be a hummingbird in search of a protein fix. Those places that shelter an abundance of small insects are excellent hunting grounds.

Once I saw a wondrous hummingbird happening right from my chaise lounge. It was high summer, and a cloud of gnats had gathered over my head. I was lying almost flat, watching the gnats dancing, when a hummingbird zoomed into the middle of the cluster. Hovering in place, the hummingbird nabbed dozens of gnats, its tongue reaching and recoiling like that of a flicker dabbing up ants.

I'm sure nature has equipped hummingbirds with the sense to know when they need more of a particular nutrient, which is probably why insect feeding seems to happen most frequently before a rainy spell. When the tree toads in my neighborhood start calling, portending afternoon thundershowers, I've noticed that the hummers also get more active in their hunt for insects. My guess is that they need the extra protein to keep them fueled during the inclement weather.

HUMMINGBIRDS AND SPIDERS Spiders seem to get the short end of the stick in their relationship with hummingbirds; not only do they serve as food but their carefully made webs are ripped down in a flash by female hummers seeking nesting materials.

Unless you pay close attention to the denizens of your garden, the only spiders you're likely to notice are the largest ones, like the enormous black-and-yellow argiopes, which weave huge webs. Zillions of other smaller spiders also roam your yard, from nocturnal wolf spiders that hunt on foot to tiny creatures that build delicate webs no bigger than a 50-cent piece.

Even though we may overlook our garden spiders, they don't escape the sharp eyes or instincts of hummingbirds. Often when I sit on my side porch in summer, a hummingbird will patrol beneath the ledge of the porch railing just inches away. While I watch, the bird plucks out the spiders, plus any delectable prey that has been caught in the web.

Magnificent Muscle

Under those pretty feathers, hummingbirds are all "dark meat"—the blood-rich muscle that powers their wings and other movements. More blood vessels mean more oxygen delivered to the muscle cells, just like a bigger air intake on a race car. Hummingbirds have oversized pectoral muscles that allow them to fly at astonishing speeds. These muscles may account for almost a third of their body weight, and would be the envy of any bodybuilder. In human terms, that would be 50 pounds of chest muscle in a 150-pound person!

If you like to stroll around your garden in the morning, you probably know the feeling of a spider web plastering itself across your face. I used to carry a stick in front of my face, sweeping it back and forth to remove such webs. Now I look more closely and duck instead because I've discovered these webs are a prized source of sustenance for hummingbirds. Because the web is out in the open, it's easy for a hungry hummingbird to hover before the web and remove each hapless insect that's been caught in it.

SPIDER SILK FOR NESTS The silk that spiders spin for their webs is vital to hummingbird nests. All species use the stuff as a major building block—the sticky strands plaster the nest securely to a tree branch or other support, and also comprise the walls of the nest. Because of its fibrous nature, the silk makes good insulation for the eggs and babies, keeping them snug on chilly or rainy nights and preventing overheating in summer sun.

If you see a female hummer spending time at a spider web, watch closely to see if she's collecting silk. I've seen the birds gather it into a clumped-up beakful, and I've also watched an even more intriguing behavior, when the female collects silk in coils. Every summer I usually spot a hummingbird collecting loops of spider webbing. The tiny bird moving back and forth maneuvers the strands like I coil a balky garden hose.

Perching
Although hummingbirds may seem to eat continually, they actually stop for a breather between bouts of feeding. Follow with your eyes as a hummer flies away from a feeder, and you're likely to see it stop at a nearby perch. Utility wires are a favorite resting place, as are dead twigs at the tops of shrubs. Even the top of the shepherd's crook that holds the feeder may serve as a perch.

Hummingbirds have extremely short legs and they never walk. Their feet are tiny black claws, useful for clinging to a perch, but worthless for hopping about on the ground.

Early hummingbird nectar feeders were made without perches. When I was a child, commercial hummingbird feeders were not available. Fans of the little buzzing birds made their own feeders from test tubes, hamster water bottles, or other homemade contraptions—none of which had a perch attached. Today, you can choose from many styles of nectar feeders, with and without perches. I supply both kinds so that my fast-flying friends can take a rest if they like while they feed. The ones with perches are favorites by a mile. They always have customers, while the perchless feeders only catch the overflow crowd.

Guarding the Territory
With their lives depending on how much nectar they can gather, it's no wonder some hummingbirds show a strong streak of defensiveness. If your nectar feeder is within a male's feeding territory, that hummingbird is likely to be the only one you see at the feeder except during migration times. Even a good food

plant can become the object of a territorial defense. Hardy fuchsia (*Fuchsia magellanica*), a wonderful shrub that blooms for months, was always a source of disputes among the feeding hummingbirds in my Oregon garden. Here in southern Indiana, it's the flaming scarlet sage (*Salvia splendens*), a common bedding annual, that is most apt to be guarded ferociously.

Ferocious is the word, too, because hummingbirds will dart after any trespasser full speed. Even I won't stand up to a hummingbird's attack. My dogs yield the scene even faster—a habit that I've put to good use. When I want to protect a particular plant from the effects of male dogs using it as a fire hydrant, I nestle a few plants of red sage around the prized plant.

Well hidden among sheltering branches, a nest of young black-chinned hummingbirds is protected from the notice of passing predators.

Hummingbird specialists divide territorial behavior into two categories, based on observations of species in Mexico. Some hummers, they discovered, were "trapliners," that traveled a wide area daily, visiting one plant after the next. These roaming species didn't stick around to defend a small area or particular plant like other hummingbirds, which were dubbed "territorialists."

You'll soon find out which of these categories the birds in your area fall into. If a single hummer chases away other visitors to the nectar feeder, you have a territorialist. If your hummers feed amicably together, it's either migration season—when hummingbirds drop their territorial defenses because they're on the move—or your species are trapliners.

Warning Calls

Listen for the distinctive voices of your hummingbirds—they use those chips and squeaks to warn intruders away from defended territories. If the verbal warning is ignored, then the hummer darts to the defense.

It's not only food that hummingbirds fight over. Their rivalries can be as bad as those of human siblings, with the birds arguing over just about anything. I've even seen them battle

Sharing doesn't come naturally to hummingbirds, which argue incessantly with each other at any prime feeding location. Often a single territorial bird will lay claim to a feeder, relentlessly chasing away all other comers. Add a few extra feeders if yours is hogged by a bully.

over a perching place. Interestingly, although an airborne intruder to a perch gets driven away immediately, I have never seen hummingbirds physically attack if both are already perched. Rather than one of the pugnacious birds rising to assault the other, they resort to verbal attacks and just scream insults back and forth.

Hummingbirds on the Roost

Like other birds, hummingbirds seek out a roost where they will be sheltered from rain, cold, and predators during the dark hours. A final flurry of feeding usually precedes their retirement for the day or before a storm. Once on the roost, though, hummingbirds exhibit very different behavior than your average robin.

Considering that their bodies burn calories faster than a forest fire, you might wonder how hummingbirds stay alive overnight, when temperatures drop and no feeding takes place. Generally, the bird can store enough calories to manage through the hours of night until daylight comes and it can begin to feed again. But in cool weather or other conditions, a special evolutionary adaptation called torpor gets hummingbirds through the night—as well as through days of rain or other inclement weather. When the sun goes down, their body temperature drops, their respiration slows, and the amount of calories they burn is greatly decreased. The metabolic rate of a torpid hummingbird drops to as little as $\frac{1}{60}$ of the usual daytime level.

Unlike songbirds, which tuck their head under a wing or into their back feathers, hummingbirds adopt an unusual posture for sleeping or torpor. When they need to preserve energy they point their bill upward at a 45-degree angle, close their eyes, and stay put.

COURTSHIP AND MATING

Think about the everyday flying skills of a hummingbird. Now imagine you were that bird, out to impress a potential mate. Oh, the acrobatics you'd do!

That's exactly how hummingbirds perform at courtship time. While the female sits nearby, acting blasé, the male bird engages in fantastic aerial maneuvers above her. He soars, he dives, he does death-defying loop-de-loops. She acts uninterested. He persists, for days if necessary, until she finally relents.

Each species of hummingbird has its own patented act. Experienced birdwatchers have learned the tricks, too, and can identify a male by the pattern and accompanying sounds of his flight. You'll find detailed descriptions of these aeronautics for each of the more common North American species in Chapter 9.

Mating is just as exciting as the courtship display. The first time I saw it, I could not believe my eyes. I thought two hummers were trying to kill each other. They were locked together in what seemed like a death grip and spinning in circles just above the ground, exactly like a Fourth of July firework.

When I approached the two to break up the "fight," I saw immediately that it was male and female ruby-throated hummingbirds locked in a mating bond. The male had his head tipped backward, exposing the brilliant color of his carmine throat as the couple whirled at extraordinary speed.

After a seemingly endless 2 minutes, the still-clinched couple rocketed upward to about 20 feet, then separated. The male swung into his exultant courtship dives, twittering shrilly, while the female preened on a nearby branch.

Nest Building
Miniatures are always fascinating, and hummingbird nests are no exception. The smallest nest of any American bird, these tiny cups are no bigger in outside diameter than the egg cup you spooned your soft-boiled breakfast egg from—and they're smaller on the inside.

The flashy gorget of a male ruby-throated hummingbird shines when the male buzzes in high-speed loops and dives to woo the female.

Although hummingbird nests may be tiny, they're quite strong. The walls are thick and stout, and the hummingbird attaches the nest securely to its support, gluing it in place with a platform of sticky spider web.

In all species, it's the female that makes this marvelous home. She alone collects strands of web, bits of lichen, and other teeny construction materials. The size and shape of the nest varies according to species, as does the list of building materials, but all depend on spider web to hold the thing together. The thick walls and air-retaining materials make hummingbird nests superbly insulated, enough to hold the heat of the mother bird even on a chilly desert or mountain night.

Some species complete the nest before laying their two white eggs inside, while other females continue decorating and strengthening their home even after laying eggs. The nest is deep from the outset, so the eggs are nestled securely from the first.

Nesting

A fine parent, the female hummingbird looks more like a murderer when she begins the task of feeding the newly hatched young. They're tiny creatures, as you'd expect, but also supremely ugly, looking like squirming blackish lumps. Imagine a baby bird that's approximately the size of a lima bean, and you've got part of the picture.

If you have no luck tracking down a hummingbird nest in the wild, visit a natural history museum to marvel at this tiny wonder of the natural world.

Now imagine the mother hummingbird inserting her rapier bill into the open mouth of a nestling. If you're lucky enough to see this, you would swear she's about to pierce its gullet with her long, pointed beak. Yet, like the great blue heron at the opposite end of the size scale, the hummingbird is extremely careful in her movements, and no babies seem to be the worse for wear after their 3 weeks of sword-feeding.

Depending on the hospitality of the climate where the various hummers live, they may raise more than one brood each year. In most areas, the nesting season usually begins around April and runs through July. The farther north the hummingbird must travel to reach nesting grounds, the later it starts raising a family, although the difference is usually only a few weeks. Baby hummingbirds take longer from egg to flight than most songbirds: about 15 to 18 days of incubation, and then another 3 weeks before the young leave the nest. Add another week of babysitting by the female after the young have fledged, for a total of 6 weeks or more invested in raising young.

Birds in more southerly areas may raise a second or even a third brood because the young have plenty of time to fledge before migration begins. In California, for instance, the black-chinned hummingbird starts her first family in early April, the second brood in June, and the third in August or September. But in Montana, she attempts only a single nest, usually in May or June. Anna's hummingbird, which lives year-round in some warm areas, begins nesting as early as February.

It can be a frightening sight to watch a mother hummingbird feed her nestlings, but don't worry—the babies are not injured by the mother's beak.

MIGRATION

Except for the Anna's hummingbird in California, our North American hummingbirds are migratory. Twice a year they make the trek—north in the spring, south in the late summer to fall.

Some travel just a hop, skip, and a jump—a couple of hundred miles. A few are marathon migrators. The familiar ruby-throated hummingbird, for instance, makes a flight as long as 2,000 miles, including a 500-mile-long leg across the Gulf of Mexico.

You've probably noticed that swallows, blackbirds, and other songbirds tend to flock together when summer nears its end. When their internal clocks say it's time to leave, the flock takes off, gathering other small groups as it moves, until eventually the numbers billow into the tens of thousands.

Hummingbirds are different. They leave their summer homes, and their winter quarters, one by one. In solitary flight, they zip across the continent. Even if a thousand of them, say, are heading for Indiana in April, they all travel alone and arrive individually.

The timing of migration varies according to how far the bird travels, the route it takes, and its final destination. You can count on the spring season beginning in February, with the Allen's hummingbird, and continuing until late April or even May.

In spring, the birds seem to be extra-hungry as they move north, and thus become even more inquisitive than usual about any red object. Once I was talking with a circle of friends on the sidewalk outside my house when a hummer zipped up and hovered just a couple of inches from my face. My friends were impressed that "my" hummingbird remembered me so well and had come to say hello. I tried to be humble, but I was secretly thrilled, too. Only later, when I caught sight of myself in a mirror, did I realize the bird was more interested in my red lip gloss than in renewing our acquaintance.

Following the Food
Hummingbirds have evolved right along with the wildflowers that nurtured them on their travels. These migrants were traveling long before there

Whether it's azaleas on a grand scale like this estate garden on the Gulf Coast in Alabama or just a single bush in a backyard garden, nectar plants are a welcome sight for hummingbirds that cross the Gulf during their migration north in the spring.

Long "spurs" on a western wild columbine blossom advertise the presence of plenty of nectar to this rufous hummingbird, which migrates northward just as the western wildflower comes into bloom. In the East, a similar species of columbine follows the same schedule with ruby-throated hummingbirds.

were any American flower gardens (or gardeners, for that matter) to supply nectar flowers. They established their migration patterns far back when the plastic we use to make their feeders was still transforming from tree ferns to petroleum. Despite all the changes we humans have made to the natural landscape, hummingbirds still follow their old patterns of migration (though they've added some new ones, too, thanks to feeders and gardens).

Hummingbirds head north at the same time the flowering currant (*Ribes sanguineum*) blooms along the Cascade Mountains of the Pacific Coast, and the red-and-yellow wild columbine (*Aquilegia canadensis*) dangles its blossoms in the New England woods. As these blossoms open, they supply essential food for the migrating birds, and the birds pollinate the plants in return—a perfectly evolved relationship. On the return trip the native late summer wildflowers beckon to hummingbirds along the way, offering bountiful nectar in return for a pollinating tickle.

It's a great system. Should unusual weather delay the blooming of their companion plants, hummingbirds can stay put or even retreat until the succession continues. With thousands of miles of flowers backing them up, the nectar drinkers have a great built-in support system.

Besides moving north or south to keep up with the flowers, hummers also zoom up and down. Some species follow the wave of wildflowers from valley floors to mountain heights, where blooms open later in the spring, as they travel.

End of the Season In late August, it's time to say goodbye to hummingbirds for most of us. The little birds pack their bags and head south, with the last individuals leaving in early September. If you visit any of the hawk migration observation points during the fall season, such as Hawk Mountain Sanctuary in Kempton, Pennsylvania, or Cape May, New Jersey, watch for passing hummingbirds, too. Although they usually fly much lower to the ground than hawks, many follow the same route. I connect spring hummingbird migration season to that of wood warblers, so when I hear the first sharp "chip!" notes of warblers and grab my binoculars, I also keep an ear cocked for the whirr of hummingbird wings.

Most of our species winter in Mexico and Central America, although they have stayed increasingly on the Gulf Coast in recent years. In warm areas of southern California, Anna's hummingbird resides year-round.

Spring migrants don't usually linger in my yard or at the feeders, but the fall crowd is more leisurely and often hangs out in increasing numbers. I often have to refill my feeders twice a day to keep up with the demand.

PREDATORS AND HAZARDS

A whole laundry list of hazards face tiny hummingbirds. When they hover near water to sip nectar from jewelweed or cardinal flower, a bullfrog may zap out its coiled tongue and swallow them whole. Fish gulp them down, too, given a chance.

But water hazards pale in comparison to the death traps on land. We humans lead the list of land hazards, thanks to our nice shiny glass windows, the site of many a fatal encounter. Car accidents take a toll, as do our beloved feline pets, who skulk around nectar feeders and gardens.

On the natural side, hummingbirds make a fine snack for hawks. I've witnessed hawks make quick work of hummingbirds on two different occasions. During fall migration, the little birds often follow the same path as their much larger predators—a potentially dangerous habit. One September day, I was watching a slim falcon called an American kestrel soar toward the lookout at Hawk Mountain Sanctuary in Pennsylvania, when a hummingbird came zipping along beneath it. Immediately the hawk dropped a few feet, casually extended a foot and grabbed the hummer in midair. Then it flew on, never missing a beat. I've also seen a peregrine falcon at Cape May, New Jersey, beat the bushes for birds. Twice the gray hunting hawk I was watching came up from its sortie with a hummingbird in its clutches.

Hummingbirds are so small in stature that even insects are enemies. An oft-told story tells of one of the little birds snared by a dragonfly. It seemed to be an even match, with both buzzing fiercely, until a human observer intervened and separated the two. Even praying mantises may nab a hummingbird now and then.

Accidents also befall hummingbirds. Their attraction to the color red can lead them to get stuck in screen doors or trapped in buildings. They can also become impaled on thistles (as can small bats) when they are seeking nectar or small insects. Hummers can become inextricably entangled in spider webs, and may also become prey for large spiders.

Hummingbirds have good reason to fear the argiope spider, a giant-size garden resident with a strong web and voracious appetite.

GETTING THE BEST VIEWS

You can watch plenty of interesting butterfly and hummingbird behavior without using binoculars, but at times, using binoculars will give you a view that magnifies their beauty tremendously. I find it best to practice observing first without binoculars. When you begin to get a feel for the actions of the hummers and butterflies in your yard, it becomes much easier to follow them with binoculars.

If you already have a pair of bird-watching or general-purpose binoculars, you may already be equipped for observing hummingbirds and butterflies. Try using your existing binocs to focus on a butterfly at a flower, or a hummingbird at a feeder. If you can get the creature into sharp detail by adjusting the focus, you're all set.

If your binoculars won't allow you to focus on butterflies and hummingbirds at close range, you may want to consider buying a second pair especially for close viewing. Selecting binoculars for viewing these fabulous visitors is different than shopping for bird-watching binocs. Instead of choosing glasses that give you the best view from a distance, you'll want a pair that allows you to get a clear look up close.

The small, lightweight plastic "compact" binoculars made by many different companies are generally ideal for hummingbird and butterfly viewing. Choose a reputable

The best way to study the subtle details of coloration on some butterflies—like this hairstreak perched on a goldenrod stem—is to focus on them with a pair of compact binoculars.

manufacturer, such as Nikon, Pentax, Canon, or other makers of good-quality equipment. Look for a pair of binoculars that use a "porroprism" system of conveying the objective to your eyes; the sales clerk or catalog will tell you which models are designed that way. Those that magnify 8 or 9 times (8× or 9×), with the bigger lens about 20 mm in size or greater, are fine for this kind of viewing—they're sold as "8×20," "9×23," etc. Expect to pay about $70 to $100 for a decent pair of binoculars that will hold up to repeated use. You can also pay $400 or more for top-quality optics that will send your friends into throes of envy.

Compact binoculars are good for focusing close up, with many models able to deliver a sharp image from about 6 feet away—which is about as close as you can usually get to a butterfly without alarming it into flight. Be sure to try them out before you buy—one pair may be much better suited to you than another.

You'll also save your arm muscles by using compact binoculars, which weigh much less than standard models. Appreciating the subtle patterns and colors of butterfly wings takes time—and that means several minutes of holding a pair of binoculars to your eyes.

PHOTOGRAPHY

Photographing butterflies is much easier than getting a shot of a hummingbird, but neither subject is exactly cooperative. Few butterflies will pose quietly while you fiddle with your camera, and hummingbirds are a catch-as-catch-can proposition.

The lovely photos you see in this book and others are the results of hours of dedication, years of experience—and many rolls of film. The more time you invest in the hobby, the more good shots you'll accumulate. But take heart—even a snapshot can give you a personally gratifying picture.

My photo albums (okay, the shoeboxes stuffed with pictures I intend to put into albums someday) include shots of swallowtails on zinnias, monarchs on butterfly bushes, and

Photographing butterflies calls for plenty of patience. Professional photographers may use a lens like this one; you should choose whichever lens you own that gives you the closest shot possible.

caterpillars on anything, as well as a few prized photos of hummingbirds at flowers—and even though you'll never see those pictures on the cover of a magazine, they still warm my heart with memories of summer gardens.

To photograph fast-moving hummingbirds, or to still fluttering butterfly wings that otherwise would appear blurred, use "fast" film, 400 ASA speed or better, which will allow you to take a picture in an infinitesimal fraction of a second and thus stop the motion of your jittery subject.

Make sure your butterflies and hummingbirds are more than just a dot of color in the photo by using a big lens or zooming in with a macro lens. Fill the frame as much as possible with the subject. My moderately priced point-and-shoot camera adjusts the lens from 28mm to 70mm with the touch of a button. I use the larger setting for closeup photos, and the smaller ones for wide garden views that include some airborne dots that I know are butterflies.

Experiment with your own camera's capabilities until you know what works best for you. A few rolls of film and developing are an inexpensive lesson that can lead to years of pleasure as you record your visitors on film.

Photographing Nests, Eggs, and Caterpillars

The butterfly life cycle, and the behavior of hummingbirds at the nest, are prime subjects for an aspiring photographer. Butterfly eggs, caterpillars, and chrysalises require a sharp eye to find the subject in the first place, and powerful lenses to magnify them to a big enough size for a photo. Use a tripod to steady the camera. You can snap away at a slow shutter speed because your subjects move about as fast as the proverbial molasses.

Hummingbird nests don't move unless they are the pendant type and the wind is blowing, but the mama bird zips in and out of the frame at autobahn speeds. You'll need fast film and a quick shutter speed to stop her motion unless you're going for the trendy blurry effect in your nature photography. You'll probably also need a boost to get to nest height. A portable deer stand platform, available from sporting-goods stores and catalogs,

Photographing a hummingbird nest means finding one first, which can be a matter of serendipity or the result of careful observation of hummingbird behavior. Be sure to keep a respectful distance that doesn't alarm the parent birds—no photo is worth an abandoned nest.

may do the trick for intrepid types. Or try a long telephoto lens aimed from a vantage point on the second floor of your house.

Keep in mind that even a prize-winning photo isn't worth upsetting a parent hummingbird to extreme agitation. If your subject seems to be telling you to back off, pay attention. Not only are you annoying a bird that needs all the help it can get, you're also opening her nest site to the notice of predators. Those predators certainly won't hesitate to rudely disturb the little family.

CHAPTER 9

A Gallery of
HUMMINGBIRDS

More than 300 species of hummingbirds add their special flashing beauty to the Western Hemisphere, which is the only part of our earth that hosts the birds. Nearly all hummingbirds live in the subtropics and tropics of Central and South America and islands off the coasts. Only a handful of species make the trek northward across the Mexican border into the United States. The 15 species you'll meet in this alphabetical gallery range from common to rare. I include the common ruby-throated hummingbird of the East and the wide-ranging rufous hummingbird of the West, as well as the beautiful blue-throated hummingbird and other seldom-seen species, whose sighting makes a red-letter day for any bird watcher.

The illustrations in this chapter show the colorations and markings of the male of each species. The females are described within each species's entry. The measurement underneath each illustration is that hummer's overall length (from tip of bill to tip of tail) in inches.

As you read about each hummingbird, you'll learn about behavior patterns and other quirks that make each species a special one. You'll also get plenty of suggestions for the nectar plants that encourage each of the birds to linger in a feeding area—aka your backyard! You'll notice a preponderance of native plants listed in the favorites for each species. That's because most researchers study the birds in the wild, and so their sightings of

the birds often occur at wildflowers of a particular region. If you live in the range of a particular hummingbird, planting some of its favorite wild foods will be a strong attraction. It's also a great way to get to know your native-plant neighbors. But a much wider selection of garden "hummingbird flowers" will also satisfy the birds. I've included some of the plants I've seen hummingbirds seek out in gardens across the country, and you too will soon have your own "favored plants" to add to the list as you watch hummers come and go in your own garden.

Conducting your own research by keeping records of the garden plants preferred by your birds is fun and easy. You can also include your observations of the calls you hear and the behavior you see, and your guess as to the reasons behind it. If you take the time to make daily notes in a journal, you'll end up with your own very personal book of hummingbird behavior. My "journal" is a bare-bones version—I scribble notes on a page stapled to the wall calendar.

No matter what type of records you keep, jotting down some information will help you know what to watch for and when. You'll be able to see how the current year's hummingbird activities in your garden stack up against those of previous years.

June 28th 2000

Was out weeding in herb garden today. Saw a red admiral basking on one of the stepping stones near the pond. What a welcome sight. I stood and watched it for about five minutes. Then it suddenly flittered off to the edge of the woods.

Red Admiral

Monarch

July 2nd 2000

Warm day. Out deadheading and pinching the early summer blooms. Looked over at the zinnias- six monarchs! One, sitting as though at attention; another basking on an open flower; and four more hovering above. I hope they'll decide to stick around. I planted butterfly weed along the driveway for them. Last year two pupated and I saw them emerge from the chrysalis.

If you have an artistic bent, try making sketches and taking notes of your hummingbird and butterfly observations in a sketch book. You'll end up with your own personal backyard nature journal.

Allen's Hummingbird
(Selasphorus sasin)

Allen's hummingbird is a beautiful, small hummingbird with soft cinnamon sides and deep rust tail and rump, set off by fiery, deep orange cheeks and throat. A metallic shimmer overlays the bronze-green head, back, and wings. The female is bronze-green topside, with pale rusty sides and a whitish throat.

Length: 3"–3½"

▶ RANGE

Allen's hummingbird breeds along the coast of California and on coastal islands, north to the Oregon boundary. It winters in northwest Mexico. Stragglers have turned up in Alabama, Louisiana, British Columbia, and other unlikely locations.

▶ HABITAT

These birds are fond of gardens and other areas of mixed vegetation and open space. They're often seen in city parks or golf courses; brushy areas with poison oak, willows, or dogwood; the bottoms of canyons; along streams and rivers; and mountain meadows. They seem to prefer humid areas where fog settles. Males stake out territories in shrubby areas, often in canyons or beside streams. Females frequent colonies of willows, blackberry thickets, and other dense vegetation.

▶ AERIAL DISPLAY

The male Allen's hummingbird starts his display with a warm-up series of shallow arcs, punctuated with buzzing and squeaking at the bottom of each swing. The bird then climbs vertically as if shot from a rubber band, zipping high into the air. He dives suddenly back toward earth, making a loud ripping sound ("vrrrp") at the base of the dive that is probably produced by air rushing through his tail feathers.

▶ NESTING

Females usually seek a nesting site in groves or woods, often selecting a live oak, eucalyptus, or tangle of vines to support the nest.

▶ COMMENTS

Look carefully to distinguish the Allen's hummingbird from the similar rufous. Although the male birds look very much the same from the front, the rufous has a rust-colored back, while Allen's wears green feathers. The female Allen's is so similar to the female rufous that only experts can tell the birds apart—by noting the slightly narrower outer tail feathers of the female Allen's. Allen's hummingbirds are attracted to all nectar flowers, especially those listed below.

FAVORED PLANTS

Agave, century plant
(*Agave americana*)

Indian paintbrushes
(*Castilleja* spp.)

California lilacs
(*Ceanothus* spp.)

Honeysuckles
(*Lonicera* spp., especially
L. involucrata)

Monkey flowers
(*Mimulus* spp.)

Tree tobacco
(*Nicotiana glauca*)

California fuchsia
(*Zauschneria californica*;
late summer through fall)

Anna's Hummingbird
(Calypte anna)

Anna's hummingbird is the most brightly colored of the western hummingbirds and one of the larger species. The male's spectacular neon pink head and throat are as bright as a fluorescent marking pen. The color changes with the light from rose red to pink. The female has a small deep pink patch surrounded by radiating dark spots on her throat. Both sexes have a pale grayish breast and bronze-green back, wings, and tail.

Length: 3½"–4"

▶ RANGE

A bird of the far West, Anna's breeds from southern Canada through Mexico and eastward into Arizona. It winters from southern California and Arizona into Mexico, occasionally northward as far as Oregon. In California, Anna's often can be seen in winter, nectaring at blossoms or feeders. Occasionally, bird watchers report spotting an Anna's hummingbird in places far beyond its normal range, including Alaska, Minnesota, and Florida. Keep watching your feeders and flowers, even if you don't live in the West—anything can happen!

▶ HABITAT

Anna's is a common bird of gardens and nectar feeders. It frequents city parks, golf courses, and anywhere nectar flowers grow. It can also be found in wooded areas, along roadsides, and in chaparral. At nesting time, males range in open habitat, while females often stick to groves of evergreen oaks and other trees.

▶ AERIAL DISPLAY

The male sings during his courtship flight as he flies upward and at the top of the climb. Then he dives to earth like an arrow, over the perched female, before reversing for another climb. Listen for the startling popping or "peek!" noise as a male Anna's hits the bottom of his pendulum dive and swings upward.

▶ NESTING

Nest sites run the gamut. The female will use practically anything that will support the nest, including utility wires; eucalyptus, oak, and other trees; and shrubs and vines.

▶ COMMENTS

Anna's is a highly vocal hummingbird, keeping up a chatter of squeaks, gurgles, and harsh, loud chittering notes. They're attracted to all nectar flowers, especially those listed below.

FAVORED PLANTS

Agave, century plant
(*Agave americana*)

Indian paintbrushes
(*Castilleja* spp.)

Eucalyptus
(*Eucalyptus* spp.)

Bush monkey flower
(*Mimulus aurantiacus*)

Tree tobacco
(*Nicotiana glauca*)

Flowering currant
(*Ribes sanguineum*)

Fuchsia-flowered gooseberry
(*Ribes speciosum*)

Indian pink
(*Silene laciniata*)

Blue curls
(*Trichostemma* spp.)

Black-Chinned Hummingbird
(*Archilochus alexandri*)

Even in full sun, this species keeps its namesake throat color. Its older common name of "purple-throated hummingbird" comes from the band of violet blue at the lower edge of the throat patch. A white collar extends onto the sides of the neck from the breast. Head, tail, wings, and back are bronze-green; breast is whitish. The female looks like the male, but sports a white throat.

Length: 3¼"–3¾"

▶ RANGE

The black-chinned is a widespread western species, breeding from British Columbia through southwest Texas and into Mexico, but appearing practically anywhere west of the Rockies from spring through fall. Bird watchers report rare sightings in many southeastern states and as far north as Nova Scotia! Black-chinned hummingbirds winter in Mexico.

▶ HABITAT

Common in areas with open space, the black-chinned is a frequent sight in gardens and at nectar feeders. It also may be seen in orchards, along rivers, in canyons and groves, on mountain slopes, or cruising through the chaparral.

▶ AERIAL DISPLAY

A master of exaggerated aerial maneuvers, the black-chinned male swoops through pen-dulum arcs of about 90 feet long. His performance is for the benefit of a female sitting just beneath the bottom of the arc. The flight may also trace a figure eight. Listen for the loud whistling noise as the male displays his prowess, probably the sound of wind rushing through his feathers. The male also sings as he flies, with sweet, long notes.

▶ NESTING

Look for the nest of a black-chinned hummingbird above a creek bed, dry or with water. The female will often plaster her nest to a crotch or saddle it to a smaller branch of a streamside tree.

▶ COMMENTS

Watch for the nervous tail motions of this species as it hovers before a flower or feeder. The female black-chinned looks just like the female Costa's and ruby-throated hummingbirds.

FAVORED PLANTS

Butterfly bush
(*Buddleia davidii*)

Texas redbud
(*Cercis canadensis* var. *texensis*)

Scarlet delphinium
(*Delphinium cardinale*)

Ocotillo
(*Fouqueria splendens*)

Honeysuckles
(*Lonicera* spp.)

Tree tobacco
(*Nicotiana glauca*)

Ironwood
(*Olneya tesota*)

Palo verde
(*Parkinsonia florida*)

Nasturtium
(*Tropaeolum majus*)

Blue-Throated Hummingbird
(Lampornis clemenciae)

The male blue-throated boasts a throat that shimmers metallic blue. A giant among North American hummingbirds, it has a solid, beefy look at over 5 inches long. Male and female share the typical bronze-green back, with dusky gray undersides and sporty white eye stripes. The big, broad tail flashes white tips when the bird spreads its tail feathers.

Length: 4½"–5"

▶ RANGE

The blue-throated hummingbird breeds in very limited areas of Texas, southeast Arizona, and occasionally southern New Mexico. It winters in Mexico. Migrants occasionally stray along the Gulf Coast of Texas, and have been seen in Denver and Utah.

▶ HABITAT

The blue-throated hummer frequents the mountains of Texas, Arizona, and New Mexico, ranging down into canyons and along streams and the Rio Grande. When you visit its breeding area in Big Bend, Texas, or the canyons of the neighboring states, you may spot it in wooded areas near water or zipping around desert slopes where agaves are abundant.

▶ AERIAL DISPLAY

I've never seen the display flight of the blue-throated and apparently, neither have the authors of the references I consulted. As with other species, it's likely to be a series of loops, swoops, and dives.

▶ NESTING

Females usually seek a nest site sheltered from above by a "roof" more solid than the usual leafy branch. The nest may be tucked under a ledge, beneath an overhanging rock, or under the eaves of a house. Undeterred by human activity, the blue-throated may nest on houses, sheds, or barns.

▶ COMMENTS

All hummingbirds are swift, direct fliers, but this one would probably win any race of its compatriots. Luckily, it's not shy around people and will often perch or feed from garden flowers just a few short steps away from a quiet human observer.

Listen for the loud "seep" call of the male. Watch for territorial battles with other species, when this large hummingbird fans its tail aggressively. In the wild and in gardens, these hummers seek both nectar and insects, which make up a big part of its diet.

FAVORED PLANTS

Agaves
(*Agave* spp.)

Gilias
(*Ipomopsis* spp.)

Lobelias
(*Lobelia* spp.)

Mints
(*Mentha* spp.)

Tree tobacco
(*Nicotiana glauca*)

Penstemons
(*Penstemon* spp.)

Salvias
(*Salvia* spp.)

Broad-Billed Hummingbird

(Cynanthus latirostris)

Despite its name, you'll have to look mighty close to notice any difference between the bill of this species and other hummers. Use color instead: Both sexes have a bright orange-red bill, which stands out against the dark body of the male bird. Female and male are the usual bronze-green on top. The female is whitish beige below. The male's green back continues in a seamless sweep, from deep emerald on breast and belly to a shining bluish green throat.

Length: 3¼"–4"

▶ RANGE

This bird is an attraction for lucky birders who live in or travel to southern Arizona, New Mexico, and southwest Texas. It winters in Mexico, but occasional birds show up in Louisiana, Utah, and California.

▶ HABITAT

Look for mesquites or agaves in this hummingbird's range for a good chance of spotting the bird in the wild. It frequents arroyos and canyons in the desert mountains and ranges onto drier slopes to forage. It also hangs out in hospitable gardens or backyards in its range.

▶ AERIAL DISPLAY

Either this bird suffers from stage fright when humans are present, or it chooses secluded areas for courtship displays. Little has been recorded about this species' show-off maneuvers during courtship, other than a reference to the male's pendulum-like flight punctuated by a high-pitched zing.

▶ NESTING

The broad-billed hummingbird cleverly camouflages her nest. The female bird often chooses a nest site on a low branch hanging just a short distance above water. Here she builds a nest that looks just like a little blob of flood debris caught in the branches! Willows, mesquites, and low branches of sycamores and hackberries—usually near water—have all served as nesting places.

▶ COMMENTS

The lack of contrast between the male's blue-green throat and deep green breast makes this a more subtly colored hummingbird than other more eye-catching species, but waiting for a good look in bright light is worth the effort. In dim light, when color is impossible to discern, look for the forked tail of the male.

In the wild and in the garden, these birds seek out nectar plants and also will nip the tiny insects attracted to flowers—even daddy-long-legs are fair game.

FAVORED PLANTS

Agaves
(*Agave* spp.)

Ocotillo
(*Fouqueria splendens*)

Prickly pears
(*Opuntia* spp.)

Penstemons
(*Penstemon* spp.)

Broad-Tailed Hummingbird
(Selasphorus platycercus)

This is the western counterpart of the ruby-throated humming-bird—common and widespread. Male and female have a green back tinged with metallic bronze. The male's underside is white and he sports a rosy red gorget—the decorative feathers at the throat. The female's nether regions are tinged with a delicate flush of orangish pink.

Length: 4"–4½"

▶ **RANGE**

This is *the* Rocky Mountain hummingbird! From the low foothills to 11,000 feet, this little bird ranges the mountains from California to Texas and northward to Idaho and Wyoming. It also turns up for usually brief visits in odd places, including the Midwest and Florida. It winters in Mexico and Central America.

▶ **HABITAT**

The broad-tailed hummer is common in mountains at any elevation and in almost any kind of habitat, from pine-oak woodlands to alder thickets, from dry slopes dotted with junipers to streamside willows or open mountain meadows. It is also common in towns, backyards, and gardens.

▶ **AERIAL DISPLAY**

Big, fast, shallow U-shaped dives are the trademark of the male broad-tailed. Sometimes a female joins a male for a brief interlude; they hover bill-to-bill as the male positions his gorget to best effect. Males also perform a "yo-yo" dance, zipping up and down or out and back short distances.

▶ **NESTING**

These hummers nest in a variety of places, often over water. Those that frequent valleys might choose a willow, alder, or cottonwood to support the tiny cupped nest, while those of higher hills seek out firs, spruces, pines, or aspens. The female often returns to the same area year after year to nest.

▶ **COMMENTS**

The male's wing feathers make a shrill whistle as air passes through them. One observer noted that the tail feathers make three "flups" at the bottom of each courtship dive.

Not a fussbudget when it comes to flowers, the broad-tailed readily visits any suitable blossoms for nectar and insects.

FAVORED PLANTS

Agaves
(*Agave* spp.)

Indian paintbrushes
(*Castilleja* spp.)

Delphiniums
(*Delphinium* spp.)

Ocotillo
(*Fouqueria splendens*)

Gilias
(*Ipomopsis* spp.)

Penstemons
(*Penstemon* spp.)

Gooseberries
(*Ribes* spp.)

Willows
(*Salix* spp.)

Salvias
(*Salvia* spp.)

Yuccas
(*Yucca* spp.)

Buff-Bellied Hummingbird

(*Amazilia yucatanensis*)

"Buff," a warm, pale orangish tan color, sometimes tinged with pink undertones, perfectly describes this small species' breast and belly. Male and female look alike and appear to be wearing a green hood that wraps around into their green back. The throat is a striking emerald green that glints like metal in full sun, and the tail is a beautiful chestnut hue.

Length: 4½"

▶ RANGE

The lower Rio Grande Valley of Texas is the only place in the United States to get a glimpse of the buff-bellied hummer. Its year-round range extends from Texas southward through eastern Mexico into the Yucatan Peninsula, from which the bird gets its species name, *yucatanensis*. A few individuals sometimes turn up in Louisiana.

▶ HABITAT

Look for the buff-bellied hummingbird along the edges of woods or in thickets or scrub in lowlands. The tiny bird is difficult to spot among the tangled vines and shrubs along the streams and gullies. It also frequents citrus groves and sometimes patches of Texas palmetto in the area.

▶ AERIAL DISPLAY

Although the buff-bellied hummingbird is still a fairly common sight, it once nested much more frequently in Texas ("an abundant summer visitor," says an account by Dr. James Merrill in 1876). Apparently no one made note of its display flight for the literature. We assume it performs aerial stunts like other hummingbirds, but if you want to learn more about the acrobatics, you'll have to visit the Rio Grande and see for yourself.

▶ NESTING

A bird after my own heart, the buff-bellied hummer adds dried flowers to the outside of its tiny nest, which it usually builds within a few feet of the ground. It builds its nest in the shrubs and small trees of its natural habitat, often attaching the nest to a skinny twig.

▶ COMMENTS

Like the broad-billed hummingbird, the buff-bellied has an orange-red beak that widens at the base. Should it grace your garden, look for this feature through binoculars. You may spot it at any nectar flowers or a feeder. Some of the plants it frequents in the wild are listed below.

FAVORED PLANTS

Agave, century plant
(*Agave americana*)

Desert willow
(*Chilopsis linearis*)

Gilias
(*Ipomopsis* spp.)

Penstemons
(*Penstemon* spp.)

Texas ebony
(*Pithecellobium flexicaule*)

Mesquite
(*Prosopis glandulosa*)

Salvias
(*Salvia* spp.)

Calliope Hummingbird
(Stellula calliope)

The Calliope is the only species in the United States with a distinctive striped throat, formed by streaks of reddish purple throat feathers against a white background. When the Calliope male displays its "bib," the colored feathers of his throat extend outward beyond his neck on both sides. The back is greenish bronze, and the underparts are whitish in both male and female.

Length: 2¾"–3¼"

▶ RANGE

This adorable little mite ranges the western mountains from the Rockies to the Cascades, reaching the Pacific at some points. It nests as far north as British Columbia and south through the mountains as far as southern California. A couple of population pockets also exist in eastern Wyoming. In winter, some birds stick around in the southerly portions of the nesting range, while others retreat southward into Mexico. Oddball individuals have turned up in the Midwest and the Southeast, including Florida.

▶ HABITAT

A bird of the heights, the Calliope is found in mountain meadows, near conifers. During migration, it may turn up in other habitats.

▶ AERIAL DISPLAY

The ultratiny Calliope male needs a big space for his big-hearted courtship display. He swoops in connected U-dives across a 20- to 30-foot course, punctuating the display with bursts of metallic buzzes from his wings. The male may also treat the female to an extended bout of buzzing.

▶ NESTING

A master of mimicry, the female Calliope can make her nest look like a pine cone or a knot of mistletoe to blend in with her nesting site. In areas filled with aspens, a female Calliope will create her nest to look like a little tangle of mistletoe, which naturally afflicts aspens.

▶ COMMENTS

The Calliope's busy little body—not counting its bill—is about the size of a nice fat bumblebee! The white "stripes" on the male's throat are actually the white bases of its unusually narrow purple gorget feathers. Its only vocal sounds are tiny chips and squeaks, plus an occasional "see-ree" call by an amorous male. The Calliope visits nectar feeders and all nectar flowers in the garden.

FAVORED PLANTS

Columbines
(*Aquilegia* spp.)

Bearberries, manzanitas
(*Arctostaphylos* spp.)

Indian paintbrushes
(*Castilleja* spp.)

Skyrocket
(*Ipomopsis aggregata*)

Monkey flowers
(*Mimulus* spp.)

Penstemons
(*Penstemon* spp.)

Gooseberries, currants
(*Ribes* spp.)

Costa's Hummingbird
(Calypte costae)

The gorget and most of the head of the male Costa's hummingbird are a magnificent deep purple. To make things even better, the purple changes color as the light shifts, flashing through every shade of the spectrum from green through violet. The backs of both male and female are the usual bronze-green, and they both have white underparts. Like the Calliope hummer, the male Costa's can flare its bib when it is excited, making the long feathers extend outward.

Length: 3"–3½"

▶ RANGE
The Costa's hummingbird breeds in the American Southwest over to the Pacific and offshore islands. The birds can be seen year-round over most of their breeding range. Infrequent strays have turned up as far north as Alaska and east to Texas, but they are rarities.

▶ HABITAT
This species is common in desert areas of the Southwest and southern California and also frequents towns and backyard gardens. It may range through chaparral and wooded areas. They often frequent the hot desert areas where cholla cactus and ocotillo grow.

▶ AERIAL DISPLAY
A deep, whooping U-shape is the signature of the male Costa's at courtship time. The bird may begin its dive from almost 200 feet up! On the way down, the high-speed flier makes an ear-splitting whistle, sustaining it for a few seconds. Listen for the unusually loud whistle in areas of suitable range—you'll hear it from a distance, long before you see the displaying bird.

▶ NESTING
Costa's females vary the shape, size, and construction of their nests to fit the available site and building materials. As is often the case with hummingbird nests, spiderwebs hold the structure together. The females favor no particular type of site, selecting trees, shrubs, cacti, yuccas, and even sagebrush to hold their homes. Even palm trees, dead cocklebur plants, and vines have been noted as nest sites. Since water is a scarce commodity in their range, when Costa's hummingbirds are found in other areas, their nests usually are far from water.

▶ COMMENTS
Costa's and black-chinned hummingbirds have similar courtship flights and are believed to be closely related. The female Costa's looks frustratingly similar to the female black-chinned and the two are discernable only by experts. The Costa's hummingbird will dine at any nectar flowers, and in the wild, you may see it at the plants listed below.

FAVORED PLANTS
Chuparosa
(*Anisacanthus thurberi*)

Desert willow
(*Chilopsis linearis*)

Scarlet delphinium
(*Delphinium cardinale*)

Ocotillo
(*Fouqueria splendens*)

Salvias
(*Salvia* spp.)

Lucifer Hummingbird
(Calothorax lucifer)

Though the word "Lucifer" may bring to mind the angel of darkness, the word itself means "light." This small hummingbird practically glows. The backs of the male and female are golden green. The male also has a brilliant purple throat, and the female's breast is washed with warm buff. Not only will you notice color on this species—that downward curving bill will catch your eye, too.

Length: 3¾"

▶ RANGE

This is an uncommon-to-rare bird in southeast Arizona, southwest New Mexico, and a tiny dab of southwest Texas. The lucifer hummingbird's breeding range is mostly in Mexico, where it also winters.

▶ HABITAT

Lucifer hummingbirds seem to show no loyalty to a particular habitat. They visit the mountains of Texas, open desert, canyons, and areas around streams, as well as gardens and feeders. In open deserts, they favor spots that offer an abundance of agaves.

▶ AERIAL DISPLAY

Lucifer males don't end their courtship flights after the female takes to her nest. They continue displaying even while she sits tight on her eggs or nestlings. She sometimes joins him in the dance. During his display, the male flies back and forth between two perches, then spirals upward until finally power-diving down to a perch. During the shuttling back and forth, the bird's wings sound like a rapidly shuffled deck of cards.

▶ NESTING

In the United States, this species nests mainly in Big Bend, Texas, though nesting north of Mexico is infrequent. Only a few other nests have been recorded in Arizona and New Mexico. Nests have been found attached to dry seedpods on the stalks of lechugilla plants, several feet above ground level, and in low shrubs.

▶ COMMENTS

More a visitor to the United States than a nesting bird, the lucifer hummingbird is always a delight. Scientists theorize that the unusual bill is designed for maneuvering insects out of long-tubed blossoms. Lucifer hummingbirds are primarily insect eaters. They feed at many plants in the garden and the wild, including the ones listed below. Instead of counting on your nectar feeder to attract a wandering lucifer, add some agaves to your garden, particularly *A. americana*, *A. chisoensis*, *A. harvariana*, and *A. lechugilla*. Look for young plants at native plant society sales, botanical gardens, or local independently owned nurseries.

FAVORED PLANTS

Agaves
(*Agave* spp.)

Eucalyptus
(*Eucalyptus* spp.)

Ocotillo
(*Fouqueria splendens*)

Tree tobacco
(*Nicotiana glauca*)

Magnificent Hummingbird
(Eugenes fulgens)

The magnificent (once known as Rivoli's) hummingbird is one of the largest species north of Mexico. The male has a glittering green body, deep purple cap, and metallic emerald green throat that positively shines against its gleaming black breast. The female is a much drabber green and lacks the gorget and purple head color. The male has a deeply forked tail, another clue to identity in dim light.

Length: 4½"–5½"

▶ RANGE

The magnificent breeds in the usual hummingbird havens of southern Arizona, southwestern New Mexico, and southwestern Texas, where mountain ranges rise from the desert floor. Its breeding territory stretches southward through Mexico all the way to Panama. In the United States, magnificent hummers are most common in their Arizona range. Birds from the States winter in Mexico.

▶ HABITAT

These birds find a hospitable home in the oak and pine forests of the mountains rising from our southwestern deserts. These forests are common along streams, in canyons, on agave-studded slopes, or in higher ponderosa pine forests. Magnificent hummers also frequent backyards within their range.

▶ AERIAL DISPLAY

No description of the display flight exists in the many reference books I consulted, but I have seen male birds in the Chiricahua Mountains of the Southwest engaging in pendulum-type loops that may have been a precursor to the flight. If you live in or plan to visit magnificent hummingbird territory during breeding season, keep your video camera handy.

▶ NESTING

The preferred site for a magnificent hummingbird's nest is up in a tree—from about 10 to 50 feet up. The female typically saddles her nest on a horizontal branch. She may use a variety of trees, both deciduous and evergreen. Maples, sycamores, alders, Douglas firs, and pines have all supported a family of magnificent hummingbirds.

▶ COMMENTS

Check the skyline for magnificent hummingbirds. Once you know what to look for, you can easily spot them at the top of a tree, as they often choose an exposed perch.

The species name, *fulgens*, means "to glitter."

FAVORED PLANTS

Thistles
(*Cirsium* spp.)

Fuchsias
(*Fuchsia* spp.)

Honeysuckles
(*Lonicera* spp.)

Red-flowered
zonal geraniums
(*Pelargonium* spp.)

Penstemons
(*Penstemon* spp.)

Salvias
(*Salvia* spp.)

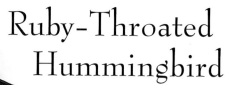

Ruby-Throated Hummingbird
(Archilochus colubris)

If you live east of the American Great Plains, this hummer brightens your garden spring through late summer—and into fall and winter in the South. From the back, the male and female sport green feathers glinting bronze in the sun. From the front, the male shows off his brilliant gorget of deep red.

Length: 3½"

▶ RANGE

The hummer of the Midwest and East, this species covers the entire right half of the United States, as well as Canada from Nova Scotia to Saskatchewan. In winter, you'll find it vacationing in Florida and from Texas into Mexico, as well as on offshore islands.

▶ HABITAT

A common, widespread species, the ruby-throated occurs just about everywhere in its range, from backyards and towns to woodlands. Its noisy humming wings and frequent squeaky calls give it away.

▶ AERIAL DISPLAY

The male's aerial pyrotechnics include wide, regular pendulum arcs before a female—or in hopes of luring one to his selected breeding territory. When a female is receptive, the two will face off in the air, hovering and rising in tandem.

▶ NESTING

The female ruby-throated hummingbird plasters her golf-ball-size nest on a thin, horizontal branch toward the outside of a tree with open space or water below it and a protecting branch just over-head. Oaks, hickories, tulip poplars, and many other deciduous trees host ruby-throated hummingbird broods.

▶ COMMENTS

Keep your feeders filled even after the bulk of fall migrants have moved on. Occasional stragglers, usually inexperienced juveniles, have been known to show up as late as November, and sugar water then will be a lifesaver.

Quite a few native plants depend on the ministrations of the ruby-throated hummingbird to achieve pollination. Think of the wildflowers in the eastern half of the country with red or orange tubular blossoms, and you'll have the start of a fine hummingbird garden. Any good "hummingbird flower" and nectar feeders will attract this avian garden delight.

FAVORED PLANTS

Horse chestnuts, buckeyes
(*Aesculus* spp.)

Trumpet vine
(*Campsis radicans*)

Eastern redbud
(*Cercis canadensis*)

Jewelweed
(*Impatiens capensis*)

Cardinal flower
(*Lobelia cardinalis*)

Bee balm
(*Monarda didyma*)

Black locust
(*Robinia pseudoacacia*)

Fire pink
(*Silene virginica*)

Rufous Hummingbird
(Selasphorus rufus)

Look for the burnished rusty orange color of the male of this species to identify our only North American hummer with a reddish back. The throat of the male is breathtaking, shining with deep orange-red color. His head is capped with feathers that gleam golden green to rust. The female has a greenish back with touches of rust on her sides and the base of her tail.

Length: 3½"–4"

▶ RANGE

The rufous is found in northwest North America; in its migrations north and south, the birds travel through every state west of the Plains. It has turned up unexpectedly in every state of the United States and every Canadian province. In winter, it retreats to Mexico. In recent years it has also adopted the states along the Gulf Coast as a winter playground.

▶ HABITAT

The rufous is at home in the vast conifer forests of Oregon and Washington and in downtown urban backyards. It also swings through chaparral, meadows, streamsides, mountain ridges, and other varied habitats.

▶ AERIAL DISPLAY

The male rufous may complete an entire oval loop in his courtship display, accompanied by a series of loud wing buzzing, then a loud whine, and finally a rattling noise.

▶ NESTING

Observers have noticed that early-season nests of rufous hummingbirds are usually placed low in conifer trees, where they are easier to keep warm, than in the exposed treetops. Later nests, however, are often sited near the tops of deciduous trees, taking advantage of breezes and the release of moisture from the leaves to avoid overheating the young. Rufous hummingbird homes have also been found in vines, tangles of tree roots, huckleberry bushes, and other places.

▶ COMMENTS

One of the first animal species to revisit the devastated areas of Mount St. Helens, Washington, after the volcanic blast, the rufous hummingbird tickled orange-suited scientists by probing the ventilating grommets of their coveralls, searching for "nectar."

Rufous hummingbirds like most nectar flowers and feeders.

FAVORED PLANTS

Crimson columbine
(*Aquilegia formosa*)

Madrone
(*Arbutus menziesii*)

Indian paintbrushes
(*Castilleja* spp.)

Cleomes
(*Cleome* spp.)

Delphiniums, larkspurs
(*Delphinium* spp.)

Penstemons
(*Penstemon* spp.)

Currants, gooseberries
(*Ribes* spp.)

Thimbleberry
(*Rubus parviflorus*)

Salmonberry
(*Rubus spectabilis*)

Violet-Crowned Hummingbird
(Amazilia violiceps)

The violet-crowned hummingbird is one of the rare treats of the Southwestern hummingbird hot spots. It is a beautiful bird with a blue-purple cap, a snowy white throat and belly, and a red bill that adds the finishing touch. It is one of the few male hummers in North America that doesn't sport an iridescent gorget. Male and female are quite similar, though the female's cap is dull green rather than violet. Both sexes have green backs.

Length: 3¾"–4½"

▶ RANGE

Count yourself lucky if you encounter this uncommon species, which ventures into very limited areas of Arizona, New Mexico, Texas, and occasionally California from its more usual Mexican haunts. Nesting records are extremely rare, limited to the Guadalupe Canyon of the Southwest. Most visits seem to be just temporary sojourns in summer. Though the extent of their winter range is still something of a mystery, the birds are found in Mexico and the Yucatan during the winter months.

▶ HABITAT

Watch for this unusual species in open woodland or along riversides, the edges of forests, and other areas with scattered trees. Nectar feeders and gardens with tempting treats may lure it in, too.

▶ AERIAL DISPLAY

As you might expect with a bird that is infrequently seen, its courtship display has not been recorded. Keep your eyes open if you're traveling through its nesting habitat, and you may be able to add to the knowledge about the behavior of this species.

▶ NESTING

The first record of a violet-crowned nest in the United States was made in 1979, in Arizona. Of the few nests found since then, all have been in sycamores, from 20 to about 36 feet from the ground. In Mexico, the bird has also been known to nest in a "thorny bush" and in oaks.

▶ COMMENTS

One of the few hummingbird species in which male and female look very much alike. The contrast between the rich color of the cap and the pure white underneath is as striking as the coloring of a tree swallow.

FAVORED PLANTS

Not much is known about the favorite plants of the violet-crowned hummingbird. They do feed at agaves (*Agave* spp.), but whether they are feasting on insects or nectar is not known for sure.

White-Eared Hummingbird

(Hylocharis leucotis)

A small white swoosh on each side of its head gives this hummingbird its name. The male has a brilliant, rich blue-violet chin and crown, with a gleaming emerald green throat. Dark metallic bronze decorates the back of its head, and brighter bronze glimmers on its greenish back, wings, and tail. The female also wears a white eyestripe, but her head is topped with bronze-green, and her throat is streaky and dotted.

Length: 3½"

▶ RANGE

Another gem of the southwest, this hummer rarely ventures any farther than southeastern Arizona in the United States, although it has also been spotted in southwest New Mexico and in west Texas. In winter, it retreats to Mexico and Guatemala.

▶ HABITAT

This forest-loving bird sticks mostly to woodlands and wooded canyons of southwestern mountains, although it may venture into more open areas to feed. The oasis-like pine and oak forests suit it perfectly.

▶ AERIAL DISPLAY

The white-eared has a lovely voice (for a hummingbird!), sounding a clear "tink-tink-tink" call for long intervals. The courtship songs are conducted en masse, in "singing assemblies." The courtship dance is centered tightly on the female, with the selected male whizzing closely around his perched partner. The dance escalates until both partners are darting about in dizzying loops and whirls, with face-to-face hovering now and then during the flight.

▶ NESTING

The white-eared female nests low, usually not more than 20 feet above the ground and often as low as 4 feet. She often uses shrubs or oaks as nesting spots; oaks figure largely in nest-making, too.

▶ COMMENTS

Because of the black patch below the stripe of the white-eared, the eyestripe stands out more boldly on its head than in other species. Plants that attract tiny insects may attract a foraging white-eared hummingbird; the birds also nab bugs on the wing in midair.

Although they also nectar at flowers, white-eared hummingbirds depend heavily on insects for a large part of their diet.

FAVORED PLANTS

Bur marigold
(*Bidens refracta*)

Firecracker flower
(*Cuphea jorullensis*)

Penstemons
(*Penstemon* spp.)

Small-flowered
red or blue salvias
(*Salvia* spp.)

CHAPTER 10

A Gallery of

BUTTERFLIES

Welcome to the beautiful world of backyard butterflies! This sampling of the main butterfly families will give you an idea of the incredible variety of winged creatures you can attract to your yard. With hundreds of species fluttering across America just looking for nectar or a plant to call home, success is simple. Start by making nectar-seekers happy by brightening your yard with flowers, a surefire draw. Like hummingbirds, butterflies vary in their preferences for nectar sources. Use the "Favored Plants" in this gallery as a starting point, but don't hesitate to plant any other flowers you like. Chances are that a butterfly will appreciate them! Choose plants that grow well in your area, and remember that weeds hold high appeal, too.

Speaking of "weeds," one of the most popular nectar plants, butterfly bush (*Buddleia davidii*), can become pesty should it leap from the garden into wild places. In my observation, it only colonizes areas that have already been disturbed by us humans, like railroad beds and empty lots, but if you don't want to take the chance of introducing a problem, call a local nature preserve, native plant society, or your county extension agent to check on the plant's tendencies in your area. As you add enticements to your yard, remember that fruit feeders, water features, and host plants will also attract more beauty on the wing. Keep your own journal of observations, and your butterflies themselves will teach you what they find most appealing.

The illustrations in this chapter show the colorations and markings of the male of each species. The females are described within each species' entry. The measurement underneath each illustration is the butterfly's wingspan in inches.

SWALLOWTAILS (Papilionidae)

Swallowtails are the beauty queens of the butterfly world. Their "tails" extend from their hindwings—a safety device that gives birds a target and protects their tender body. Their caterpillars are often boldly striped and usually adorned with big scary eyespots and rank-smelling "horns," called osmeterium, to frighten off predators.

Pipevine Swallowtail
(Battus philenor)

These butterflies have a distinctive flight pattern—their fast, jerky movements are unusual for such a large butterfly. Pipevines can look dull and uninteresting until the sun strikes them just right to make their beautiful blue overlay flash with color. Pipevine swallowtail caterpillars ingest toxins from the Dutchman's pipe (*Aristolochia* spp.) vines they eat, making them unappealing to predators.

Wingspan: 2¾"–3⅜"

▶ RANGE
The pipevine swallowtail has a large range covering eastern Canada south to Florida, west to Nebraska, through Texas into Arizona and California, and north to Oregon. The range is expanding as gardeners add pipevines to their gardens.

▶ CATERPILLAR
The pipevine swallowtail caterpillar is large and rusty black, studded with a fearsome array of black or red projections that should make any bird think twice before sampling this un-delicious morsel.

▶ HOST PLANTS
Pipevines are the mainstay for this species. It uses Dutchman's pipe (*Aristolochia macrophylla*) and snakeroot (*A. serpentaria*) throughout most of its range, and in the West, it uses the native pipevines—California pipevine (*A. californica*) and swan flower (*A. longiflora*). Note that swan flower is a fairly rare native plant; you probably won't find it for sale at nurseries.

▶ COMMENTS
Male pipevine swallowtails gather at mud puddles. Swallowtails feed at many flowers, including their favorites, listed below.

FAVORED PLANTS
Milkweeds
(*Asclepias* spp.)

Butterfly bush
(*Buddleia davidii*)

Honeysuckles
(*Lonicera* spp.)

Common zinnias
(*Zinnia elegans*)

Eastern Black Swallowtail
(*Papilio polyxenes*)

The black swallowtail is one of the most common swallowtails and is a frequent visitor to home gardens. It inhabits gardens and wild spots across the eastern two-thirds of the country. Gardeners sometimes scorn black swallowtail caterpillars as "parsley worms," thanks to their habit of using parsley—plain or curly—as a host plant. They are easy and gratifying to raise to adulthood. Poke the caterpillar gently behind its head and you will see and smell the orange "horns" that the larva erects as a defense mechanism. Many similar species of swallowtails range in the West, including the western black swallowtail, the desert swallowtail, and the Oregon swallowtail.

Wingspan: 2⅝"–3½"

► **RANGE**
The black swallowtail makes its home east of the Rockies from southern Canada south to Mexico.

► **CATERPILLAR**
This caterpillar is a beautiful creature with a white to pale green body slashed by striking black bands and yellow to orange dots.

► **HOST PLANTS**
The caterpillar chows down on members of the carrot family, including Queen Anne's lace (*Daucus carota*) and parsley (*Petroselinum crispum*), and also some members of the citrus family, such as rue (*Ruta graveolens*).

► **COMMENTS**
Many flowers tempt these butterflies. As with all large butterflies, the black swallowtail favors common zinnias (*Zinnia elegans*). They also feed often at the plants listed at right.

FAVORED PLANTS

Milkweeds
(*Asclepias* spp.)

Butterflyweed
(*Asclepias tuberosa*)

Butterfly bush
(*Buddleia davidii*)

Eupatoriums
(*Eupatorium* spp.)

Phlox
(*Phlox* spp.)

Ironweeds
(*Vernonia* spp.)

Wingspan: 2⅝"–3"

Anise Swallowtail
(*Papilio zeliacon*)

The most common swallowtail west of the Rockies, this beautiful big butterfly has broad bands of yellow decorating its topside. The male and female look very much the same. At least five large swallowtails carry a similar color scheme—black and yellow—accented with spots of blue on their hindwings that look as if they've been sprinkled with loose powder and dabbed with bits of bright orange, especially on the undersides. You can always tell the anise by the wide, bold bands of yellow.

▶ RANGE

The anise swallowtail lives west of the Rocky Mountains to the Pacific Coast, south into Mexico and north into Canada.

▶ CATERPILLAR

The caterpillars are tiny at first, but soon mature into big green specimens with bold black stripes and rows of orange dots.

▶ HOST PLANTS

The anise swallowtail gets its name from the diet of its caterpillars. They feed mainly on licorice-scented fennel (*Foeniculum vulgare*), a ferny herb from the Mediterranean that has be-come a problematic weed in many parts of the West. Other plants in the parsley family and citrus family also serve as host plants, including angelicas (*Angelica* spp.) and cow parsnip (*Heracleum sphondylium*). These stout, super-size plants add dramatic architecture to the garden. (But be careful in working with cow parsnip—it can cause an irritating rash.) The caterpillars eat leaves, buds, flowers, and stems.

▶ COMMENTS

The anise swallowtail feeds at many nectar flowers, including those listed at right.

FAVORED PLANTS

Asters
(*Aster* spp.)

Yarrows
(*Achillea* spp.)

Butterfly bush
(*Buddleia davidii*)

Coreopsis
(*Coreopsis* spp.)

Mints
(*Mentha* spp.)

Oregano
(*Origanum vulgare*)

Scabiosa
(*Scabiosa* spp.)

Verbenas
(*Verbena* spp.)

Zinnias
(*Zinnia* spp.)

Giant Swallowtail
(*Heraclides cresphontes*)

Humongous is the word for this monster-sized swallowtail, which can stretch as wide as 5½ inches from wingtip to wingtip! It's a beauty, but not beloved by commercial or backyard citrus growers in its range who suffer from the appetite of its caterpillars for citrus foliage. If the sheer size of this butterfly doesn't grab your attention, you'll surely notice the distinctive horizontal bar of yellow across its wings. A lookalike species, the Thoas swallowtail, overlaps part of its range in the extreme South.

The giant swallowtail is easy to identify from a distance by its trademark flight, which is slow and sailing, often going for long stretches with wings outstretched instead of flapping.

Wingspan: 3⅜"–5½"

▶ RANGE

Although often thought of as a southern species, the giant swallowtail roams across almost the entire eastern half of the country, from Canada to Mexico. It's usually restricted within that area to places where its host plants thrive.

▶ CATERPILLAR

Masterful protective coloration makes the big, plump caterpillar unappealing to birds—it looks like the biggest bird dropping you ever saw! Should this ruse fail, the caterpillar can pop out a pair of red horns that give off a blast of strong scent.

▶ HOST PLANTS

Backyard orange trees, a patio pot of dwarf lemon, or 100 acres of navel oranges are all fair game to the giant swallowtail. Besides citrus, the larvae also have a taste for related plants, such as prickly ash (*Zanthoxylum americanum*), rue (*Ruta graveolens*), and hop tree (*Ptelea trifoliata*).

▶ COMMENTS

This lovely creature feeds at many nectar flowers, including the ones listed here.

FAVORED PLANTS
Milkweeds (*Asclepias* spp.)
Bougainvilleas (*Bougainvillea* spp.)
Lantanas (*Lantana* spp.)
Honeysuckles (*Lonicera* spp.)
Azaleas (*Rhododendron* spp.)

Tiger Swallowtail
(*Pterourus glaucus, P. rutulus*)

If you have flowers in your yard, you're probably already familiar with the tiger swallowtail. This is one of the most common and widespread species of butterflies, and it's just as noticeable as the equally familiar monarch. Male tiger swallowtails are eye-catching yellow with the splashes of blue and orange found in other swallowtails.

Two very similar species, the eastern (*P. glaucus*) and western (*P. rutulus*) tiger swallowtails, pretty much blanket the country. Eastern tiger females may be yellow or brownish black. In areas where pipevine swallowtails are found, the female eastern tiger is often a copycat of this species, adopting its dark coloring to keep from being eaten. Look closely when the wings are backlit and you'll see faint traces of the tiger stripes that give this butterfly its name.

Wingspan: 3⅛"–5½"

▶ RANGE
The eastern species inhabits areas from Alaska to the Atlantic Ocean, south to Texas and Florida. The western species covers the area west of the Rockies, from Washington to California.

▶ HOST PLANTS
Although they look alike, the eating habits of these butterflies' larvae are different. The eastern species dines on tuliptree (*Liriodendron tulipifera*), wild cherries (*Prunus* spp.), willows (*Salix* spp.), birches (*Betula* spp.), and ashes (*Fraxinus* spp.). The western counterpart seeks out willows (*Salix* spp.), poplars and aspens (*Populus* spp.), and alders (*Alnus* spp.).

▶ CATERPILLAR
That's no bird dropping on that leaf, it's a young tiger swallowtail caterpillar. Within a week, the larvae take on a lovely green color, adding big eyespots and a fearsomely large head end to their arsenal of protective tricks.

▶ COMMENTS
The nectar flowers listed at right—and a host of others—will keep them coming back for more.

FAVORED PLANTS
Butterflyweed
(*Asclepias tuberosa*)

Butterfly bush
(*Buddleia davidii*)

Purple coneflower
(*Echinacea purpurea*)

Eupatoriums
(*Eupatorium* spp.)

Blazing stars
(*Liatris* spp.)

Oregano
(*Origanum vulgare*)

Ironweeds
(*Vernonia* spp.)

Zinnias
(*Zinnia* spp.)

Two-Tailed Tiger Swallowtail
(*Pterourus multicaudatus*)

Two tails on each wing are better than one, if you're a big butterfly trying to outwit a bird. One nip of a beak, and you still have three tails to spare. These tempting appendages divert attention from your vital body parts. Another giant of a butterfly, this species can top 5 inches across.

Wingspan: 3⅜"–5⅛"

▶ RANGE

A western species, the two-tailed tiger swallowtail ranges from British Columbia to Baja, California, and Texas.

▶ CATERPILLAR

If you find a folded leaf of one of this species' host plants, it may be hiding a feeding caterpillar. The two-tailed swallowtail caterpillar starts out the color of a Granny Smith apple and takes on a reddish hue just before maturity. Should a curious human or predator peel open the leaf, the caterpillar depends on its eyespots and humped shape to ward off danger.

▶ HOST PLANTS

These caterpillars find plenty of nourishment in the abundant foliage of wild cherries (*Prunus* spp.) and ashes (*Fraxinus* spp.). In Texas, they often feed on hop tree (*Ptelea trifoliata*). You'll spot this native shrub or small tree, also known by the charming name of "stinking ash," along hedgerows and streams.

The caterpillars may occasionally eat privets (*Ligustrum* spp.) and shadblows (*Amelanchier* spp.).

▶ COMMENTS

The two-tailed tiger swallowtail feasts at many nectar flowers, including its favorites, listed at right.

FAVORED PLANTS

Milkweeds
(*Asclepias* spp.)

Asters
(*Aster* spp.)

Butterfly bush
(*Buddleia davidii*)

Blazing stars
(*Liatris* spp.)

Lobelias
(*Lobelia* spp.)

Cardinal flower
(*Lobelia cardinalis*)

Honeysuckles
(*Lonicera* spp.)

Oregano
(*Origanum vulgare*)

Lilacs
(*Syringa* spp.)

Zinnias
(*Zinnia* spp.)

Spicebush Swallowtail
(*Pterourus troilus*)

Give me the old-fashioned romantic names, rather than the information-imparting modern monikers! This lovely butterfly was known in days gone by as the "green-clouded swallowtail" thanks to the soft blue-green coloring of its hind-wings. Today it's identified by the favorite food of its caterpillars. Still, by any name, this large, dark swallowtail is a sight to behold.

Wingspan: 3½"–4½"

▶ RANGE

The spicebush swallowtail ranges through eastern North America to the Rockies, but it is most plentiful in the East and Midwest.

▶ CATERPILLAR

Look carefully at a spice-bush shrub and you may spot a rolled-up leaf that, on closer inspection, is held together with silken threads. Inside hides the yellow-green spicebush swallowtail caterpillar, safe from the hungry eyes of birds. It has bright eye-spots outlined in darker color, and a humped appearance.

▶ HOST PLANTS

The aromatic shrub or small tree called spicebush (*Lindera benzoin*) is tops on the host plant list for this species, although it often munches on sassafras (*Sassafras albidum*) and redbay and other bays (*Persea* spp.).

▶ COMMENTS

The spicebush butterfly ea-gerly seeks nectar at many tempting nectar flowers. It finds the ones listed at right especially enticing.

FAVORED PLANTS

Anise hyssop
(*Agastache foeniculum*)

Milkweeds
(*Asclepias* spp.)

Butterfly bush
(*Buddleia davidii*)

Buttonbush
(*Cephalanthus occidentalis*)

Purple coneflower
(*Echinacea purpurea*)

Eupatoriums
(*Eupatorium* spp.)

Lantanas
(*Lantana* spp.)

Ironweeds
(*Vernonia* spp.)

Common zinnias
(*Zinnia elegans*)

Palamedes Swallowtail
(*Pterourus palamedes*)

If you ever go exploring in the steamy swamps of Florida and Georgia, keep a lookout for this butterfly. It will quickly catch your eye as it flies along the edges of woods and thickets or rises slowly to treetop height. Rivaling the giant swallowtail in size, it checks in at as much as 5½ inches across its widespread wings. At first glance, it looks very much like the eastern and western black swallowtails, except for the smudged effect of the yellow band on its hindwings. Notice also the rounded look to its front wings, another distinguishing characteristic.

Wingspan: 3⅛"–5½"

▶ RANGE
The palamedes swallowtail lives in the southeast and eastern United States from Maryland through Florida along the Atlantic coast, and west along the Gulf of Mexico to Texas.

▶ CATERPILLAR
Twice the usual number of eyespots may make predators think twice before gulping down this quadruple-eyed caterpillar. Otherwise, it is a pretty spring green.

▶ HOST PLANTS
The palamedes swallowtail caterpillar favors shrubs and trees that are native to its swampy homelands: redbay (*Persea borbonia*), which is a close relative of the avocado (*P. americana*); the shiny-leaved, white-flowered sweet bay (*Magnolia virginiana*); and the aromatic sassafras tree (*Sassifras albidum*).

▶ COMMENTS
In its natural haunts and in garden pools, the blue flowers of the aquatic plant called pickerel weed (*Pontederia cordata*) sustain the palamedes swallowtail. It also seeks out the plants listed below.

FAVORED PLANTS

Eupatoriums
(*Eupatorium* spp.)

Lantanas
(*Lantana* spp.)

Pentas
(*Pentas lanceolata*)

Pickerel weed
(*Pontederia cordata*)

Azaleas
(*Rhododendron* spp.)

Wingspan: 2⅜"–3½"

Zebra Swallowtail
(Eurytides marcellus)

A swallowtail of another color, the well-named zebra is a nervous sort. This butterfly seems to be super-wary, unlike its yellow-and-black kin, which share generally calm natures. It flits quickly from one flower to another and rarely allows a human observer to approach closely. Even when perched at a flower, its wings keep up an almost constant quivering. Its exaggerated tails make it quickly recognizable in flight. Note also its sharply triangular wings.

▶ RANGE

Although its range covers most of the eastern part of the country from the Great Lakes east to New England and south to Florida and the Gulf, the zebra swallowtail is much more common in the South than in the northern parts of its range.

▶ CATERPILLAR

The head end of the zebra swallowtail caterpillar has a humped look like its swallowtail relatives. The segments of its bright green body are marked with yellow lines, with a couple of black stripes near the head.

▶ HOST PLANTS

Look for zebra swallowtails wherever their host plant, the pawpaw (*Asimina triloba*), grows. Gardeners have recently become enamored with this unusual tropical-tasting native American fruit and as they add pawpaws to their gardens, the zebra swallowtail caterpillar can move into areas where it formerly found no appropriate host for its progeny. Unfortunately, we gardeners aren't planting pawpaws fast enough to replace those that development is destroying in wilder haunts.

▶ COMMENTS

The zebra swallowtail feeds at many nectar flowers, including those listed here.

FAVORED PLANTS

Milkweeds
(*Asclepias* spp.)

Tickseed sunflower
(*Bidens aristosa*)

Butterfly bush
(*Buddleia davidii*)

Eupatoriums
(*Eupatorium* spp.)

Ironweeds
(*Vernonia* spp.)

Common zinnias
(*Zinnia elegans*)

WHITES AND SULPHURS (Pieridae)

Expect to see lots of these bright, white or yellow butterflies dancing in your garden: They're abundant anywhere flowers beckon. With about five dozen species in North America, this family includes some of the most common garden butterflies.

Spring White
(*Pontia sisymbrii*)

Wingspan: 1¼"–1½"

The dainty spring white is one of the first butterflies to brighten the landscape in the spring in its range. It's a western representative of a number of similar species. The male is usually a cooler white than the female. Dark veins on the undersides of its wings are characteristic of most of the native types of these species. Many similar butterflies dance in various habitats: Becker's white in sagebrush, the Florida white in shady southern thickets, the West Virginia white of the Appalachians, the pine white in western mountains, and the Chiricahua pine white in the desert mountains of the Southwest.

▶ **RANGE**
Look for the spring white (once called the California white) in the West, from the rocky grasslands of the Great Basin to the mountain slopes of the Rockies and Sierra Nevada.

▶ **CATERPILLAR**
The small caterpillar is yellow with strong black stripes.

▶ **HOST PLANTS**
The spring white's larvae have an instinctive taste for the peppery tang of plants in the mustard family. They devour bright purple twist flowers or jewel flowers (*Streptanthus* spp.) and rock cresses (*Arabis* spp.).

▶ **COMMENTS**
Just about anything in the garden will attract these petite butterflies. They like a good big patch of damp mud or manure, and especially plants with daisylike, clustered, or spikes of small flowers, including herbs.

Cabbage White
(*Artogeia rapae*)

This small white butterfly is an imported species, once commonly known as the European cabbage butterfly (or incorrectly as the cabbage moth). You're likely to be just as familiar with its caterpillars as with the adult: They're the well-camouflaged bright green larvae that hide along the stems of broccoli heads and in other cabbage-family crops. This dainty butterfly is a sociable creature and often congregates with other whites and sulphurs at flowerbeds or mud puddles.

Wingspan: 1¼"–1⅞"

▶ **RANGE**

Although it is native to Eurasia, this successful colonizer now occupies all of North America, from mid-Canada south, and also inhabits parts of Hawaii.

▶ **CATERPILLAR**

This caterpillar is bright green with stripes of yellow on its sides and back.

▶ **HOST PLANTS**

Lots of plants in the cabbage family are prime fodder for the caterpillars of the cabbage white, including cabbage, broccoli, and mustard. Nasturtiums (*Tropaeolum* spp.) may also serve as a host. I like to grow a few broccoli plants in my flowerbeds for these guests. The tightly budded broccoli heads open into sunny yellow flowers that provide lots of nectar for many kinds of butterflies. I don't mind cabbage white caterpillars in my broccoli as long as I'm not planning to eat it!

▶ **COMMENTS**

The cabbage white will enjoy just about any flowers of varied shapes and sizes in your garden.

FAVORED PLANTS

Yarrows
(*Achillea* spp.)

Hyssops
(*Agastache* spp.)

Dahlias
(*Dahlia* spp.)

Dame's rocket
(*Hesperis matronalis*)

Lavenders
(*Lavandula* spp.)

Sedums
(*Sedum* spp.)

Marigolds
(*Tagetes* spp.)

Verbenas
(*Verbena* spp.)

Zinnias
(*Zinnia* spp.)

Checkered White
(*Pontia protodice*)

The checkered white was once much more common than it is today. It has suffered from competition by a foreign invader—the cabbage white butterfly, imported from Europe—and from the adulteration of the natural landscape. Once called the "common white," this butterfly may be better described as the not-so-common white. For every several dozen cabbage whites you see, you're apt to see just one or two checkered whites. Some butterfly experts disagree on the reason for the downturn in population

Wingspan: 1¼"–1¾"

in some areas, noting that in other regions the checkered white is more than holding its own. These experts theorize that human-caused habitat changes rather than the invasion of the cabbage white may be the real reason for population shifts.

▶ **RANGE**

The checkered white ranges over nearly all of the United States and lower Canada, except for the Pacific Northwest. It is less common in the East than in the Midwest and West.

▶ **CATERPILLAR**

The pretty caterpillar has a bluish cast and a soft, almost velvety look. It's decorated with black dots and yellow stripes running lengthwise down its body.

▶ **HOST PLANTS**

The checkered white caterpillar isn't fussy about its food—as long as it belongs to the huge cabbage or mustard family. It eats many kinds of mustards, from garden broccoli and cabbage to wild cress. Native plants and those from other countries are equally welcome in the diet.

▶ **COMMENTS**

No specialist, the checkered white visits hundreds of kinds of flowers for nectar, including clovers and the ones listed at right.

FAVORED PLANTS

Butterfly bush
(*Buddleia davidii*)

Chrysanthemums
(*Chrysanthemum* spp.)

Wild chicory
(*Cichorium intybus*)

Salvias
(*Salvia* x *sylvestris*— 'May Night' in my garden)

Sedums
(*Sedum* spp. and hybrids)

Verbenas
(*Verbena* spp. and hybrids)

Zinnias
(*Zinnia* spp.)

Wingspan: 1½"–1¾"

Creamy Marblewing
(*Euchloa ausonides*)

The creamy marblewing and its relatives—the pearly, Olympia, and northern marblewings—get their name from the subtle coloring of their underwings, which are thickly veined and barred with soft color, like a block of beautiful marble. Four species appear in springtime in the West and a few other areas.

"Now you see it, now you don't" is the motto of the marblewings. Look carefully: Their brief appearance, small size, and inconspicuous coloring blend in superbly against the greenery of plants. Use your binoculars to appreciate their understated beauty—they are worth an up-close look!

▶ RANGE

Marblewings live in the western mountains and in the Great Lakes area where they roam the shore and nearby dunes. The Olympia species appears as far east as West Virginia.

▶ CATERPILLAR

Caterpillar coloring varies among the species, but is generally green with darker flecks and white, yellow, or gray longitudinal stripes. Like the larvae of the related European cabbage white butterfly, the caterpillars of the marblewing species eat not only leaves but also buds, flowers, and stems of their host plants.

▶ HOST PLANTS

Like many other members of the whites and sulphurs family, marblewing caterpillars are mustard eaters. They munch on wild and weedy mustards like jewel flowers (*Streptanthus* spp.) and black mustard (*Brassica nigra*), as well as vegetable and flower plants of the cabbage family such as broccoli, cabbage, dame's rocket (*Hesperis matronalis*), and rock cresses (*Arabis* spp.) that they find in gardens.

▶ COMMENTS

Almost any nectar flower will get the attention of the marblewings in your area. Since most species are on the wing only briefly in spring, try early bloomers. The flowers of mustards of all kinds are also ideal, so don't be too quick to pull out your garden's "weeds."

FAVORED PLANTS

Chives
(*Allium schoenoprasum*)

Rock cresses
(*Arabis* spp.)

Dame's rocket
(*Hesperis matronalis*)

Clovers
(*Trifolium* spp.)

Violets
(*Viola* spp.)

Falcate Orangetip
(*Anthocharis midea*)

For me, this little butterfly epitomizes all
the best things about butterflies—it's a
surprising beauty, easy to spot near one
of my favorite wildflowers, and it arrives
in early spring when other, flashier butterflies are few and far between. At first
glance the falcate orangetip appears to be an
insignificant little white butterfly, but its dash of
dramatic orange makes me feel as if I've spotted
a hidden treasure. I invariably see it flitting about
near a little white-flowered nosegay called cut-leaved
toothwort (*Dentaria laciniata*), which this butterfly relies on to host its caterpillars.

Wingspan: 1⅜"–1½"

"Falcate" means "hooked," and refers to the curved projection at the tip of each
forewing. Both male and female have these hooks, but only the male flaunts beautiful
orange wingtips.

▶ RANGE
This little treasure ranges
through the eastern United
States from New England
to Wisconsin and south to
the Gulf Coast.

▶ CATERPILLAR
The small, dark green caterpillar looks great under a
magnifying glass, when
even my far-sighted,
middle-aged eyes can
clearly see its stripes of
yellow, green, and blue and
its longitudinal orange and
white stripes. Try raising
this caterpillar inside, just

to delight in the ingenuity
of its chrysalis—it looks
just like a green thorn fas-
tened to a stem.

▶ HOST PLANTS
Mustards! Members of the
mustard or cabbage family
provide fodder for the
caterpillars of the falcate
orangetip, from the
common but attractive
weed called shepherd's
purse (*Capsella bursa-
pastoris*) to the ornamental
rock cresses (*Arabis* spp.)
spilling over your rock
garden.

▶ COMMENTS
Mustards seem to be an all-
in-one food source for this
species: While the caterpillars munch the plant, the
butterflies sip from the
flowers. They are also often
seen on dandelions.

FAVORED PLANTS
Virginia bluebells
(*Mertensia virginica*)

Clovers
(*Trifolium* spp.)

Violets
(*Viola* spp.)

Common Sulphur
(*Colias philodice*)

This delightful little butterfly is the most common of the yellow butterflies that brighten summer days. It is easy to distinguish the male and female of this species. While the male's lemony wings display a dramatic solid black border, the female wears a band of black broken with yellow dots. When the butterfly closes its wings, as it usually does when feeding or puddling, no black edges are visible. Look closely and you'll see two pretty silver spots on the hindwings outlined in deep pink-red. In my garden, this butterfly is one of the last still flying at the end of the season—I sometimes see it even after a night with frost.

Wingspan: 1⅜"–2"

▶ **RANGE**

The common sulphur ranges across North America, except in Florida.

▶ **CATERPILLAR**

This small caterpillar is very hard to see due to its bright, clover green color. Light stripes on its side and a dark stripe down the back increase its ability to hide among the leaves. Should you manage to spot one, avoid jostling the plant, or the caterpillar will instantly drop to the ground and disappear from view.

▶ **HOST PLANTS**

The yellow and orange sulphur butterflies use legumes for their host plants. This species is particularly partial to clovers (*Trifolium* spp.).

▶ **COMMENTS**

Common sulphurs feed at most common garden flowers and wildflowers. As with other sulphurs, a great way to make the common happy is to create a mud puddle for congregating.

FAVORED PLANTS

Yarrows
(*Achillea* spp.)

Hyssops
(*Agastache* spp.)

Butterfly bush
(*Buddleia davidii*)

Purple coneflower
(*Echinacea purpurea*)

Mints
(*Mentha* spp.)

Oregano
(*Origanum vulgare*)

Salvias
(*Salvia* spp.)

Clovers
(*Trifolium* spp.)

Orange Sulphur
(*Colias eurthymeme*)

Our brightest orange butterfly, this beautiful creature will catch your eye from across the garden when it comes fluttering to your flowers. To fully appreciate its fantastic color, focus close-range binoculars on it as it feeds and look for the delicate pink fringe that provides a slightly feathered edge to its wings. Like other sulphurs, the intensity of the wing color may vary from one individual to another, with some showing rich orange and others tending toward golden yellow.

Wingspan: 1⅝"–2⅜"

▶ RANGE
The orange sulphur ranges across North America but is observed most frequently in the southern half of the country. It is seldom seen in the steamiest parts of Florida or along the Northwest coast.

▶ CATERPILLAR
The small caterpillar is green with attractive pink and white stripes.

▶ HOST PLANTS
Once called the alfalfa butterfly, this species often lays its eggs on that pretty purple-flowered farm crop and roadside weed (*Medicago sativa*). In years past, it sometimes posed a threat to farmers, especially in the Imperial Valley of California, where hungry caterpillars chewed their way through many an alfalfa field. The caterpillars also use clovers (*Trifolium* spp.) and other legumes as host plants.

▶ COMMENTS
Like other sulphurs, this species will enthusiastically visit a host of garden flowers and wildflowers. Practice your camera skills with this species; it often lingers at a flower for a long time.

FAVORED PLANTS

Yarrows
(*Achillea* spp.)

Chives
(*Allium schoenoprasum*)

Asters
(*Aster* spp.)

Butterfly bush
(*Buddleia davidii*)

Mints
(*Mentha* spp.)

Goldenrods
(*Solidago* spp.)

Marigolds
(*Tagetes* spp.)

Clovers
(*Trifolium* spp.)

Dogface
(*Zerene cesonia*)

Finding the dog on the wings of this butterfly can take some imagination, but keep looking and you'll spot the profile of a hound's head (some folks see a poodle) in the markings on this species' open wings. The black borders of the wings are the background, and the head is the golden orange part on the forewing. See the dark "eye?" Examine several dogface butterflies and you'll see that the shape of the dog varies from one specimen to the next.

Wingspan: 1⅞"–2½"

▶ RANGE
A southern species, this butterfly usually resides from southern California to Florida, although it is a wanderer and can show up as far north as Canada.

▶ CATERPILLAR
Just as variable in markings as the adults, the caterpillars share a basic green color. They may be marked with stripes, bands, or dots of other colors.

▶ HOST PLANTS
This species of sulphurs uses clovers (*Trifolium* spp.) and other legumes, including lead plant (*Amorpha canescans*) and false lead plant (*A. fruticosa*) as host plants.

▶ COMMENTS
Most sulphur species look nearly alike when their wings are closed, as they are when the butterfly is feeding. To find out whether you're hosting the interesting "Fido face," stick around and wait until the butterfly flits to another blossom, giving you a brief glimpse of its identifying markings. The dogface visits many flowers, including those listed at right.

FAVORED PLANTS

Butterflyweed
(*Asclepias tuberosa*)

Asters
(*Aster* spp.)

Butterfly bush
(*Buddleia davidii*)

Scabiosa
(*Scabiosa* spp.)

Goldenrods
(*Solidago* spp.)

Clovers
(*Trifolium* spp.)

Verbenas
(*Verbena* spp.)

Cloudless Giant Sulphur
(*Phoebis sennae*)

In the tropics, many butterflies exhibit just one color, although usually with a sheen of iridescence. More northerly butterflies are nearly all marked with at least two different colors. This species is as close to the tropical look as our butterflies get. It's a large member of the sulphurs, with lovely, clear yellow wings that look like a primrose flower on the wing. It was once called by the wonderfully descriptive name of "brimstone butterfly" (brimstone being an old nickname for the mineral sulphur).

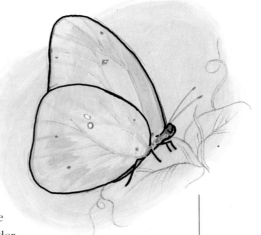

Wingspan: $2\frac{1}{8}$"–$2\frac{3}{4}$"

▶ RANGE
The cloudless giant sulphur is a true tropical butterfly, ranging into South America but also delighting observers in North America in the extreme South. It frequently wanders into the Midwest and as far as eastern Canada.

▶ CATERPILLAR
This caterpillar can be yellow, chartreuse, or green with striped sides and dots across its back. It conceals itself by "sewing" a leaf together with silk to create a protective feeding tent, making it difficult to spot.

▶ HOST PLANTS
This species' larvae prefer legumes as host plants. Sennas (*Cassia* spp.) are tops on the menu, but the adult butterflies also choose partridge pea (*C. fasciculata*) and that old sulphur standby, clovers (*Trifolium* spp.), to nourish the young'uns.

▶ COMMENTS
Many flowers get the attention of these beautiful butterflies, including its favorites, listed at right.

FAVORED PLANTS

Tickseed sunflower
(*Bidens aristosa*)

Butterfly bush
(*Buddleia davidii*)

Dahlias
(*Dahlia* spp.)

Sedums
(*Sedum* spp.)

Marigolds
(*Tagetes* spp.)

Mexican sunflower
(*Tithonia rotundifolia*)

Ironweeds
(*Vernonia* spp.)

Zinnias
(*Zinnia* spp.)

Sleepy Orange
(*Eurema nicippe*)

When you see this pretty butterfly in the hot days of summer, you'll think "sleepy" is definitely a misnomer. It flits about as if it's had a few too many cups of coffee! In cooler weather, however, it is definitely slower on the wing. In some years, populations swell to large numbers, especially at the mud-puddle social clubs that sulphur butterflies frequent. The male is easy to identify—it's our only black-bordered orange butterfly—but females, whose color may lean more toward yellow, are easy to confuse with other species.

Wingspan: 1⅜"–1⅞"

▶ RANGE

A mostly southern species, the sleepy orange sticks mainly to the South and Southwest. It shows up in much fewer numbers east of the Rockies and occasionally in the Northeast.

▶ CATERPILLAR

Small and green, the caterpillar displays stripes along its sides with black, white, and yellow markings that help camouflage it among the foliage. The chrysalis looks like the triangular insect called a leafhopper.

▶ HOST PLANTS

The sleepy orange is a sulphur, so its caterpillars eat legumes, favoring clovers (*Trifolium* spp.) and sennas (*Cassia* spp.).

▶ COMMENTS

Many low-growing flowers are favorite nectar sources of the sleepy orange. Or, delight the sleepy orange by giving it a damp patch of earth or manure-mix mud puddle to hang out at with others of its kind. If the mud is a regular attraction, the numbers of sleepy orange butterflies it draws can mount to a flock of many dozens.

FAVORED PLANTS

Chives
(*Allium schoenoprasum*)

Tickseed sunflower
(*Bidens aristosa*)

Lavenders
(*Lavandula* spp.)

Sweet alyssum
(*Lobularia maritima*)

Mints
(*Mentha* spp.)

Oregano
(*Origanum vulgare*)

Marigolds
(*Tagetes* spp.)

Clovers
(*Trifolium* spp.)

Verbenas
(*Verbena* spp.)

Dwarf Yellow
(*Nathalis iole*)

Just plain cute, this miniature yellow butterfly is the smallest of the family of whites and sulphurs. Formerly called the dainty yellow, it's usually less than an inch. Like many other species of its family, the dwarf yellow is an emigrant making periodic treks northward into territory far outside its usual range. An observer in 1874 described an emigration to Bermuda: "Early in the morning several persons living on the north side of the main island perceived, as they thought, a cloud coming over from the northwest, which drew nearer and nearer to shore. . . . Fishermen out near the reefs . . . stated that numbers of these insects fell upon their boats, literally covering them."

Wingspan: ¾"–1⅛"

►**RANGE**

The dwarf yellow resides in the extreme South and Southwest from southern California to the Gulf states. Mass emigrations are a wondrous sight, with thousands of the tiny yellow wings on the move heading as far north as Canada.

►**CATERPILLAR**

The itty-bitty caterpillar, only about ½ inch long, is dark green, striped longitudinally with purple, black, and yellow.

►**HOST PLANTS**

An aberration among sulphurs, the dwarf yellow uses plants in the daisy family and the pink family instead of legumes to host its caterpillars. Most are weeds, such as common chickweed (*Stellaria media*) and shepherd's needle (*Bidens pilosa*), but the marigolds (*Tagetes* spp.) in your garden may also nourish a brood.

►**COMMENTS**

The dwarf yellow feeds at many garden flowers, as well as many wildflower "weeds."

FAVORED PLANTS

Yarrows
(*Achillea* spp.)

Asters
(*Aster* spp.)

Butterfly bush
(*Buddleia davidii*)

Lantanas
(*Lantana* spp.)

Lavenders
(*Lavandula* spp.)

Marigolds
(*Tagetes* spp.)

Clovers
(*Trifolium* spp.)

Verbenas
(*Verbena* spp.)

Zinnias
(*Zinnia* spp.)

GOSSAMER WINGS (Lycaenidae)

This large family includes the aptly named blues and coppers, as well as the hairstreaks, a group of butterflies that have thin, threadlike "tails" projecting from their hindwings. All are nectar drinkers; the blues are also fond of clustering at mud puddles and manure. Many gossamer wings are very small butterflies—look closely to spot this clan.

American Copper
(Lycaena phlaeas)

As bright as a copper kettle, this is one of the most common species in North America. Males and females look very much alike but may vary in their coloring, depending on where they live and when they hatched. One of the smallest butterflies, the American copper flies low to the ground, so it's easy to miss. They can be aggressive toward passersby, darting out to challenge trespassers on their territory.

Wingspan: ⅞"–1⅛"

▶ **RANGE**
Members of this species range through most of the United States but are most common in the northern half of the country.

▶ **CATERPILLAR**
The larva looks more like a slug than like a typical caterpillar. It may be green or rosy pink in color.

▶ **HOST PLANTS**
Two of the most common weeds in America serve as the usual host plants of this species—sheep sorrel (*Rumex acetosella*) and curly dock (*R. crispus*). Look for these plants along the roadside and in backyards. High in the mountains, the species uses mountain sorrel (*Oxyria digyna*) to nourish its progeny.

▶ **COMMENTS**
Coppers seem to be particularly drawn to tiny flowers in my garden—especially in the mint patch in late summer when those fragrant plants are in full bloom. They also love asters.

FAVORED PLANTS

Anise hyssop
(*Agastache foeniculum*)

Eupatoriums
(*Eupatorium* spp.)

Euphorbias
(*Euphorbia* spp.)

Oregano
(*Origanum vulgare*)

Chaste tree
(*Vitex agnus-castae*)

Bronze Copper
(*Hyllocaena hyllus*)

Double the size of the American copper and "tarnish" the metal, and you have the bronze copper, discernible from its smaller kin by its darker color as well as its bigger stature. While many of the coppers are wide-ranging in their habits and found in varied habitats, this species is usually seen near the wet places or moist roadsides and meadows where its host plants thrive. Like other coppers, it frequently perches motionless on grasses and other plants. In full sun, look for the purple iridescent gleam overlaying the male's dark coppery forewings.

Wingspan: $1\frac{1}{4}"-1\frac{3}{8}"$

▶ RANGE
The American copper lives mainly in the northern part of the country from Canada as far south as Kansas and along the Atlantic Coast. It also is found in Mississippi.

▶ CATERPILLAR
Like other coppers, the caterpillars of the bronze copper resemble slugs rather than the usual "worm." They are lime green with a single stripe down the back.

▶ HOST PLANTS
The female lays her eggs on curly dock (*Rumex crispus*) and various knotweeds (*Polygonum* spp.), especially near marshes, streams, and other wet places.

▶ COMMENTS
Plants of the Composite, or daisy, family are tops with the bronze copper, along with other roadside weeds and garden flowers. In the mountain West, where a European invader called knapweed has become a pest in native grasslands, I've spent several delightful hours watching these beautiful butterflies visit one purplish pink flower head after another, probing the fuzzy bachelor's button–like blossoms with their delicate proboscises.

FAVORED PLANTS
Milkweeds
(*Asclepias* spp.)

Asters
(*Aster* spp.)

Centaureas, including bachelor's buttons, sweet sultan, mountain bluet, yellow knapweed, and others
(*Centaurea* spp.)

Thistles
(*Cirsium* spp.)

Euphorbias
(*Euphorbia* spp.)

Wingspan: 1"–1¼"

Purplish Copper
(*Epidemia helloides*)

Telling one copper from the next is a job for experienced butterfly watchers or for those with plenty of patience because many of the species look almost alike at first glance. Luckily, they have a habit of sitting still long enough to allow a good look with field guide in hand. To identify this species, check the hind edge of the wing for a telltale zigzag marking. The purple sheen that gives it its name appears only on the male and is visible only in good sunlight.

►RANGE
The most common copper in California and often seen in the Northwest, this species ranges eastward to the Great Lakes and the Midwest. It is most common in the Far West.

►CATERPILLAR
This bright caterpillar is a lovely spring green with yellow stripes along the back and diagonally on the sides.

►HOST PLANTS
Cultivate a few stout weeds in your garden if you live within the range of this beautiful butterfly. Sheep sorrel (*Rumex acetosella*), curly dock (*R. crispus*), and other *Rumex* species are host plants, as are many knotweeds (*Polygonum* spp.)

►COMMENTS
This is a summer to early fall butterfly, on the wing from the summer solstice to the Indiana summer days of September. Look for it at flowers with clusters of small blossoms.

FAVORED PLANTS

Yarrows
(*Achillea* spp.)

Butterflyweed
(*Asclepias tuberosa*)

Knotweeds
(*Polygonum* spp.)

Goldenrods
(*Solidago* spp.)

Clovers
(*Trifolium* spp.)

Brazilian vervain
(*Verbena bonariensis*)

Great Purple Hairstreak
(*Atlides halesus*)

"Great," which means "big" in animal names, is a relative term when you're talking about a group of butterflies that usually check in at about an inch and a half across. "Purple" is also in the eye of the beholder—to my eye, this butterfly is blue. It's a beautiful creature with shining iridescent color as pretty as a sapphire ring or the small songbird called an indigo bunting. Notice the two tails on each of its hindwings, which may serve to distract the attention of birds from more vital parts.

Wingspan: 1¼"–1½"

► **RANGE**
The great purple hairstreak roams across the southern half of the country, occasionally ranging northward.

► **CATERPILLAR**
This caterpillar is green with a longitudinal yellow stripe on the sides and a single dark stripe down the back.

► **HOST PLANTS**
The caterpillars of the purple hairstreak have a limited menu, feeding only on mistletoes (*Phoradendron* spp.). Mistletoes are parasitic plants that live on trees of many species, from oaks and cottonwoods to needled junipers. Mistletoes flourish in many areas, especially the South.

► **COMMENTS**
Many nectar flowers tempt the purple hairstreak. At right are some of its special favorites. A fast flier, the great purple hairstreak moves swiftly from one blossom to another. Watch how the male shines various hues of blue as the light shifts across its wings.

FAVORED PLANTS

Hyssops
(*Agastache* spp.)

Eupatoriums
(*Eupatorium* spp.)

Sunflowers
(*Helianthus* spp.)

Mints
(*Mentha* spp.)

Oregano
(*Origanum vulgare*)

Goldenrods
(*Solidago* spp.)

Verbenas
(*Verbena* spp.)

Brown Elfin
(*Incisalia augustinus*)

Elfins are nondescript, drab-brown little butterflies that are easily overlooked—but worth noticing because they appear early in spring. This is the most common of the elfins and the most widely distributed, covering most of the country except the South. It's a warmer color than many of its kin, varying from rusty orange to mid-brown to grayish brown.

Wingspan: ¾"–1⅛"

▶ RANGE
The brown elfin ranges from Canada south to California and east to Virginia.

▶ CATERPILLAR
The green caterpillar, marked with red-and-yellow crosswise stripes, eats not only the foliage but also the buds and flowers of its host plants.

▶ HOST PLANTS
An unusual list of food plants, mostly native woodland shrubs, satisfies the caterpillars of this species. Blueberries (*Vaccinium* spp.), mountain laurel (*Kalmia angustifolia*), azaleas (*Rhododendron* spp.), California lilacs (*Ceanothus* spp.), manzan-itas (*Arbutus* spp.), plus the parasitic white-and-orange vining weed called dodders (*Cuscuta* spp.) all may serve as host plants.

▶ COMMENTS
Because the brown elfin is usually found in a wooded habitat, its known nectar favorites are flowers that thrive in shady situations. They favor ericaceous (heath family) shrubs, including those listed at right. In spring, I make a habit of checking pussywillows in full flower. They sometimes attract brown elfins and other close kin. If your garden is near a woods, elfins are likely to visit other nectar flowers, too.

FAVORED PLANTS

Rock cresses
(*Arabis* spp.)

Bearberry
(*Arctostaphylos uva-ursi*)

Mustards
(*Brassica* spp.)

Bachelor's buttons
(*Centaurea cyanus*)

Wintergreen
(*Gaultheria procumbens*)

Dame's rocket
(*Hesperis matronalis*)

Blueberries
(*Vaccinium* spp.)

Olive Hairstreak
(*Mitoura grineus*)

I think "emerald hairstreak" would be a much better name for this lovely little butterfly, which is a striking bright green, not the dull color its name suggests. The olive is flashiest beneath its wings, unlike most other hairstreaks, which have drably colored undersides. It also lacks the dab of red or orange often seen on the undersides of the more somberly colored species. On top, it's dark to golden brown. It sports the typical skinny tail projections of its kin.

Wingspan: ⅞"–1"

▶ RANGE
You may spot this green butterfly throughout most of the eastern half of the country to the Great Lakes and New England.

▶ CATERPILLAR
The caterpillar is the same shade as the needled foliage of cedars—its host plants—a deep green. It has lighter-colored markings on its side that help camouflage it.

▶ HOST PLANTS
Development, roadside mowing, and farming tend to remove this pretty butterfly's host plants, the Eastern red cedar (*Juniperus virginiana*) and the southern red cedar (J. *silicicola*). This has caused a decline in the populations of the olive hairstreak, but as cleared land goes fallow, the red cedar often returns, welcoming the butterfly back.

▶ COMMENTS
The olive hairstreak feeds on many flowers. Its favorites are listed at right.

FAVORED PLANTS

Hyssops
(*Agastache* spp.)

Tickseed sunflower
(*Bidens aristosa*)

Butterfly bush
(*Buddleia davidii*)

Purple coneflower
(*Echinacea purpurea*)

Sunflowers
(*Helianthus* spp.)

Sedums
(*Sedum* spp.)

Mexican sunflower
(*Tithonia rotundifolia*)

Zinnias
(*Zinnia* spp.)

Wingspan: 1"–1¼"

California Hairstreak
(*Satyrium californica*)

So many butterflies, so many plants. The diversity of plant life in America means a diversity in butterfly life, too. While a few species adapt to make use of widespread and common host plants, others are much more specialized in their needs and fill separate ecological niches. In the West, where the California hairstreak overlaps the range of the very similar Acadian hairstreak, the species are separated by their host plant preferences. The California sticks to dry country, where its host plants, the oaks and California lilacs (*Ceanothus* spp.), flourish. The Acadian, which raises its next generation on willows (*Salix* spp.), doesn't stray far from water, where these moisture-loving plants thrive.

▶ RANGE
The California hairstreak ranges in the West from British Columbia to southern California and east to the Rockies.

▶ CATERPILLAR
As usual in the world of butterflies, the California hairstreak caterpillar displays very effective camouflage. Its skin is the same brown as the twigs of its host plants, with dashes of white and gray.

These added touches help make it look even more like sunlit bark.

▶ HOST PLANTS
This species chooses California lilacs (*Ceanothus* spp.) and oaks (*Quercus* spp.) for its caterpillar food sources.

▶ COMMENTS
Plants with clusters of small flowers appeal to the California hairstreak. Try a few of the plants

below to tempt this brown beauty.

FAVORED PLANTS
Milkweeds
(*Asclepias* spp.)

Butterflyweed
(*Asclepias tuberosa*)

California lilacs
(*Ceanothus* spp.)

Sunflowers
(*Helianthus* spp.)

Red-Banded Hairstreak
(Calycopis cecrops)

It's easy to overlook the hairstreaks, even though there are dozens of species ranging in various habitats across the country. These small, mostly brownish butterflies aren't flashy enough, like the bright yellow sulphurs, to catch your eye when they're on the wing. Although they're not showstoppers, their wing markings have a delicate, subtle beauty. This species earns its name from the thin band of bright red color on its underwings. Notice the blue spot on its hindwing, a frequent marking of the hairstreak group.

Wingspan: ¾"–1"

▶ RANGE
Most common in the South, this species ranges from the Northeast south to Florida and Texas.

▶ CATERPILLAR
The tiny caterpillar is dark brown with black stripes along its back and, like some hairstreak species, has brown hair over its body.

▶ HOST PLANTS
The caterpillars feed on shining sumac (*Rhus copallina*). In more southerly parts of their range, they also eat crotons (*Codiaeum* spp.). The caterpillars have the highly unusual habit of eating dead foliage, not fresh leaves. They feed on the dropped leaves beneath their host plants, another good reason not to be too tidy about garden cleanup.

▶ COMMENTS
Think fuzzy when it comes to attracting the red-banded and other species of hairstreaks; clusters of "fuzzy" flowers seem to hold high appeal, as do those listed below.

FAVORED PLANTS

Blue mist
(*Caryopteris* × *clandonensis*)

California lilac
(*Ceanothus* spp.)

Buttonbush
(*Cephalanthus occidentalis*)

Eupatoriums
(*Eupatorium* spp.)

Sumacs
(*Rhus* spp.)

Sedums
(*Sedum* spp.)

Wingspan: 1"–1¼"

Gray Hairstreak
(*Strymon melinus*)

"Common hairstreak" is another name for this species, which tells you that this one is apt to be in your garden frequently. In fact, sometimes it visits gardens and farms to the point of peskiness. Its caterpillars have a taste for such crops as beans, strawberries, hops, corn, and cotton—which can put them at odds with backyard gardeners or commercial growers.

► **RANGE**
This common butterfly lives all across North America.

► **CATERPILLAR**
The E.T. of caterpillars, this species can extend its head like a gooseneck lamp. The caterpillar stretches it out from its little green sluglike body so that its jaws can reach inside a seedpod while its body remains outside.

► **HOST PLANTS**
Sometimes called the cotton square borer or the bean lycaenid, the larvae of the gray hairstreak feed on the developing seedpods of beans and other legumes, plus corn, cotton, mints, strawberries, hops, and mallows (*Lavatera* spp.). Oaks may get a nibble, too. If you have a long growing season, try planting a row of cotton or transplanting a few cotton plants among your flower garden. The blossoms look like silky, dark-eyed hollyhock flowers, and the plants are likely to attract this pretty butterfly.

► **COMMENTS**
Many flowers attract the gray hairstreak, including those listed at right.

FAVORED PLANTS

Yarrows
(*Achillea* spp.)

Butterflyweed
(*Asclepias tuberosa*)

California lilacs
(*Ceanothus* spp.)

Eupatoriums
(*Eupatorium* spp.)

Sunflowers
(*Helianthus* spp.)

Mints
(*Mentha* spp.)

Oregano
(*Origanum vulgare*)

Goldenrods
(*Solidago* spp.)

Veronicas
(*Veronica* spp.)

Western Pygmy Blue
(*Brephidium exilis*)

You can guess from the name that this is a tiny butterfly. It's the tiniest of the western butterflies and one of the smallest of all North American species, checking in at just about ½ inch across, give or take a few millimeters. Like most blues, the male and female look different, with the female having less blue to boast of than the male. With wings closed, both sexes are a nondescript, speckled grayish brown.

Wingspan: ⅜"–¾"

▶ RANGE
This butterfly ranges from Oregon to California, east to the Plains and Texas. Butterflies of this species occurring north of the Southwest may be emigrants, since this species is prone to wandering. Along the Gulf Coast and east into Florida, the similar eastern pygmy blue takes over.

▶ CATERPILLAR
The tiny caterpillar is creamy light green with yellow lengthwise stripes. Look closely and you'll see minute brown bumps on its segmented body.

▶ HOST PLANTS
Hatching from a beautiful aquamarine-colored egg, the itty-bitty caterpillars eat plants in the goosefoot family (Chenopodiaceae), which are mostly weedy plants like lamb's-quarters (*Chenopodium* spp.) and oraches or saltbushes (*Atriplex* spp.).

▶ COMMENTS
Although this is an abundant butterfly, it's easy to miss because of its small size. Look for it flying slowly among any garden flowers, including mints and herbs.

FAVORED PLANTS

Butterfly bush
(*Buddleia davidii*)

Eupatoriums
(*Eupatorium* spp.)

Lavenders
(*Lavandula* spp.)

Mints
(*Mentha* spp.)

Oregano
(*Origanum vulgare*)

Goldenrods
(*Solidago* spp.)

Clovers
(*Trifolium* spp.)

Wingspan: ⅝"–1"

Marine Blue
(*Leptotes marina*)

Don't be fooled by the name—this is not a seafaring butterfly. "Marine" describes the beautiful blue-lavender color of this species rather than its homeland, which can be far from the sea. An abundant butterfly, it's so small that it often slips in and out of the garden unnoticed, like most of the other species in the gossamer wing family. The female has less blue on her upper wings; she's marked with brown and violet.

▶ RANGE
The marine blue ranges from the Central Pacific coast through Texas and north into the Midwest. Like some other species of the tiny blues, in summer it succumbs to wanderlust, and then emigrates outside its normal breeding range.

▶ CATERPILLAR
Caterpillars vary in color—they may be green or brown—but like other larvae of blue butterflies, they are shaped more like slugs than the usual cylindrical caterpillar shape.

▶ HOST PLANTS
Legumes are tops on the menu for this species. Fe-males seek a wide variety of plants as hosts from locoweeds (*Astragalus* spp.) and alfalfa (*Medicago sativa*) to ornamentals. In the garden, plant native wisterias (*Wisteria frutescens* and *W. macrostachya*), sweet peas (*Lathyrus* spp.), and leadworts (*Plumbago* spp.) to attract egg-laying females.

▶ COMMENTS
The marine blue is partial to plants with clustered blossoms or spikes of small flowers, which describes many herbs.

FAVORED PLANTS

Yarrows
(*Achillea* spp.)

Chives
(*Allium schoenoprasum*)

Lavenders
(*Lavandula* spp.)

Mints
(*Mentha* spp.)

Oregano
(*Origanum vulgare*)

Goldenrods
(*Solidago* spp.)

Dandelion
(*Taraxacum officinale*)

Clovers
(*Trifolium* spp.)

Eastern Tailed Blue
(*Everes comyntas*)

Combining the delicate thready tail of a hairstreak butterfly with the diminutive size and pretty color of the blues, this species is one of the most beautiful butterflies—although it takes a sharp eye to appreciate it. When it closes its wings, a dab of bright orange near the tails will catch your eye. When the male's wings are open, the rich color of its black-bordered wings is breathtaking. Females are variable in color and in spring may be deep brown.

Wingspan: ¾"–1"

▶ RANGE
This is a common and abundant species over the entire eastern two-thirds of the continent.

▶ CATERPILLAR
Like the caterpillars of other blues, this one is tiny, well camouflaged, and variable in color. Give yourself an A+ in the vision department if you manage to discern its pink-striped green body.

▶ HOST PLANTS
Flowers of legumes are the favorite food of this species' caterpillar, a good argument for letting a patch of clover flourish without mowing in a discreet corner of your yard. If you find a caterpillar munching on the flowers of the beans in your garden, this may be the culprit.

▶ COMMENTS
Plant an herb garden to attract many of the blue butterflies, including the eastern tailed blue. Flowers with clusters or spikes of small blossoms are favored, but other nectar plants, including those listed at right, also attract attention.

FAVORED PLANTS

Yarrows
(*Achillea* spp.)

Butterfly bush
(*Buddleia davidii*)

Dame's rocket
(*Hesperis matronalis*)

Lavenders
(*Lavandula* spp.)

Mints
(*Mentha* spp.)

Oregano
(*Origanum vulgare*)

Dandelion
(*Taraxacum officinale*)

Zinnias
(*Zinnia* spp.)

Spring Azure
(*Celastrina ladon*)

One of my favorite delights of spring, this little butterfly is on the wing as soon as the first flowers bloom. In my yard, that's often chickweed and henbit, a couple of weeds that do a good job of sneaking into garden beds. Look near the ground to see this butterfly—like its kin in the group of blues, it often flies low on its search for nectar or a hospitable mud puddle. The species is a quick-change artist, showing variation in color depending on the time of year it hatched and its homeland. An early American butterfly observer and collector, Samuel H. Scudder, described this species as "a violet afloat."

Wingspan: ¾"–1¼"

▶ **RANGE**
The spring azure is common across North America.

▶ **CATERPILLAR**
When I first spotted a few ants busily running over and around a tiny pinkish caterpillar that was eating the middle of a dogwood flower, I thought they were attacking. A look through a magnifying glass showed me that the ants were actually protecting the caterpillar from an infinitesimal predatory fly that was planning to use the caterpillar's body as a host for its own eggs. Further watching showed the ants' stake in this game: The caterpillar secreted honeydew from its body—ambrosia to the ants. Like other blues, the spring azure caterpillar may occur in different colors, in this case pink to green.

▶ **HOST PLANTS**
These little caterpillars don't eat much: just a nibble of the flowers of many plants, including dogwoods (*Cornus* spp.), viburnums (*Viburnum* spp.), California lilacs (*Ceanothus* spp.), and blueberries (*Vaccinium* spp.).

▶ **COMMENTS**
Flowering herbs are perfect for the spring azure because of their small flowers and their blossoms in many-flowered clusters or spikes.

FAVORED PLANTS

Hyssops
(*Agastache* spp.)

Chives
(*Allium schoenoprasum*)

Lavenders
(*Lavandula* spp.)

Mints
(*Mentha* spp.)

Oreganos
(*Origanum* spp.)

Rosemaries
(*Rosmarinus* spp.)

Dandelion
(*Taraxacum officinale*)

Thymes
(*Thymus* spp.)

Common Blue
(*Icaricia icaroides*)

Arguments over classification of butterflies have been going on ever since the first collectors set out with their nets, and the often-confusing group of blues gets plenty of attention. Lepidopterists once grouped the common blue with the spring azure, but it now rates its own Latin name and boasts more than a dozen subspecies. Regardless of what it's called, this is a pretty, easily spotted butterfly. Females may be blue or brown.

Wingspan: 1"–1⅜"

▶ **RANGE**

The common blue is an abundant butterfly with many variations. It lives in the western half of the country.

▶ **CATERPILLAR**

The half-inch caterpillar is green with a coat of whitish hair that allows it to blend in well with the often hairy stems or foliage of lupines.

▶ **HOST PLANTS**

Plant species of lupines (*Lupinus* spp.) that are native to your region if you want to increase populations of the common blue in your geographically appropriate backyard. The female may choose one of more than three dozen species of lupines as a host plant, depending on location.

▶ **COMMENTS**

Think small when planning a menu for the common blue. Like its relatives, this lovely creature seems to prefer clusters or spikes of tiny flowers. Many garden flowers and herbs are suitable nectar sources. Let some clover grow in your lawn or garden, too, and don't be too quick to uproot flowering weeds; the blue butterflies prize the weeds as nectar sources.

FAVORED PLANTS

Rock cresses
(*Arabis* spp.)

Dame's rocket
(*Hesperis matronalis*)

Lavenders
(*Lavandula* spp.)

Mints
(*Mentha* spp.)

Dandelion
(*Taraxacum officinale*)

Thymes
(*Thymus* spp.)

Clovers
(*Trifolium* spp.)

Acmon Blue
(*Icaricia acmon*)

This butterfly used to be known by the beautiful name "emerald-studded blue." You have to have really good eyesight to see the emerald on this butterfly—tiny metallic dots that top a row of black spots on the edge of the hindwing. The only time I got a satisfyingly long look at the jewelry of this butterfly was when I found the discarded wings of a few individuals by some English daisies. A crab spider had claimed the daisy as its hunting ground and dispatched the blue butterflies when they arrived to dine. If you don't have a crab spider to "aid" your observations, watch the butterfly as it nectars to get the best look. This species has a wonderful habit of flitting its hindwings back and forth, giving you a split-second glance at the metallic green as bright in the sun as a hummingbird's feathers.

Wingspan: ¾"–1"

▶ RANGE
A mostly western species, the acmon blue ranges from the Pacific Coast to the beginning of the Great Plains. It is also found in a few midwestern states.

▶ CATERPILLAR
The small caterpillar is a hairy little guy with a whitish fuzz covering its dull yellowish body.

▶ HOST PLANTS
Weeds are prime fodder for the caterpillars of this species, which chow down on wild buckwheats (*Erio-gonum* spp.), locoweed (*Astragalus* spp.), deerweed (*Lotus dendroideus*), and knotweeds (*Polygonum* spp.). The caterpillars also favor native lupines (*Lupinus* spp.), and it is worth cultivating a few in your garden to boost the number of these butterflies in your own yard.

▶ COMMENTS
Cultivate an herb garden to bring this low-flying butterfly into close viewing range. Many herbs are ideal nectar sources. The acmon blue also frequently visits other garden flowers as well as weeds in bloom.

FAVORED PLANTS

Chives
(*Allium schoenoprasum*)

Lavenders
(*Lavandula* spp.)

Mints
(*Mentha* spp.)

Oreganos
(*Origanum* spp.)

Rosemaries
(*Rosmarinus* spp.)

Thymes
(*Thymus* spp.)

METALMARKS (Riodinidae)

Metalmarks flood the tropics in huge numbers, with perhaps up to 900 often brightly colored species flitting about in the warm sun of Central and South America. But north of the border, the family is represented by only about two dozen species, which all look pretty much alike. They're small butterflies with a checkered pattern of brown and dull orange. The "metal" is on the wings—small, glinting, silvery spots in some species.

Mormon Metalmark
(*Apodemia mormo*)

This western butterfly is one of the most strikingly colored metalmarks and is eye-catching in flight. Though it measures in at only about an inch in width, you may notice it flitting about because of its fast flapping and bright flecks against a dramatic dark background. Unlike others of this group, the light spots on these wings are white, not silver.

Wingspan: ¾"–1¼"

▶ RANGE
The mormon metalmark is found in the dry West, from eastern Washington to Baja, California, east to the Great Basin and Texas. A small population in British Columbia is classified as a rare, threatened species.

▶ CATERPILLAR
Dark gray with a faint flush of purple, the caterpillar sprouts widely spaced tufts of hairs down its body.

▶ HOST PLANTS
The caterpillars of this species thrive on buck-wheats (*Eriogonum* spp.).

▶ COMMENTS
This pretty butterfly flies low to the ground and has a predilection for yellow flowers, which are usually the predominant color in its dryland habitat.

FAVORED PLANTS

Rock cresses
(*Arabis* spp.)

Desert marigold
(*Baileya multiradiata*)

Mustards
(*Brassica* spp.)

Rabbitbrush
(*Chrysothamnus viscidiflorus*)

Senecios
(*Senecio* spp.)

SNOUT BUTTERFLIES (Libytheidae)

There are only two species representing this family on this continent. The snouts get their name from a long "beak" (a pair of mouthparts called palpi) that extend beyond the front of their body, giving them a Pinocchio look. This is easy to see on a perching butterfly. Snouts are common, abundant backyard butterflies. They nectar at flowers, visit mud puddles, and perch on garden plants, opening their wings flat in the sun.

Snout Butterfly
(*Libytheana bachmanii*)

Notice the unusually shaped tips of the forewings of this butterfly and its similarly designed southern relative. These wing tips plus the snout make the two snout species easy to recognize. The southern snout butterfly is a paler, duller orange color. Anywhere hackberries (*Celtis* spp.) thrive, you are likely to find snouts, but during their emigrations they can appear almost anywhere.

Wingspan: 1⅝"–1⅞"

▶ RANGE
The snouts are common from New England to the Rockies and south to Mexico. Their breeding range is limited to areas where hackberry trees grow.

▶ CATERPILLAR
The caterpillar is hackberry-leaf green with stripes down the side and a paler belly. It is shaped like a smaller version of a swallowtail caterpillar with a hump near its head.

▶ HOST PLANTS
Hackberry, hackberry, hackberry! To snouts, the choice of host plant is easy. All of the trees commonly called hackberries (*Celtis* spp.) nourish their caterpillars.

▶ COMMENTS
Many flowers appeal to snout butterflies, including fruit-tree flowers.

FAVORED PLANTS
Butterfly bush
(*Buddleia davidii*)

Brazilian vervain
(*Verbena bonariensis*)

Common zinnias
(*Zinnia elegans*)

BRUSH-FOOTED BUTTERFLIES (Nymphalidae)

Moving up in size from the tiny gossamer wings and weird-looking snouts, the brush-footed butterfly family includes most of the middle-size butterflies that keep our summer gardens alive with beautiful colored wings. Hackberries, fritillaries, crescentspots, anglewings, viceroys, and many other familiar garden butterflies are in this family.

Gulf Fritillary
(Agraulis vanillae)

From the top, the Gulf fritillary bears little resemblance to other fritillaries, but when it closes its wings you'll see spangled silver and brown. Its vivid color and long wings look like a little piece of the Tropics, and it is indeed a lover of warm regions. It hasn't adapted to withstand the winter cold in many parts of North America, so its range is limited, although it does occasionally wander and may survive mild winters.

Wingspan: 2½"–2⅞"

▶ RANGE
This species lives along the Gulf of Mexico, in central and southern California, and shows up as far north as the Great Lakes to New York.

▶ CATERPILLAR
This caterpillar is rusty orange with wicked-looking spines on its body. Backward-curving spines on its head no doubt help it repel predators.

▶ HOST PLANTS
The vines called passionflower (*Passiflora* spp.) feed this species' caterpillars. The tough but beautiful purple passion flower or maypops (*P. incarnata*) is a vigorous, hardy vine great for covering a chain-link fence or a sturdy trellis.

▶ COMMENTS
Any nectar flowers serve as dinner for this species.

FAVORED PLANTS

Asters
(*Aster* spp.)

Pentas
(*Pentas* spp.)

Verbenas
(*Verbena* spp.)

Zinnias
(*Zinnia* spp.)

Wingspan: 3"–3⅜"

Zebra
(*Heliconius charitonius*)

You can't miss this butterfly—it's a big one and a beauty. Its elongated wings are shaped differently than most other North American butterflies. It's sometimes classified in the Heliconian family, a tropical tribe that includes many of the most gorgeous butterflies on earth. The striking zebra is as black as coal, with contrasting bands of light yellow across its elegant wings. It's a slow, dreamy flier, drifting through woodlands and gardens most of the day and preferring shaded edges or paths to open spaces. At night, zebras gather in group roosts by the dozens. They cling to Spanish moss, dead branches, or other vegetation, forming chains of one butterfly upon another until the morning sun sends them back into the air.

▶ RANGE

The trademark butterfly of the Everglades and Walt Disney World, this species lives in the Southeast, south to Texas and the Gulf. It occasionally straggles out of its normal territory to California and eastward to the Plains states.

▶ CATERPILLAR

Black spines say "Keep away!" to any predator that might think of making a meal of the big white caterpillar. One way to spot a chrysalis is to keep your eyes open for an adult male butterfly nearby; appar-

ently males are able to discern the presence of a female just before she hatches.

▶ HOST PLANTS

As with many tropical species, passionflower vines (*Passiflora* spp.) are the food of choice for its caterpillars. Maypops (*P. incarnata*) has intricate flowers as beautiful as any of the tender, tropical species but withstands cold winters.

▶ COMMENTS

Many flowers will tempt the beautiful zebra to your

garden. Plant flowers that thrive in a shady spot, the kind of habitat these butterflies prefer. The butterflies also eat pollen.

FAVORED PLANTS
Butterfly bush (*Buddleia davidii*)
Impatiens (*Impatiens walleriana*)
Lantanas (*Lantana* spp.)
Pentas (*Pentas lanceolata*)

Diana
(*Speyeria diana*)

The butterfly shown here is a male; the female has black and blue wings. No wonder early butterfly collectors were fooled into thinking the male and female of this species were two separate kinds of butterfly altogether! It wasn't until 1864 that William H. Edwards finally pegged the female as the mate of the orange and black male. Ed-

Wingspan: 3"–3⅞"

wards managed to capture both male and female in the same patch of western ironweed (*Vernonia fasciculata*) in Kanawha County, West Virginia. Scientists believe the female evolved the black-and-blue coloring to mimic the pipevine swallowtail, a species distasteful to birds because of the chemicals it ingests as a caterpillar. Never very common, the Diana has suffered from logging that destroys its wooded homelands. Although it prefers woods, it does venture afield to find nectar and its other favorite food, manure.

▶ RANGE

This is a species of the East, Midwest, and Southeast, ranging from Maryland and Pennsylvania to the mountains of Georgia and the Carolinas, and occasionally as far west as Oklahoma.

▶ CATERPILLAR

Most caterpillars of this large family are spiny little devils, and the Diana is no exception. It is black with many branched spines that show a bit of orange at their base.

▶ HOST PLANTS

Once known as the Diana fritillary, the caterpillars share with other fritillaries a predilection for violets (*Viola* spp.).

▶ COMMENTS

Ironweeds (*Vernonia* spp.) are still a favorite a century and a half after Edwards' famed discovery. The Diana is particularly fond of manure. Horse manure has an inoffensive odor, or try wetted bagged, composted manure.

FAVORED PLANTS

Purple coneflower
(*Echinacea purpurea*)

Eupatoriums
(*Eupatorium* spp.)

Joe-Pye weed
(*Eupatorium purpureum*)

Coneflowers
(*Rudbeckia* spp.,
but not 'Goldsturm', which
appears to be unappealing to
nectar-seeking butterflies)

Ironweeds
(*Vernonia* spp.)

Common zinnias
(*Zinnia elegans*)

Great Spangled Fritillary
(*Speyeria cybele*)

It's big ("great"), it's flashy with silver spots beneath its wings ("spangled"), and it's dotted like a pair of dice ("fritillary," from the Latin, *fritillus*), but to most backyard butterfly enthusiasts, this species is simply that big, flashy orange-and-black butterfly that adds some spice to the garden whenever it deigns to visit. Females are paler than the males, leaning toward a pale gold rather than pumpkin orange. Like other fritillaries, many of which are confusingly similar in color though not as big as this 3-inch species, the great spangled is a fast flier, never pausing long in one place. I know fall is on the way when the great spangled fritillaries start flocking to my garden. Although I may see an occasional specimen throughout the season, the late-summer hatch increases their numbers just in time for peak bloom of the prairie flowers they like best.

Wingspan: 2⅛"–3"

▶ RANGE
This beautiful species ranges across most of the United States and north into eastern Canada, but isn't found in the deep South or the extreme Southwest.

▶ CATERPILLAR
A horde of scary-looking barbed spines stud the plump black body of the large caterpillar.

▶ HOST PLANTS
Violets (*Viola* spp.) are the only item on the menu for the caterpillars of this species. They feed at night.

▶ COMMENTS
Many nectar flowers tempt the great spangled fritillary to gardens. Some of its favorites are listed at right.

FAVORED PLANTS

Milkweeds
(*Asclepias* spp.)

Butterfly bush
(*Buddleia davidii*)

Purple coneflower
(*Echinacea purpurea*)

Eupatoriums
(*Eupatorium* spp.)

Joe-Pye weed
(*Eupatorium purpureum*)

Ironweeds
(*Vernonia* spp.)

Common zinnias
(*Zinnia elegans*)

Atlantis Fritillary
(*Speyeria atlantis*)

One of the medium-size fritillaries, this beautiful species ranges from sea to shining sea, although it's absent from most of the Midwest and South. It varies in color depending on where it lives, with the silver spots on the undersides of its wings sometimes absent, sometimes just partly shining, and sometimes full-fledged silver. The intricate patterns on its topside are beautiful to look at through close-range binoculars. The butterfly often feeds with wings closed and erect, so you'll have a better view of the pretty silver spots on the undersides of the wings—if the butterflies in your locale display the spots. Many species of fritillaries are similarly colored, with only subtle differences to distinguish them.

Wingspan: 1¾"–2⅝"

▶ **RANGE**
The Atlantis fritillary roams from Alaska to the Atlantic Coast, then diagonally to the Southwest. It is also found in the eastern mountains, south to Virginia.

▶ **CATERPILLAR**
The somber black or black-purple caterpillar is decorated with a street-punk collection of orange spines.

▶ **HOST PLANTS**
There's an easy pattern with host plants of the fritillaries: Violets (*Viola* spp.) are the bill of fare.

▶ **COMMENTS**
Many nectar flowers attract the fritillaires, including those listed at right.

FAVORED PLANTS

Butterfly bush
(*Buddleia davidii*)

Purple coneflower
(*Echinacea purpurea*)

Eupatoriums
(*Eupatorium* spp.)

Joe-Pye weed
(*Eupatorium purpureum*)

Ironweeds
(*Vernonia* spp.)

Common zinnias
(*Zinnia elegans*)

Pearly Crescentspot
(*Phyciodes tharos*)

A small golden orange-and-black butterfly, this species is one of our most "frequent fliers," ranging across the continent and abundant just about everywhere. Look carefully when the butterfly pauses with its wings closed and erect, and you'll spot the pale crescent near the edge of its hindwings. This perky butterfly often flies fairly low, visiting one patch of flowers after another, but it also rises to greater heights to seek a perch. There it sits for long stretches of time, wings outspread but ready to dart into the air after any passerby. These encounters don't always have a happy ending. More than once, I've seen this species pick a fight with a passing bird, which instantly switched to pursuer and snatched the butterfly in midair.

Wingspan: 1"–1½"

▶ RANGE
The pearly crescentspot is common across America, except for the Pacific Coast. Several other species of crescentspots roam North America, and all of them are somewhat similar in color.

▶ CATERPILLAR
Small, dark, and spiny, the caterpillars drop to the ground immediately when disturbed while feeding. Even brushing against the plant and jostling the leaves is enough of a warning to cause the cater-pillars to "disappear" by falling to the ground below.

▶ HOST PLANTS
Asters (*Aster* spp.) are an all-purpose plant for this butterfly. The caterpillars chow down on the foliage, feeding in groups, and the adults eagerly visit the very same plants for nectar.

▶ COMMENTS
The pearly crescentspot feasts at many nectar flowers. Blossoms belonging to the daisy family are always a big hit with these little butterflies.

FAVORED PLANTS

Asters
(*Aster* spp.)

Purple coneflower
(*Echinacea purpurea*)

Euphorbias
(*Euphorbia* spp.)

Snow on the mountain
(*Euphorbia marginata*)

Goldenrods
(*Solidago* spp.)

Ironweeds
(*Vernonia* spp.)

Common zinnia
(*Zinnia elegans*)

Bordered Patch
(*Chlosyne lacinia*)

This is a butterfly that never seems to look the same twice. Not only do the male and female often look entirely different, individuals that hatch from the same batch of eggs may also show little resemblance. This species is one of the checkerspot group, which are usually marked with distinctive, contrasting blocks of color that live up to the name, though this species doesn't have the characteristic markings. Most checkerspots inhabit areas where their host plants grow, but this species ranges widely and is the most abundant checkerspot.

Wingspan: 1⅝"–1⅞"

▶ RANGE
This butterfly ranges from southern California to Texas and south into South America.

▶ CATERPILLAR
Just like the adults of this species, the caterpillars vary in color. They may be black, orange, or a striped combination of those colors. (The chrysalis, as you may have guessed, also shows the same variability of color as every other stage of this butterfly's life.)

▶ HOST PLANTS
If you're an allergy sufferer, say thank you to the next bordered patch butterfly you see—giant ragweed (*Ambrosia trifida*) is one of this caterpillar's favorite host plants. The adults may also lay their eggs on sunflowers (*Helianthus annuus*) and other members of the aster family.

▶ COMMENTS
This butterfly visits many nectar flowers, including those listed at right.

FAVORED PLANTS

Asters
(*Aster* spp.)

Cornflowers
(*Centaurea* spp.)

Rabbitbrush
(*Chrysothamnus viscidiflorus*)

Coneflowers
(*Echinacea* spp. and *Rudbeckia* spp.)

Eupatoriums
(*Eupatorium* spp.)

Ironweeds
(*Vernonia* spp.)

Zinnias
(*Zinnia* spp.)

Wingspan: 1⅝"–2½"

Baltimore Checkerspot
(*Euphydras phaeton*)

The Baltimore checkerspot, or Baltimore, as it's also called, is famous because of the appetite of its caterpillars, which were once believed to eat one and only one plant. Although that plant, turtlehead (*Chelone glabra*), is not widespread in the wild, it has become increasingly popular in gardens. If you plant it, you may become a host to a new brood of Baltimore checkerspots. The male and female look alike, but populations in various areas show some variation in color, although they are still mainly orange and black. Sharing a name with another orange-and-black winged creature—the Baltimore oriole—is no coincidence. Both were named for Lord Baltimore, whose heraldic colors were the same as those of the songbird and the butterfly.

▶ RANGE
This colorful butterfly's range stretches from Canada through the Great Lakes to New England, south into Arkansas and Georgia. It likes particularly wet places such as sphagnum bogs, where turtlehead flourishes.

▶ CATERPILLAR
Orange stripes and many spines decorate the bristly black caterpillars, which feed as a group. Look for the distinctive chrysalises when the caterpillars leave the host plants. They are white with dark markings and look just like a bird dropping suspended from a leaf or other surface.

▶ HOST PLANTS
Turtlehead (*Chelone glabra*) is tops, but gerardias or false foxgloves (*Agalinis* spp., also called *Gerardia* spp.), white ash (*Fraxinus americana*), and the common lawn weed, English plantain (*Plantago lanceolata*), are also used. Caterpillars make a nest of silk over a branch of the plant like tent caterpillars and feed within.

▶ COMMENTS
Try one of these plants to entice the Baltimore to your yard.

FAVORED PLANTS
Milkweeds (*Asclepias* spp.)
Roses (*Rosa* spp.)
Chickweed (*Stellaria* spp.)
Viburnums (*Viburnum* spp.)

Question Mark
(*Polygonia interragationis*)

Wingspan: 2³⁄₈"–2⁵⁄₈"

As a lover of the written word, I'm definitely fond of the "literary" butterflies: the question mark and its relative, the comma. The question mark butterfly has its "punctuation marks" on the underside of the hindwing, delicately inscribed as if someone had used a fine brush dipped in silvery white paint to apply the mark. The marking looks rather like a semicolon—it actually resembles the Greek interrogation point, not the English one. In years gone by, the species was known as the interrogation butterfly, which makes me picture it wearing a tiny trench coat and asking "Whodunnit?" Even before being called the interrogation butterfly, this butterfly was called the violet-tip butterfly. (Notice the fine lavender edging on the open wings and the coloring of the lower wingtips). Imagine how well camouflaged this anglewing is when its wings are closed. In the wooded areas it frequents, it disappears when at rest against a tree trunk.

► **RANGE**
The question mark is common from east of the Rockies across the eastern two-thirds of the continent.

► **CATERPILLAR**
Bristling with whitish spines, the blackish caterpillar is less than appetizing to most predators.

► **HOST PLANTS**
The caterpillars favor a diet of elm tree foliage (*Ulmus* spp.), although they'll often use hackberries (*Celtis* spp.), hops, and plants in the nettle family as host plants.

► **COMMENTS**
Don't bother trying to tempt the question mark or other anglewings with flowers. These gourmets prefer rotten fruit, and they'll eagerly visit fermented fruit even though it makes them tipsy. They will come eagerly for fruit on a plate or still on the tree. The dropped fruit of ornamental crabapples is a favorite. They also dine on sap and the liquid from carrion and manure. Spraying a bit of water on paving or rock may also attract them.

Wingspan: 1¾"–2"

Comma
(*Polygonia comma*)

This common and abundant anglewing butterfly is marked with a perfect silvery white comma on its underside. The chrysalis of this species and the closely related question mark (which both feed on hops) are fantastic objects. They're dark in color, but marked with knobs and spikes that shine as if made of silver and gold. The amount of "metal" markings varies. This butterfly was once called the hop merchant because according to long-ago hops growers, the coloring of its chrysalis determined the price of the hops crop. When the chrysalises were especially lustrous, the hops would sell at a high price. Similarly, when the metallic decorations were skimpy, the hops crop allegedly was worth less. I have to wonder if the old-timers were right. Perhaps some chemical in the foliage of the hops induces the formation of the markings? You can conduct your own experiments by growing hops yourself! It's a pretty vine with delicate foliage and lasting, papery strings of seedpods that look good in a vase or on a trellis. A hops vine grows fast and is likely to cover your arbor the second year after planting.

▶ RANGE

The comma butterfly is common in the eastern half of North America, except for the deep South, where it doesn't venture.

▶ CATERPILLAR

The spiny, dark-colored caterpillars often make a protective tent by "stitching" a leaf together with silk so that they are shielded from view. They often feed in groups and, if caught out in the open on a leaf, will instantly drop to the ground if disturbed.

▶ HOST PLANTS

The caterpillars feed on hops (*Humulus lupulus*), a vine that provides the makings for beer but is also a pretty plant for the garden. Nettles, false nettles, and elms (*Ulmus* spp.) are also host plants.

▶ COMMENTS

Like other anglewings, commas won't be attracted to flowers no matter how delicious their nectar. They prefer to feed at soft or rotting fruit and also drink sap and the liquid from manure and carrion. You may even see them feeding upon fresh bird droppings. Wet rocks or paving will also get the attention of this moisture-loving species.

Zephyr Anglewing
(*Polygonia zephyrus*)

Wingspan: 1¾"–2"

Many of the anglewing butterflies look frustratingly alike, being a tawny golden orange with ragged wing edges that look like a dead leaf when closed. This one even bears a silvery comma mark on its underwings, making it doubly difficult to distinguish from some other species. It helps to know that this is the most likely species you'll see if you live in or near any of the western mountain ranges. Another surefire way to identify it is by the diet of the adults: Unlike most other anglewing species, they often nectar at flowers. The zephyr gets its name from its fast, agile flight. Like most anglewings, it usually hangs out in or near woods, although it will leave the shelter of the trees to feed.

▶ RANGE
The zephyr is abundant from the eastern Rockies north to Canada and south to Mexico, and west through the Sierras and Cascades to the Pacific Coast.

▶ CATERPILLAR
The blackish caterpillar looks very much like that of other anglewings, armored with a coat of bristly spines. When disturbed, the caterpillar may curl up as if to present the most unappealing spiny morsel to a possible predator.

▶ HOST PLANTS
Elms (*Ulmus* spp.), currants (*Ribes* spp.), and rhododendrons (*Rhododendron* spp.)—all native plants of the western mountains—are used as host plants by the zephyr anglewing. As with other anglewings, the caterpillars may live even on seedling trees of its favorite host species.

▶ COMMENTS
Plant asters (*Aster* spp.) of any kind to attract this butterfly. They also visit many other nectar flowers, including those listed at right.

FAVORED PLANTS

Asters
(*Aster* spp.)

Butterfly bush
(*Buddleia davidii*)

Blue mist
(*Caryopteris* × *clandonensis*)

Coneflowers
(*Echinacea* spp. and *Rudbeckia* spp.)

Eupatoriums
(*Eupatorium* spp.)

Zinnias
(*Zinnia* spp.)

Mourning Cloak
(*Nymphalis antiopa*)

This butterfly gets its name from Victorian England: Picture a Victorian woman in the long black gown of grief with her petticoat peeking out below the hem, and you'll be able to make the connection to this lovely species. In America, the edge of the mourning costume is actually yellow or yellowish white rather than the pure white it is in England. Only up close will you notice the beautiful blue spots that also decorate this butterfly's open wings. When the wings are closed, you'll notice the uneven edges and the camouflage coloring. One of the earliest butterflies to be seen each year, the mourning cloak hibernates as an adult and comes out to sun itself on warm days, even in winter.

Wingspan: 2⅞"–3⅜"

▶ RANGE
The mourning cloak ranges across North America except for the Deep South.

▶ CATERPILLAR
The spiny black caterpillars, enlivened with red dots and orange legs, feed en masse. That makes them easy targets for the brilliantly colored fiery searcher beetle, which runs about frenetically in search of juicy caterpillars. Look up to find the workings of mourning cloak caterpillars: well-eaten leaves or denuded branches signal their prescence. Don't worry; the tree will suffer no harm.

▶ HOST PLANTS
Mourning cloak larvae prefer tree leaves. Elms (*Ulmus* spp.), poplars (*Populus* spp.), hackberries (*Celtis* spp.), and willows (*Salix* spp.) are the usual host plants. The females lay their eggs in masses and the caterpillars may seem frighteningly numerous when they first emerge. Don't reach for the pesticide! Let nature take its course, and parasitic and predatory insects will soon do away with many of them.

▶ COMMENTS
Mourning cloaks are not flower feeders, although I have seen one of these butterflies inserting its proboscis into pussywillow catkins. Tempt them with soft and rotting fruit, or look for them where sap drips from trees. Plants infested with aphids also attract the mourning cloaks: The butterflies dine on the sticky-sweet honeydew secreted by the aphids, which collects on leaves beneath the pesty insects. The butterflies will also visit carrion, manure, and wet rocks or paving.

Red Admiral
(*Vanessa atalanta*)

An unmistakable butterfly, the red admiral is also one of the most endearing, thanks to its habit of settling on your shoulder or hat while you stroll the garden. While I love the look of this butterfly with wide-open wings, I'm just as enthralled by the beautiful blue, pink, and brown marbled patterns on its underside. A pugnacious sort, the red admiral often darts after other butterflies—and my dogs! I've even seen it chasing a hummingbird investigating the same flower the butterfly was sipping from.

Wingspan: 1¾"–2¼"

▶ RANGE
This is a common and abundant species over the entire continent except the very far North.

▶ CATERPILLAR
Dark and spiny, the caterpillar looks very much like those of the comma, the question mark, or the mourning cloak.

▶ HOST PLANTS
Stinging nettle (*Urtica dioica*) is a weedy plant that grows in thick colonies, looking almost like a bed of mint—but don't touch! Those stinging hairs will leave your skin fiery red with pain and itching. Still, if you have an out-of-the-way corner where you can grow a small patch, they're worth cultivating for the sake of more red admirals in the garden. False nettle (*Boehmeria cylindrica*) is also used as a host plant and lacks the sting of true nettles. You can also plant hops (*Humulus lupulus*), an attractive vine for a trellis, to attract these pretty butterflies.

▶ COMMENTS
The red admiral puts the butterfly bush (*Buddleia davidii*) at the top of its food preference list, but it will also visit flowers that provide a perch and reachable nectar.

FAVORED PLANTS

Asters
(*Aster* spp.)

Tickseed sunflower
(*Bidens aristosa*)

Coneflowers
(*Echinacea* spp. and *Rudbeckia* spp., but not *R.* 'Goldsturm', which has little or no appeal to butterflies)

Eupatoriums
(*Eupatorium* spp.)

Sedums
(*Sedum* spp. and cvs., including 'Autumn Joy')

Verbenas
(*Verbena* spp. and hybrids)

Chaste tree
(*Vitex agnus-castus*)

Zinnias
(*Zinnia* spp.)

Painted Lady
(*Vanessa cardui*)

The most widespread of the three species of look-alike painted lady butterflies, this one was formerly known as the cosmopolite because it resides just about everywhere in North America. The West Coast lady, on the other hand, usually remains in (you guessed it) the West Coast. The American painted lady, once called the Virginia lady, is more common in the East. All of these ladies are real beauties, but you'll need close-focusing binoculars or a hand lens to truly admire the complex coloring of their undersides. From the topside, you can see the resemblance between these species and their close relative, the red admiral. All of the ladies are emigrant butterflies, which make one-way excursions periodically traveling far from their usual homes.

Wingspan: 2"–2¼"

►RANGE
The painted lady ranges across North America.

►CATERPILLAR
Caterpillars may be yellowish through green to rosy purple, but they are always spiny when mature.

►HOST PLANTS
Once called the thistle butterfly, the painted lady can often be seen nectaring at the fluffy flowers of these spiny plants or seeking a place to lay eggs on their foliage. The females use many other plants to lay their eggs, including asters and other daisies of the family Compositae, as well as those in the mallow family (Malvaceae). If an army of tiny green caterpillars suddenly turns the hollyhocks in your garden to lace, you may soon host a fresh batch of young painted ladies.

►COMMENTS
Many flowers appeal to the nectar-loving painted lady, especially those listed here. They favor thistles in the wild.

FAVORED PLANTS

Asters
(*Aster* spp.)

Tickseed sunflower
(*Bidens aristosa*)

Butterfly bush
(*Buddleia davidii*)

Mexican sunflower
(*Tithonia rotundifolia*)

Brazilian vervain
(*Verbena bonariensis*)

Chaste tree
(*Vitex agnus-castus*)

Common zinnia
(*Zinnia elegans*)

Buckeye
(*Junonia coenia*)

Eyespots are the distinctive hallmark of the buckeye butterfly. Both the top sides and undersides of the wings feature big staring "eyes," rimmed in deep brown and yellow and even accented with a light "pupil" on the forewings. (Decide for yourself whether or not the "eyes" look like those of an antlered male deer.) Pretty orange stripes add to the appeal of this wideranging butterfly. In late summer to fall, buckeyes move southward in amazing numbers. One day when in a store parking lot, I unexpectedly found myself in the middle of an incredible stream of wings. Passing buckeyes flapped all around me, tickling my legs and arms.

Wingspan: 2"–2½"

▶ **RANGE**
Buckeyes range across the United States and Canada, especially during emigration movements.

▶ **CATERPILLAR**
As pretty in a caterpillar sort of way as its winged parents, the buckeye larva has a colorful body marked with black, blue, white, and tawny orange and is armed with prickly looking bristles.

▶ **HOST PLANTS**
Buckeyes choose a varied menu of host plants. The common lawn weed plantain (*Plantago* spp.)

is a favorite, as are gerardias (*Agalinins* spp.) and other plants in the genus *Scrophularia*. The female may also choose to lay her eggs on vervains and other members of the verbena family, and succulents in the stonecrop family.

▶ **COMMENTS**
Butterfly bush (*Buddleia davidii*) is always most popular with buckeyes in my gardens (as it is with so many butterflies), but they will also nectar at many other garden flowers, including those listed here.

FAVORED PLANTS

Anise hyssop
(*Agastache foeniculum*)

Tickseed sunflower
(*Bidens aristosa*)

Goldenrods
(*Solidago* spp.)

Verbenas
(*Verbena* spp.)

Brazilian vervain
(*Verbena bonariensis*)

Ironweeds
(*Vernonia* spp.)

Chaste tree
(*Vitex agnus-castus*)

Zinnias
(*Zinnia* spp.)

White Admiral
(*Limenitis arthemis*)

This species belongs to a group of butterflies once known as the Sovereigns, which included the titled members the admirals and the viceroy. They are large butterflies with striking markings that will catch your eye as soon as they flutter into view. Look for pretty, usually red-spotted undersides when these butterflies pause with wings closed. At first glance, this butterfly looks deep brown, but you may catch a glimpse of a purple sheen as its wings catch the sun—the reason for its old name of "banded purple." Strong-smelling manure draws the lovely white admiral, and the butterflies gather in groups to sip delicately on piles of the pungent stuff.

Wingspan: 2⅞"–3⅛"

▶ **RANGE**

This titled creature lives in only a limited region around the Great Lakes, east to the Atlantic Coast, and north to Newfoundland.

▶ **CATERPILLAR**

The oddly shaped caterpillars of the white admiral are full of humps and bumps, not to mention a protruding pair of spiny horns at the front end. They assume many weird, uncaterpillarlike positions during their daytime rest periods, perhaps to confuse predators into thinking these lumpy white and brown things are really big bird droppings.

▶ **HOST PLANTS**

Caterpillars feed on several trees common in their natural homelands: birches (*Betula* spp.), willows (*Salix* spp.), and poplars (*Populus* spp.). They usually eat at night. Like other admirals, the caterpillars of this species overwinter inside a rolled-up leaf.

▶ **COMMENTS**

Make a manure pile from horse manure or composted cow manure and wet with a hose to attract this beautiful butterfly. A mud puddle or wet rocks and paving may also tempt it from its usual forested haunts into your backyard. You can also try spritzing foliage or tree bark with a solution of 3 parts sugar and 1 part water to mimic the aphid honeydew that this species enjoys eating.

Red-Spotted Purple
(*Basilarchia astyanax*)

This is my favorite butterfly of all, for two reasons: It's a beauty with the blue coloring I like best, and it is unafraid of human activity. In my yard, these butterflies behave almost like pets. My red-spotted purples not only know where to find the fruit and mud puddles in my yard, they also have learned that at 10 A.M. on summer mornings, I hose down a small area of old brick to make them a drinking station.

Wingspan: 3"–3⅜"

They often flutter along companionably when I haul the hose around the corner to their "butterfly bath." I love to see the contrast when the butterfly suddenly opens its wings to reveal the velvety black and glistening blue topside.

▶ RANGE
Red-spotted-purple land covers roughly the eastern two-thirds of the country, with the species also ranging into Arizona and in the North into Canada.

▶ CATERPILLAR
This is a lumpy-looking larva with the same less-than-streamlined shape as the white admiral caterpillar. It also has that "appealing" bird-dropping look, a great defense against foraging birds.

▶ HOST PLANTS
When wild cherries (*Prunus* spp.) grow from bird-planted seeds in my flowerbeds, I let them grow for several years just to tempt egg-laying red-spotted purples, which often use the trees as host plants. Willows (*Salix* spp.), poplars (*Populus* spp.), hawthorns (*Crataegus* spp.), and apples (*Malus* spp.) also host the caterpillars. Look for chewed leaves to track down the surprisingly hard-to-find caterpillar.

▶ COMMENTS
Never mind flowers for the red-spotted purple: Fruit is what it likes best, the rottener the better. It will also drink fruit juice, as I discovered when I poured out a bottle of grape juice that had gone bad. Within minutes, the saturated soil was full of butterflies jostling each other for the juiciest parts. The reason I'd poured out the juice was because it had fermented—but this tippling species enjoys wine even more than fruit juice. Sap, carrion, and manure also charm the red-spotted purple.

Wingspan: 2⅝"–3"

Viceroy
(*Basilarchia archippus*)

The viceroy is famed for riding the orange-and-black coattails of the well-known monarch, an almost lookalike species. Birds are reluctant to attack the monarch because it tastes bad. Bitter chemicals remain in its body from its milkweed-eating caterpillar life, and birds quickly learn to associate that yucky taste with the distinctive color of the monarch. By donning the same color scheme, the viceroy boosts its chances of survival—even though it never eats a bite of milkweed. To check your own observation powers, look for the curving black line across each hindwing of this species—that detail is missing in the monarch. You may also notice a difference in flight style between viceroys and monarchs. As they move from one part of your yard to another, monarchs are leisurely fliers, while viceroys flap frantically, then sail briefly.

▶ **RANGE**

The viceroy ranges across much of North America, except along the Northwest Pacific coast.

▶ **CATERPILLAR**

Find a big bird dropping clinging to a twig of willow, and you may have spotted a viceroy caterpillar. Its mottled brown-and-white color, lumpy shape, and contortionist posture make it easy to overlook among the foliage.

▶ **HOST PLANTS**

The female viceroy will frequently lay her eggs on willows (*Salix* spp.) and poplars (*Populus* spp.), but she may also choose fruit trees such as cherries, plums, and apples to house her progeny.

▶ **COMMENTS**

Viceroys are attracted to many nectar flowers in addition to those listed at right. They may also show interest in fruit or sap.

FAVORED PLANTS

Asters
(*Aster* spp.)

Butterfly bush
(*Buddleia davidii*)

Joe-Pye weeds
(*Eupatorium purpureum*)

Goldenrods
(*Solidago* spp.)

Verbenas
(*Verbena* spp. and hybrids)

Ironweeds
(*Vernonia* spp.)

Weidemeyer's Admiral
(*Basilarchia weidemeyerii*)

Both the Weidemeyer's admiral and white admiral are big, dark butterflies with a dramatic white band across the wings. The location of the band on the wing is the key to identifying which species you're looking at. Weidemeyer's is the admiral species that enlivens the scenery of the Rocky Mountain area's slopes, meadows, and water-

Wingspan: 2¾"–3⅜"

sides. It's aggressive and will often chase swallowtails and other butterflies. Even dragonflies don't escape its notice. One summer, I watched a determined Weidemeyer's along an Idaho stream make life miserable for every dragonfly that came zipping along. The dragonflies got plenty of practice in evasive maneuvers in the face of those big, flashy butterfly wings. In between parries, the butterfly rested on a log over the stream. As soon as an intruder happened by, however, it instantly took up the chase.

▶ RANGE

Weidemeyer's admirals live in the Rocky Mountains and other western mountain ranges. Their range spreads from Canada west to Oregon, east to the Dakotas, and south to New Mexico.

▶ CATERPILLAR

Like other admiral caterpillars, the caterpillar of this species is white mottled with gray, and it has a lumpy appearance.

▶ HOST PLANTS

The most popular host plants are the quaking aspen (*Populus tremuloides*) of the western mountains, famed for its glowing gold fall color, and the willows (*Salix* spp.) that line watercourses. Other species of poplars (*Populus* spp.) also host the caterpillars.

▶ COMMENTS

Tree sap, carrion, and flower nectar are the menu of this species.

FAVORED PLANTS

Milkweeds
(*Asclepias* spp.)

Rabbitbrush
(*Chrysothamnus viscidiflorus*)

Euphorbias
(*Euphorbia* spp.)

Snowberries
(*Symphocarpus* spp.)

Verbenas
(*Verbena* spp.)

Brazilian vervain
(*Verbena bonariensis*)

Lorquin's Admiral
(*Basilarchia lorquini*)

West of the Weidemeyer's range, Lorquin's admiral picks up the slack, giving the northwest quadrant of the country its own version of a big, dark butterfly with flashy white wing bands. A good-size butterfly at about 2½ inches across, it's the smallest of the admiral group. The color combination of this butterfly is easy to confuse with its related California sister, whose range overlaps this species near the Pacific coast. Like the white-banded Weidemeyer's admiral, it's usually at home near watercourses. Like most admirals, the male Lorquin's spends much time perched, waiting for a female to happen by.

Wingspan: 2¼"–2¾"

▶ RANGE
Lorquin's roams throughout British Columbia, through southern California, and east to Idaho.

▶ CATERPILLAR
Displaying the typical "admiral" shape and color, this caterpillar has a humped back and a pair of bristly spikes behind its head. The blotchy yellowish and brownish color maintains the bird-dropping effect common to the larvae of this group of butterflies. When winter nears, the caterpillar rolls itself up inside a leaf, binding it with silk, to make a snug "hibernaculum" in which to spend the winter.

▶ HOST PLANTS
The caterpillars feed on willows (*Salix* spp.), poplars (*Populus* spp.), and cherries (*Prunus* spp.).

▶ COMMENTS
Shrubs with nectar-rich flowers appeal to this butterfly. The rest of its diet consists of nutrients and moisture delicately collected from animal manure and fresh bird droppings.

FAVORED PLANTS

California buckeye
(*Aesculus californica*)

Yerba santa
(*Eriodictyon californicum*)

Privets
(*Ligustrum* spp.)

Ruddy Daggerwing
(*Marpesia petreus*)

The gorgeous orange color of this butterfly screams for attention when it flaps nearby, opening and closing its duller underwings to reveal its bright topside. Like swallowtails, daggerwings have long extensions on their hindwings. This species also has unusual downward curving tips ("hooks") on its forewings. The ruddy daggerwing is on the wing year-round in the warm areas where it makes its home and is often found perched on muddy ground with other "puddle club" butterflies.

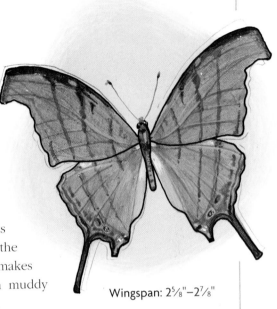

Wingspan: 2⅝"–2⅞"

▶ RANGE
This warm-weather lover resides in the United States from Florida to Texas and southward into Central America. Along with the zebra, it's one of the easiest butterflies to spot when you explore the Everglades and other great swamps of the deep South.

▶ CATERPILLAR
Echoing the color of the adult butterfly, the caterpillar is a beautiful rusty color, marked with yellow-and-black lines and spots for an ornately decorated effect. Its front end sports a pair of fierce-looking bristles, and its back is hairy.

▶ HOST PLANTS
Figs and other plants in the genus *Ficus* sustain the new brood of the ruddy daggerwing, as does the cashew nut tree (*Anacardium occidentale*).

▶ COMMENTS
If you're lucky enough to live in ruddy-daggerwing territory or if you're camping in the area, put out rotting fruit or make a mud puddle to attract this beauty.

FAVORED PLANTS

Milkweeds
(*Asclepias* spp.)

Scarlet milkweed
(*Asclepias curvassica*)

Purple milkweed
(*Asclepias humistrata*)

Swamp milkweed
(*Asclepias incarnata*)

Florida milkweed
(*Asclepias longiflora*)

White milkweed
(*Asclepias perennis*)

Cordias
(*Cordia* spp.)

Lantanas
(*Lantana* spp.)

Goatweed Butterfly
(*Anaea andria*)

It's hard to get very close to this richly colored butterfly—it takes alarm and skitters off with rapid flight before you even notice it's there. If you happen upon one, notice the excellent protective coloration at work here. When the goatweed's wings are closed in resting position, this species looks just like a leaf. Hindwing tails and hooked front wing tips help create the illusion. This species can serve as an indicator of the weather in past seasons: When it pupates during a dry spell, the butterflies that emerge are lighter in color than if pupation had occurred during a wet season.

Wingspan: 2⅜"–3"

▶ RANGE

Although this species represents a large family of tropical butterflies, it occurs as far north as Michigan, south to Colorado east of the Rockies, and east to West Virginia. It avoids most of Florida but continues its range to the Gulf and down through Mexico.

▶ CATERPILLAR

Tiny paler bumps cover the grayish caterpillar, though you'll rarely see it. Its habit of hiding within a rolled-up leaf "stitched" together with silk keeps it away from prying eyes and hungry predators. Another peculiar habit makes this caterpillar even less appealing: It sticks its own droppings to its back with dabs of silk.

▶ HOST PLANTS

This species gets its name from the plants its caterpillars eat: goatweeds or crotons (*Codiaeum* spp., formerly called *Croton* spp.), which most northerners know better as houseplants than as pest plants. In Florida, this butterfly is declining due to the development of its pine and scrub habitats, where its Florida host plant, silver croton (*C. argyranthemum*), once flourished.

▶ COMMENTS

Nectar flowers hold no attraction for this species, which prefers to dine on rotting fruit, sap, and manure.

Hackberry Butterfly

(*Asterocampa celtis*)

This butterfly was once lumped together with the goatweed and a few other species in a category called the emperors, separate from the "sovereign" group that includes the viceroy and the admirals. This is not an eye-catching species, but it is a friendly one—and one of the most common butterflies of late summer and fall. Often you'll find one

Wingspan: 1¾"–2¼"

of these little guys riding around on your gardening hat or delicately sipping sweat from your skin. If you're honored with such a visitor, notice what a light touch the butterfly uses with its proboscis—its tickle is hardly noticeable as it probes your arm.

▶ RANGE

This butterfly frequents most of the eastern half of the country wherever hackberry trees grow, from the northern Plains states and eastern Canada to Florida and Texas.

▶ CATERPILLAR

Butterfly experts call caterpillars like the hackberry "sluglike." They are flattened in shape like a stretched-out garden slug, rather than neatly cylindrical like the typical caterpillar. The hackberry caterpillar is a pretty spring green with yellow-and-lime lengthwise stripes. A pair of horns sticks up on the head end, and a pair of "tails" gives the hind end an unusual forked look.

▶ HOST PLANTS

A well-named species, the hackberry butterfly's larvae eat only the leaves of hackberry trees (*Celtis* spp.). Even seedling trees are used as caterpillar nurseries.

▶ COMMENTS

The fruit plate is tops on the menu for hackberry butterflies. I have never seen a hackberry visit a flower for nectar, although my yard is filled with dozens of these butterflies every year. They zero in on soft and rotting fruit of any kind. Crabapples that drop their fruit in fall appeal to this butterfly, as well as to red-spotted purples, question marks, and commas. Mud and manure puddles and wet paving or rocks will also bring them winging in. They also enjoy carrion, fresh manure, and sap. I sometimes see one of these butterflies siphoning nectar from the drinking holes of a hummingbird feeder.

Tawny Emperor

(*Asterocampa clyton*)

Another crowned head of the emperor group, this species can be tricky to distinguish from the hackberry butterfly. Check the forewings to make sure: Hackberry has a pair of large, distinct black eyespots, while the tawny emperor lacks these spectacles. This species also shows a richer burnt orange color on its open wings than the drabber hackberry. Just to make things tricky for butterfly watchers, the tawny emperor may vary in its color, with some individuals showing a more golden color and others tending toward a burnished chestnut hue. Its eating habits, both as caterpillar and adult, are also very similar to the hackberry butterfly. A widespread and very adaptable butterfly, this species is at home in both wild woods and city neighborhoods.

Wingspan: 1⅞"–2⅜"

▶ RANGE
The tawny emperor overlaps the hackberry butterfly's range, covering the eastern half of the country but not ranging quite as far north or west.

▶ CATERPILLAR
A lookalike to the hackberry caterpillar, this is another bright, spring green slug-type with yellow lengthwise stripes. Like the hackberry, this larva wears a pair of caterpillar antlers on its head and has an odd forked "tail."

▶ HOST PLANTS
Love those hackberries! In fact, hackberries (*Celtis* spp.) are the only thing that will suffice as host plant for this species.

▶ COMMENTS
The tawny emperor does not visit flowers for nectar. Follow the same meal plan as for the hackberry butterfly, and your tawny emperors will be content. Rotting fruit, sap, manure, and carrion are the delectables dear to its heart, though you may want to stick to an offering of over-ripe fruit.

SATYRS/BROWNS (Satyridae)

The browns are a subtly colored group of butterflies dressed in solid brown or gray-brown with darker eyespots along their wings. Most species stick to shady, wooded areas. These butterflies rarely visit flowers because nectar isn't a preferred food. Attract them instead with a mud puddle or a dappled shade garden.

Eyed Brown
(*Satyrodes eurydice*)

The small eyed brown spends most of its time along the edges of woods and in meadows. It is fairly quick to move into a yard that holds plenty of shade trees, shrubs, and paths and other open spaces. Eyed browns will also seek out a sunny spot for basking. Fool them by laying a white handkerchief in your shady garden—they're likely to be tempted into investigating the light-colored spot.

Wingspan: 1⅝"–2"

▶ RANGE
Most common in the Northeast, this species and the closely related Appalachian brown (*Satyrodes appalachia*) are found across the eastern two-thirds of the country, from Canada to Florida.

▶ CATERPILLAR
Almost impossible to see against the leaves of host plants, the caterpillar is grass green with yellow longitudinal stripes and two small horns on its head.

▶ HOST PLANTS
The caterpillars munch on grassy, clump-forming sedges (*Carex* spp.).

▶ COMMENTS
I've seen eyed browns occasionally (but very rarely) on the butterfly bush (*Buddleia davidii*), but they don't seem to be interested in flowers. More often, I spot them at a sap leak on the bark of various trees. When my klutzy human feet come blundering through the meadow garden, I often see them flittering away from the path of my boots with a lilting, weakly flapping flight.

Carolina Satyr
(Hermeuptychia sosybius)

As softly colored as a little gray mouse, the Carolina satyr is one of about 50 American species similar in appearance and habits that occupy distinct ecological niches across the country. This one, as its name suggests, is a species of the Southeast, and it is abundant there. Some satyrs (notably the smoky eyed brown of the Prairie states), have suffered from our destruction of their natural habitat, but the Carolina satyr is going strong, apparently able to find plenty of the grassy, moist areas it likes best still thriving along the coasts. It's one of the smallest satyrs, only an inch and a half in wingspan. A lookalike species, the Hermes satyr of Texas, is the subject of argument among butterfly classifiers, with some voting to give it its own species and others wanting to lump it together with the Carolina.

Wingspan: 1⅛"–1⅝"

▶ **RANGE**
The Carolina satyr is common along the Atlantic and Gulf Coasts from New Jersey to Florida and east to Texas. It also follows the Mississippi north to Kentucky.

▶ **CATERPILLAR**
Just as you'd expect for a caterpillar that dines on grass, this species is bright, light green with lengthwise stripes and a soft fuzz on its body.

▶ **HOST PLANTS**
Grasses are what fill the stomachs of the Carolina satyr's caterpillars. Carpet grass and centipede grass are the mainstays of the caterpillar diet, but some may also munch on St. Augustine grass and other species.

▶ **COMMENTS**
The Carolina satyr usually does not visit flowers for nectar. Attract it with an offering of overripe pears, melon, or other fruit, and look for it at leaking sap spots on your backyard trees or at stumps. You may even spot it searching for sap at a stack of firewood.

MILKWEED BUTTERFLIES (Danaidae)

The beloved monarch is the flagbearer of this group. Milkweed butterflies are famed for being repugnant to birds. As caterpillars, they chow down on plants in the milkweed family, whose sap contains bitter toxins that taste bad to birds. When the caterpillar transforms into a butterfly, it retains those chemicals in its body. Even though these large morsels on the wing may look tempting, birds avoid them.

Monarch
(*Danaus plexippus*)

Quick, name a butterfly! "Monarch" is bound to be in the number-one spot, thanks to its wide range, big size, bright color, and abundance. This is the miracle migrator: It travels in huge numbers from Mexico and the coast of California twice a year, although the same butterfly doesn't make the entire trip. New generations hatched along the way perform the feat on different legs of the journey (see page 169).

Wingspan: 3½"–4"

▶ RANGE
Monarchs range across the country, north into southern Canada, and south into Mexico.

▶ CATERPILLAR
The familiar monarch caterpillar has a big, plump body striped crosswise with black and yellow and a pair of thready projections at each end. The chrysalis is a translucent jade green work of art, with black lines and metallic gold dots.

▶ HOST PLANTS
Milkweeds (*Asclepias* spp.) and dogbanes (*Apocynus* spp.) feed monarch larvae. I was pleased to discover when I moved to Indiana that one of my favorite wild plants, the vigorous honeyvine (*Synanchum laeve*) that decorates my fence, is used as a host plant.

▶ COMMENTS
Besides flowers, monarchs also feed on rotting fruit, sap, and carrion.

FAVORED PLANTS

Milkweeds
(*Asclepias* spp.)

Asters
(*Aster* spp.)

Butterfly bush
(*Buddleia davidii*)

Sedums
(*Sedum* spp.)

Verbenas
(*Verbena* spp. and hybrids)

Ironweeds
(*Vernonia* spp.)

Wingspan: 3"–3⅜"

Queen
(*Danaus gilippus*)

The queen is a southern species, smaller and darker brown than the monarch. The population found in the deep Southwest was once called Bates' queen, but is now considered part of this species (though taxonomists continue to debate the classification). In areas frequented by the queen, that sneaky viceroy butterfly may adopt the coloring of this butterfly instead of the usual subject of its mimicry, the monarch. Both disguises will work to ward off birds because the caterpillars of the queen (and later the winged adults) also harbor distasteful chemicals from a milkweed diet in their plump bodies. Not as abundant as the monarch, the queen is always a treat to spot in the garden or afield.

▶ RANGE

The queen rules in the extreme South from southern California along the Gulf to Florida. It may stray as far north as the Great Plains and occasionally show up in Midwest states.

▶ CATERPILLAR

Deep brown and lemony yellow stripes decorate this caterpillar, which also has two pairs of dark, thready projections on its head and a single pair aft.

▶ HOST PLANTS

Queens feed on milkweeds, particularly on species of *Asclepias* and *Sarcostemma*.

▶ COMMENTS

Queens visit many nectar flowers, including the tasty ones listed at right. Look for the queen in open, sunny areas—like your flower garden!

FAVORED PLANTS

Asters
(*Aster* spp.)

Butterflyweed
(*Asclepias tuberosa*)

Butterfly bush
(*Buddleia davidii*)

Eupatoriums
(*Eupatorium* spp.)

Mexican sunflower
(*Tithonia rotundifolia*)

Verbenas
(*Verbena* spp. and hybrids)

Ironweeds
(*Vernonia* spp.)

Zinnias
(*Zinnia* spp.)

SKIPPERS (Hesperiidae)

Quick, erratic butterflies, skippers' distinctive shape makes them easy to identify—at least as far as family membership. Sorting out the skippers is another matter. More than 250 similar-looking species flutter about North America.

Silver-Spotted Skipper
(*Epargyreus clarus*)

The silver-spotted skipper is one of the most common backyard butterflies, and it's a highly visible member of the family, thanks to its larger size and flashy coloring. Use binoculars to admire the silvery sheen of its white wing patch.

Wingspan: 1¾"–2⅜"

▶ RANGE
This is a common and abundant butterfly from Canada through Central America.

▶ CATERPILLAR
The caterpillar is lime green mottled with darker blotches and lines. It conceals itself by making a drawn-together tent of leaves while feeding.

▶ HOST PLANTS
The female uses legumes as host plants, from the beans in your vegetable patch to the wisteria on your arbor. My dogs' nemesis, the stick-tights called beggar's ticks or tick trefoil (*Desmodium* spp.), which cause me hours of careful combing, are used by the silver-spotted skipper.

▶ COMMENTS
Many nectar flowers will tempt silver-spotted skippers. In late summer to early fall, silver-spotted skippers outnumber every other species of butterfly in my garden.

FAVORED PLANTS

Asters
(*Aster* spp.)

Blue mist
(*Caryopteris* × *clandonensis*)

Eupatoriums
(*Eupatorium* spp.)

Salvias
(*Salvia* spp.)

Verbenas
(*Verbena* spp.)

Ironweeds
(*Vernonia* spp.)

Chaste tree
(*Vitex agnus-castus*)

Wingspan: 1½"–2"

Long-Tailed Skipper
(*Urbanus proteus*)

Imagine a cross between an elegant swallowtail and a short, fat skipper, and what you've got is the long-tailed skipper. The beauty queen of the family, this pretty butterfly has a lovely iridescent glimmer on its wings and head. Unfortunately, its caterpillars have a rapacious appetite for beans, which has earned it the ire of farmers and backyard gardeners. When nectaring, it holds its front wings vertically, while the hind wings jut out at right angles.

▶ RANGE
The long-tailed skipper is a mostly southern species, ranging from southern California to the Gulf and Florida. It occasionally wanders as far north as Connecticut or into the Midwest, but it's most abundant in the Southeast.

▶ CATERPILLAR
Unless you investigate closely, you may never see this greenish caterpillar with its speckles and stripes of yellow and black. It feeds in relative privacy by rolling itself within a leaf to feed.

Farmers know it as the "bean-leaf roller."

▶ HOST PLANTS
Beans are the prime food of these larvae, but other plants also host the hungry caterpillars, including legumes, mustards, and even cannas (*Canna* spp.).

▶ COMMENTS
Offer nectar flowers of almost any sort and you'll please this butterfly. Watch for the shine of iridescent color on its wings as it nectars.

FAVORED PLANTS

Asters
(*Aster* spp.)

Butterfly bush
(*Buddleia davidii*)

Centaureas
(*Centaurea* spp.)

Lantanas
(*Lantana* spp.)

Sedums
(*Sedum* spp. and hybrids)

Mexican sunflower
(*Tithonia rotundifolia*)

Verbenas
(*Verbena* spp. and hybrids)

Ironweed
(*Vernonia* spp.)

Common Checkered Skipper

(Pyrgus communis)

Most skippers are fairly nondescript little butterflies, and this one is a good representative of the family. It's an abundant and widespread species, although you may not recognize different individuals as the same butterfly species because their markings vary greatly from one to the next.

Wingspan: ¾"–1¼"

▶ RANGE

The common checkered skipper skips across the United States, north into southern Canada and south into Mexico.

▶ CATERPILLAR

The small tan caterpillar is striped lengthwise with brown and white.

▶ HOST PLANTS

Plants in the mallow family—including common weeds like the low grower called cheeses, as well as garden plants like holly-hock (*Alcea rosea*) and hibiscus (*Hibiscus* spp.)—are the host plants for the tiny caterpillars of the checkered skipper.

▶ COMMENTS

I can't think of a flower in my garden I have not seen a checkered skipper investigating! At first you're likely to completely overlook these butterflies because they are so small and inconspicuous. Once you spot your first one, though, you'll discover there are many more than you would imagine!

FAVORED PLANTS

Asters
(*Aster* spp.)

Butterfly bush
(*Buddleia davidii*)

Blue mist
(*Caryopteris* × *clandonensis*)

Coneflowers
(*Echinacea* spp.)

Eupatoriums
(*Eupatorium* spp.)

Sunflowers
(*Helianthus* spp.)

Lantanas
(*Lantana* spp.)

Goldenrods
(*Solidago* spp.)

Verbenas
(*Verbena* spp. and hybrids)

Ironweeds
(*Vernonia* spp.)

Wingspan: 1"–1⅜"

Sachem
(*Atalopedes campestris*)

Across the southern third of the country, the small, bright sachem is a common companion in the summer garden. It's a butterfly with frequent wanderlust, indulging in one-way trips that take it as far as Oregon and New York. Notice the large black spot on the top side of the male's forewing. That's the stigma, or sex patch, a characteristic shared by the males of many skipper species. The stigma varies in size and color from species to species.

▶ RANGE

This skipper lives across the southern third of the country and may emigrate northward in summer almost to Canada.

▶ CATERPILLAR

Greenish brown but rarely seen, this caterpillar hides in a sheltering tent it makes at the base of the grass.

▶ HOST PLANTS

I'm happy to report the sachem caterpillar favors Bermuda grass, a tough lawn grass that can quickly overpower flowerbeds with its deep, spreading roots and vigorous growth. Still, despite its best efforts, the Bermuda grass in my yard grows on unperturbed. Other members of the grass family (Poaceae) are also on the menu.

▶ COMMENTS

You may have sachem visiting many nectar flowers in your garden. It can be a real challenge to sort out the skippers, but you can enjoy their perky habits whether or not you can call them by name.

FAVORED PLANTS

Asters
(*Aster* spp.)

Tickseed sunflower
(*Bidens aristosa*)

Butterfly bush
(*Buddleia davidii*)

Eupatoriums
(*Eupatorium* spp.)

Coneflowers
(*Rudbeckia* spp.)

Goldenrods
(*Solidago* spp.)

Verbenas
(*Verbena* spp. and hybrids)

Ironweeds
(*Vernonia* spp.)

Zinnias
(*Zinnia* spp.)

Yellowpatch Skipper
(*Polites coras*)

Another widespread species, this bright little butterfly is a common visitor to gardens, especially in the eastern part of the country, where it is most abundant. Roughly a dozen other skipper species look almost the same, but

Wingspan: ¾"–1"

don't worry if you can't make a positive identification: All skippers are fun to observe, even if you aren't sure who's who among them. Like many small butterflies, the yellowpatch is adept at seeking out the tiny flowers of weeds. It seems to be particularly fond of the chickweed in my garden, which makes me feel a bit more kindly toward that pesky plant myself.

▶ **RANGE**
This butterfly makes its home in southern Canada from the Pacific to the Atlantic and south to Arizona and Georgia.

▶ **CATERPILLAR**
Unusually dark, the yellowpatch skipper caterpillar is a somber maroon color blotched with brown.

▶ **HOST PLANTS**
Grasses are tops with this species.

▶ **COMMENTS**
Many flowers attract the yellowpatch skipper;

among them are the ones listed at right. Look for yellowpatch skippers flying in low, short bursts from flower to flower. Once perched at a nectar source, they often linger for several minutes, a habit they share with many other members of the skipper clan.

FAVORED PLANTS

Butterfly bush
(*Buddleia davidii*)

Blue mist
(*Caryopteris* ✕ *clandonensis*)

Eupatoriums
(*Eupatorium* spp.)

Joe-Pye weed
(*Eupatorium purpureum*)

Lavenders
(*Lavandula* spp.)

Goldenrods
(*Solidago* spp.)

Verbenas
(*Verbena* spp. and hybrids)

Ironweeds
(*Vernonia* spp.)

GIANT SKIPPERS (Megathymidae)

Sounds unbelievable, but the giant skippers can reach speeds of 60 miles an hour! These big butterflies have triangular wings like the true skippers. Scientists are still sorting out the family, which exists only in the Americas. Much remains to be learned about these butterflies because they're so difficult to observe at their superfast speed.

Wingspan: 2"–2⅞"

Yucca Giant Skipper
(*Megathymus yuccae*)

Giant, indeed—this skipper reaches almost 3 inches in width! Couple that with high-velocity flight that could keep up with auto traffic on an interstate, and you have one amazing butterfly. Most of the giant skippers are found in the Southwest, but this big butterfly ranges wider, penetrating the Southeast and the Rockies—wherever yuccas are found.

▶ **RANGE**
Found in semi-arid and desert areas, the yucca giant skipper ranges from the Great Basin east to the Carolinas, south to Baja, California, and along the Gulf to Florida.

▶ **CATERPILLAR**
Young caterpillars hatch from eggs laid at the tip of a yucca leaf, then munch their way into the leaf itself, eating all the way down into the root. They protect themselves by spinning a silken trap-door cover through which they can emerge as adults.

▶ **HOST PLANTS**
You can guess from the name of this species what food its caterpillars prefer! Yuccas (*Yucca* spp.) are the only item on the list.

▶ **COMMENTS**
Adult yuccas do not feed, although males may congregate at mud and sip up moisture.

RESOURCES AND RECOMMENDED READING

Bird and Butterfly Supplies

You can find feeders and supplies at discount stores, garden centers, and wild-bird or nature specialty shops. Fast-dissolving superfine sugar, which melts instantly in cold water, is available at well-stocked supermarkets.

Check the Internet for supplies, or look at ads in magazines such as *Bird Watcher's Digest* or *Audubon*. You may also want to shop from the mail-order firms listed below.

Droll Yankees, Inc.
27 Mill Road
Foster, RI 02825
Phone: (800) 352-9164
Fax: (401) 647-7620
E-mail: custserv@drollyankees.com
Web site: www.drollyankees.com

Duncraft, Inc.
102 Fishersville Road
Concord, NH 03303-2086
Phone (800) 593-5656
Fax: (603) 226-3735
E-mail: info@duncraft.com
Web site: www.duncraft.com

Wild Bird Centers of America
Phone: (301) 229-9585
Fax: (301) 320-6154
E-mail: info@wildbirdcenter.com
Web site: www.wildbirdcenter.com
A chain with stores in many cities

Wild Birds Forever
27212 State Highway 189
Blue Jay, CA 92317
Phone: (800) 459-2473
Fax: (909) 336-6683
Web site: www.wildbirdsforever.com

Wild Birds Unlimited
Phone: (888) 302-2473
Fax: (317) 571-7110
Web site: www.wbu.com
A chain with stores in many cities

Organizations and Programs

American Bird Conservancy
1250 24th Street NW, Suite 400
Washington, D.C. 20037
Phone: (888) BIRD-MAG (247-3624)
E-mail: abc@abcbirds.org
Web site: www.abcbirds.org
A nonprofit organization that builds coalitions of conservation groups, scientists, and the public in order to identify and protect important sites for bird conservation.

Backyard Wildlife Habitat Program
National Wildlife Federation
8925 Leesburg Pike
Vienna, VA 22184-0001
Phone: (703) 790-4000
Web site: www.nwf.org
Information on developing a wildlife-friendly backyard. You can apply to be certified as an official Backyard Wildlife Habitat site. The National Wildlife Federation also has programs to encourage schoolyard, workplace, and community habitat programs.

Hummer/Bird Study Group, Inc.
P.O. Box 250
Clay, AL 35048-0250
Phone: (205) 681-2888
Fax: (205) 681-1339
Web site: hummingbirdplus.org
A nonprofit organization whose goal is to study and preserve hummingbirds and other neotropical immigrants.

The Hummingbird Society
P.O. Box 394
Newark, DE 19715
Phone: (800) 529-3699
Fax: (302) 369-1816
Web site: www.hummingbird.org
A nonprofit organization that works to disseminate information and protect the habitat of hummingbirds.

National Audubon Society
700 Broadway
New York, NY 10003
Phone: (212) 979-3000
Fax: (212) 979-3188
Web site: www.audubon.org
Founded in 1905, one of the biggest non-profit conservation organizations, active worldwide in all kinds of conservation issues as well as birds. Join a local branch to meet other birders, participate in bird counts, and enjoy other bird-related activities.

National Bird-Feeding Society
P.O. Box 23L
Northbrook, IL 60065-0023
Phone: (847) 272-0135
Fax: (847) 498-4092
Web site: www.birdfeeding.org
Organization devoted to bird feeding.

North American Butterfly Association
4 Delaware Road
Morristown, NJ 07960
Web site: www.naba.org
A nonprofit organization working to increase public enjoyment and conservation of butterflies.

The Xerces Society
4828 S.E. Hawthorne Boulevard
Portland, OR 97215
Phone: (503) 232-6639
Fax: (503) 233-6794
Web site: www.xerces.org
An international nonprofit organization that focuses on public education about butterflies and other invertebrates and conservation projects.

Seeds and Plants

To locate a source for uncommon plants (especially native plants), search for the plant by common or botanical name on the Internet; there are many purveyors of seeds and plants of even the most unusual species, with new sites constantly added. To make sure your order will not contribute to the decline of species in the wild collected by unscrupulous dig-and-run resale merchants, e-mail the supplier before ordering and ask how the company acquires its seed and/or plants. Reputable suppliers will be happy to reassure you about their methods.

Another good place to buy unusual plants is at seed and plant sales held by native plant societies. Ask for contact information for your state's society from a nature center or state park. Botanic gardens also hold plant sales.

Boothe Hill Wildflowers
921 Boothe Hill
Chapel Hill, NC 27514
Phone: (919) 967-4091
Seeds and plants of native and naturalized flower species

Busse Gardens
17160 245th Avenue
Big Lake, MN 55309-9716
Phone: (800) 544-3192
Fax: (612) 263-1473
E-mail: customer.service@bussegardens.com
Web site: www.bussegardens.com
Reliable and beautiful perennial plants that can take cold (but also thrive in milder gardens)

Forestfarm
Ray and Peg Prag
990 Tetherow Road
Williams, OR 97544-9599
Phone: (541) 846-7269
Fax: (541) 846-6963
Web site: www.forestfarm.com
More than 2,000 plants, including wildflowers, perennials, and an outstanding variety of trees and shrubs

J. L. Hudson
Star Route 2, Box 337
La Honda, CA 94020
Large collection of woody, perennial, herb, and vegetable seeds

Kurt Bluemel, Inc.
2740 Greene Lane
Baldwin, MD 21013-9523
Phone: (800) 248-7584
Fax: (410) 557-9785
E-mail: bluemel@aol.com
Web site: www.bluemel.com
Specializes in ornamental grasses

Louisiana Nursery
5853 Highway 182
Opelousas, LA 70570
Phone: (337) 948-3696
Fax: (337) 942-6404
E-mail: dedurio@mns.com
Web site: www.louisiananursery.org
Offers vines hummingbirds adore, as well as many other trees, shrubs, and perennials

Niche Gardens
1111 Dawson Road
Chapel Hill, NC 27516
Phone: (919) 967-0078
Fax: (919) 967-4026
E-mail: orders@nichegdn.com
Web site: www.nichegdn.com
Generous-sized plants of grasses, nursery-propagated wildflowers, perennials, and herbs

Plant Delights Nursery
9241 Sauls Road
Raleigh, NC 27603
Phone: (919) 772-4794
Fax: (919) 662-0370
E-mail: office@plantdel.com
Web site: www.plantdel.com
Specializes in perennial plants

Prairie Moon Nursery
Route 3, Box 163
Winona, MN 55987
Phone: (507) 452-1362
Fax: (507) 454-5238
E-mail: pmnrsy@luminet.net
Web site: www.prairiemoonmursery.com
An outstanding variety of native prairie grasses and wildflowers; also lots of seeds

Prairie Nursery, Inc.
P.O. Box 306
Westfield, WI 53964
Phone: (800) 476-9453
Fax: (608) 296-2741
Web site: www.prairienursery.com
An excellent source of native wildflowers and grasses, many of them ideal for bird gardens

Shooting Star Nursery
444 Bates Road
Frankfort, KY 40601
Phone: (502) 223-1679
Offers plants and seeds of native grasses, flowers, and shrubs

Thompson & Morgan, Inc.
P.O. Box 1308
Jackson, NJ 08527-0308
Phone: (800) 272-7333
Fax: (888) 466-4769
Web site: www.thompson-morgan.com/gardening

Tripple Brook Farm
37 Middle Road
Southampton, MA 01073
Phone: (413) 527-4626
Fax: (413) 527-9853
E-mail: catalog-request@tripplebrookfarm.com
Web site: www.tripplebrookfarm.com
Lively catalog of wildflowers, fruits, and shrubs

We-Du Nurseries
Route 5, Box 724
Marion, NC 28752
Phone: (828) 738-8300
Fax: (828) 738-8131
E-mail: wedu@wnclink.com
Web site: www.we-du.com
Impressive selection of wildflowers and perennials, including lots of woodland plants

Wildlife Nurseries
P.O. Box 2724
Oshkosh, WI 54903-2724
Phone: (920) 231-3780
Fax: (920) 231-3554
Excellent, informative listing of plants and seeds of native plants that attract birds and other wildlife

Woodlanders, Inc.
1128 Colleton Avenue
Aiken, SC 29801
Phone/fax: (803) 648-7522
E-mail: woodlanders@woodlanders.net
Web site: www.woodlanders.net
A fantastic collection of native plants, plus other good garden plants. It's a list only, no pictures or descriptions, so if you're a new-comer to plants, pull out a plant encyclo-pedia to consult as you go.

Books

Armitage, Allan M. *Herbaceous Perennial Plants,* 2nd ed. Champaign, IL: Stipes Publishing Company, 1997.

Austin, O. L., Jr. *Birds of the World.* New York: Golden Press, 1961.

Burrell, C. Colston. *A Gardener's Encyclopedia of Wildflowers.* Emmaus, PA: Rodale, 1997.

David, L. I. *A Field Guide to the Birds of Mexico and Central America.* Austin, TX: University of Texas Press, 1972.

Dirr, Michael A. *Manual of Woody Landscape Plants: Their Identification,* 5th ed. Champaign, IL: Stipes Publishing Company, 1998.

Ellis, Barbara. *Taylor's Weekend Gardening Guides—Attracting Birds & Butterflies.* New York: Houghton Mifflin, 1997.

Glassberg, Jeffrey. *Enjoying Butterflies More.* Marietta, OH: Bird Watcher's Digest Press, 1995.

Johnsgard, Paul A. *The Hummingbirds of North America.* Washington, DC: Smithsonian Institution Press, 1997.

Kress, Stephen W. *National Audubon Society: The Bird Garden.* New York: DK Publishing, 1995.

Mikula, Rick. *Garden Butterflies of North America.* Minocqua, WI: Willow Creek Press, 1997.

Newfield, Nancy. *Enjoying Butterflies More.* Marietta, OH: Bird Watcher's Digest Press, 2001.

Ottesen, Carole. *The Native Plant Primer.* New York: Harmony Books, 1995.

Roth, Sally. *Attracting Birds to Your Backyard.* Emmaus, PA: Rodale, 1998.

Roth, Sally. *Natural Landscaping.* Emmaus, PA: Rodale, 1995.

Sunset Staff. *An Illustrated Guide to Attracting Birds.* Menlo Park, CA: Sunset Publishing Corporation, 1990.

Tekulsky, Matthew. *The Hummingbird Garden.* Boston, MA: Harvard Common Press, 1999.

Terres, John K. *The Audubon Society Encyclopedia of North American Birds.* New York: Random House Value Publishing, 1995.

Tripp, Kim E., and J. C. Raulston. *The Year in Trees.* Portland, OR: Timber Press, 1995.

Tyrell, Esther Quesada. *Hummingbirds: Their Life and Behavior.* New York: Crown Publishers, Inc., 1985.

Xerces Society and the Smithsonian Institution. *Butterfly Gardening.* San Francisco, CA: Sierra Club Books, 1998.

Special Out-of-Print Titles

Many old natural history books contain fascinating accounts of nature. I find it interesting that many of the old accounts have apparently never been bettered; some information in them is still used in some modern reference books, such as the *Audubon Society Encyclopedia of North American Birds* (see above), which draws on A. C. Bent's series of books on North American birds, published from about 1910 through the 1930s.

While these books are out of print now, it's not too difficult to track down a copy at a reasonable price, thanks to book searches and auctions on the Internet. You can also ask a local bookshop to search for out-of-print books. Here are some of my favorite out-of-print titles.

Bent, Arthur Cleveland. *Life Histories of American Birds* series.

Some are available in reprint editions from Dover Press or Ayer Company Publishers; others are out of print.

Chapman, Frank M. *Handbook of Birds of Eastern North America.* New York: D. Appleton and Company, 1895.

Comstock, John Henry. *Insect Life: An Introduction to Nature Study and a Guide for Teachers, Students, and Others Interested in Out-of-Door Life.* New York: D. Appleton and Company, 1897.

Fabre, J. H. *The Life of the Caterpillar*. New York: Dodd, Mead, and Company, 1918.

Gould, J. *A Monograph of the* Trochilidae, *or Family of Hummingbirds*. London: Taylor and Francis, 1849–1861.

Holland, W. J. *The Butterfly Book: A Popular Guide to a Knowledge of the Butterflies of North America*. New York: Doubleday, Page & Company, 1916.

Kellogg, Vernon. *American Insects*. New York: Henry Holt and Company, 1906.

Mathews, F. Schuyler. *Field Book of American Wild Flowers*. New York: G. P. Putnam's Sons, 1902.

Pough, Richard H. *Audubon Bird Guide: Eastern Land Birds*. New York: Doubleday & Company, Inc., 1946.

Weed, Clarence M. *The Nature Library: Butterflies*. New York: Doubleday, Page & Company, Inc., 1917.

Field Guides

Field guides are essential tools when you're learning to identify butterflies and hummingbirds. Many of them are also jam-packed with tidbits of interesting information about the lives of these fascinating creatures. Look at several field guides before you choose one and pick the one that seems most comfortable to your style of learning. Notice the "field marks" that the guides point out—the colors on wings or body, the behavior you might see. Then, the next time you spot an unfamiliar butterfly or hummingbird, you'll discover it's much easier to flip to the right part of the book to identify it.

The Audubon Society Field Guide series. New York: Alfred A. Knopf.
   A regional set of guides for both birds (including hummingbirds) and butterflies; uses photos instead of illustrations, which can make it a bit tricky to identify live birds and butterflies.

Dunn, Jon L. *National Geographic Field Guide to the Birds of North America* (revised and updated). National Geographic Society, 1999.
   Detailed color illustrations, range maps, and species descriptions, including information on behavior and vocalizations.

Mitchell, Robert T., and Herbert S. Zim. *Butterflies and Moths: A Guide to the More Common American Species*. New York: Golden Books, 1987.
   In my opinion, the best butterfly field guide. Excellent, accurate illustrations of butterflies (and moths)—and their caterpillars, a nice extra that most field guides don't include.

Peterson, Roger Tory [birds] and Paul Opler [butterflies]. *The Peterson Field Guide* series. Boston: Houghton Mifflin Co.
   A set of regional guides that include books for both birds (including hummingbirds) and butterflies. The birds are drawn in less lifelike poses than in the Golden Press guide, but noticeable "field marks" are clearly pointed to with arrows. The butterfly guides are illustrated with photos.

Robbins, Chandler S., Bertel Bruun, and Herbert S. Zim. *A Guide to Field Identification: Birds of North America*. New York: Golden Press, 1983.
   Shows hummingbirds (as well as other American birds) in lifelike poses and on a plant where you're likely to see them. Range maps are included with each bird's entry. The book includes all hummingbirds of North America.

Magazines

Backyard Bird News and
Bird Watcher's Digest
P.O. Box 110
Marietta, OH 45750
Web site: www.birdwatchersdigest.com

Birds and Blooms
5400 South 60th Street
Greendale, WI 53129

Organic Gardening
Rodale Inc.
33 East Minor Street
Emmaus, PA 18098
Web site: www.organicgardening.com

ACKNOWLEDGMENTS

This book has been a joint project from the beginning. Thanks go first to my mother, Mary Bohus Roth, who gave me her love of the wonderful outdoor world and all the creatures in it. I also thank her friend Stephan Sauerzopf, who I knew only as "The Flower Man" for the first 20 years of my life. Like my mother's family, he was not far removed from the old country, where he learned how to make beautiful gardens out of nothing. I can still picture him and my mother lifting a handful of soil in spring and sharing a deep sniff with eyes closed. Their gardens were always alive with songbirds, hummingbirds, bugs, bees, and butterflies.

I'm grateful to Fern Bradley, who guided this book from start to finish, no easy task when you're dealing with an author who'd rather be out looking at nature than sitting at her desk. Thanks also to Sue Burton, who kept me laughing with her observations on daily life while smoothing my written words with tact and polish. I owe a debt to Sarah Dunn for her eagle eye and remarkable command of the fine points of the English language. Sarah Wolfgang Heffner made sure all the plant names in this book are correct, so that you can track the plants down at garden centers or in catalogs. Claudia Curran made sure my instructions for projects actually worked (friends who have tried to follow my passed-along recipes know how valuable this was!). Thanks also to Michele Raes, whose eye for beauty graces the pages and cover of this book. Of course, should any mistakes turn up, they're all mine.

A big thank-you to my wonderful family of friends: Pati, Paul, Debbe, Heidi, Paul, Lynn, Randy, Beth, Tracy, Larry, Mike—you don't know how much the dinners, conversations, field trips, e-mails, and phone calls have meant. I love you all. Thanks to Fred for late-night chili dogs at the always surprising Fred's Bar (where else would an ex-Marine and an earring-bedecked 20-something get involved in a lively discussion about pruning roses?). To my music-loving friends Tracy, Beth, Mike, John, Danny, Robert, Keith, Randy, Dan, Dave, Steve, Bob, Gerd, John, David, Barbara, Larry, Jill, P.J., Becky, DeMarco, JeanAnn, Kendall, and everybody else who's ever made me want to sing or dance, a standing ovation for the many good days and nights of making music.

Finally, thanks to all of you who share the joy of hummingbirds, butterflies, and all the other wonders of the natural world. Isn't it wonderful when every day holds the promise of new discoveries! May all of your gardens always be filled with life and love.

PHOTO CREDITS

INDEX

Note: Page references in *italic* indicate illustrations and photographs. Page references in **boldface** indicate tables.

USDA PLANT HARDINESS ZONE MAP

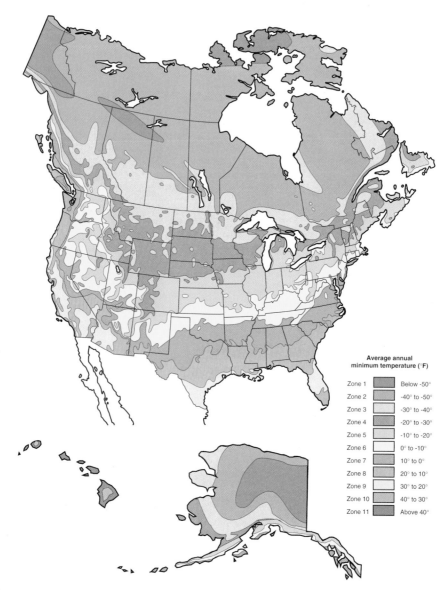

Average annual minimum temperature (°F)

Zone 1	Below -50°
Zone 2	-40° to -50°
Zone 3	-30° to -40°
Zone 4	-20° to -30°
Zone 5	-10° to -20°
Zone 6	0° to -10°
Zone 7	10° to 0°
Zone 8	20° to 10°
Zone 9	30° to 20°
Zone 10	40° to 30°
Zone 11	Above 40°

This map was revised in 1990 and is recognized as the best indicator of minimum temperatures available. Look at the map to find your area, then match its pattern to the key above. When you've found your color, the key will tell you what hardiness zone you live in. Remember that the map is a general guide; your particular conditions may vary.